WALTER   FLORINE

FLORINE STETTHEIMER

Portrait of My Mother, 1925, oil on canvas. A work particularly admired by Henry McBride, who referred to the wit of its devices, this was one of Florine Stettheimer's later portraits but she never painted more serenely or with more genuine affection; it serves as a key to the imperturbable and original graces of her art. *Coll. Mrs. Julius Ochs Adler*

FLORINE STETTHEIMER

A Life in Art

BY PARKER TYLER

Farrar, Straus and Company • *New York*

First Printing, 1963
Copyright © 1963 by FARRAR, STRAUS AND COMPANY, *Inc.*
Library of Congress catalog card number 63-19561
Published simultaneously in Canada by Ambassador Books, Ltd., Toronto
Manufactured in the U.S.A.
Designed by PATRICIA DE GROOT

CONTENTS

ILLUSTRATIONS

*Works of art are given below in Italic type, photographs in Roman;
the former are by Florine Stettheimer unless otherwise noted.*

*Prelude in the Form
of a Cellophane Squirrel Cage*

T WAS Avery Hopwood who introduced Fania and me to
the Stettheimers when they returned to New York in 1914,
driven hitherward by rumors of war, from their long sojourn in Germany. We met Ettie first, "Ettie with her sharp
tongue," Avery adjured us, but we became acquainted with the
elegant Carrie and the enchanting Florine almost immediately
after. The mother appeared last of all. We presently discovered
that each sister had her own favorites among the males, but we

became intimate friends of the entire family, a condition that persisted, through three town residences and an indefinite number of summer houses, until every one of the ladies was dead.

I have, long since, published a paper about all the ladies, but, as this is a book about Florine, this time I will write more specifically about her. Whenever I remember Florine, I think about portulacca and zinnias, both of which appear in assorted colors; these were the flowers that she grew at the various summer dwellings that she occupied with her family. I also vividly recall the cellophane flowers, imagined and executed by the artist herself, looming from tall glass vases, with which, much later, she embellished her studio in the Beaux Arts apartment building.

It is a pleasure to bring to mind the furniture in white and gold she had designed for her bedroom in the François I building, the Alwyn Court, where she slept occasionally, adjacent to her mother and her two famous sisters, Ettie (whose literary pseudonym was Henrie Waste) and Carrie, the duenna of the doll house. On Seventy-sixth Street she had decorated the vast dining room in gray and yellow, with one of her paintings of a reclining maiden over the mantelpiece. Further, somewhere in the room, stood a screen in Chinese style, in which a different sister occupied each of three panels. She had offered to design the décors for the entire apartment at Alwyn Court, to which they presently moved, but Ettie and Carrie harbored exclusive tastes and protested volubly against this attempt to usurp their rights. So, finally, her efforts at decoration were restricted to her white and gold bedroom.

Her bedroom in her studio was more informal, but fabulous in her prodigal employment of white lace, cellophane, and crystal blossoms. I am happy to remember how she made stiff paper do her bidding when she arranged the drapes at the window in the dining room of her studio. No one who saw it can ever forget the huge Robert Henri period classical nude she always kept hanging on the most prominent wall of her studio. This nude, which informed observers how conventionally she had begun to paint, was dazzlingly at variance with the brilliant contemporary fantasies which, with the aid of a palette knife, she had imagined on canvas, fancies as evanescent as dew and as exquisite as the dawn.

Her studio overlooked the greenery of Bryant Park, which she invariably referred to as "My Garden." Visualizing how she was dressed, I think of Venice in the Cinquecento; her figure in rich satins or velvets made the exact silhouette of that early Venetian extravagance of taste; everything was suggested except the mask. Sitting with her in her studio, I recall her talking endlessly about Marcel Proust, whose *À la Recherche du Temps perdu* she read volume by volume in attentive rotation, and when she had finished it, she began *Swann's Way* and reread all the volumes consecutively.

In our own apartment hang many memories of Florine; in my library is her dramatic portrait of me; the colors of our apartment on East Nineteenth Street are employed and a very slender vision of me is seated on a chair in the center of a circular green rug, brightened by a wreath of red roses. In the drawing room over the credenza, hangs one of the more brilliant of Florine's flower paintings, glowing with marigolds, daisies, delphiniums, and purple and gold iris, a painting of which I never tire, and which Ellen Glasgow tried in vain to buy before I assumed possession. In this connection it is well to remember that Florine always arranged grandiose floral decorations for the table when the Stettheimers gave dinners. In the hallway leading to the bedrooms a decided rarity looms: a carefully painted picture of a baby with her mouth open as if to coo. When Florine presented this to me it was the cover of a white satin handkerchief case. "I painted this for my mother when I was eight years old," she explained. I have caused this novelty to be framed and it is much admired by visitors. In the studio where I make photographs, on the wall near the window, is the unfinished portrait Paulet Thévenaz painted of Florine. She never cared for this. I always did. Furthermore, so far as I knew, only two other portraits of her exist; she was very rarely photographed and refused even to be photographed by me, although Ettie and Carrie both accepted that ordeal with alacrity.

Florine was a completely self-centered and dedicated person: she did not inspire love, or affection, or even warm friendship, but she did elicit interest, respect, admiration, and enthusiasm for her work in art.

It amazes me, fresh from a rereading, that Parker Tyler has been able to create such a remarkable book about Florine and her family. Although Parker knew Florine only slightly, he has assembled his facts with so much ingenuity and used his imagination so successfully that all the Stettheimers exist in the round in these pages and Florine herself appears even a trifle bigger than life size. He must have achieved this admirable end by osmosis or extreme sensitivity and he has even employed metaphysical means in the process of completing his true picture. He has touched on all the corners of her life and artistic endeavor with taste, talent, and a good deal of tact, although facts hitherto unavailable have come to light. I had never known her exact age before, for example. I congratulate Parker on his assiduity in accumulating material, on his persistence in tracking it down, and for his unusual ability to present it to the reader.

Carl Van Vechten
May 23rd, 1963, New York

FLORINE STETTHEIMER

case. Her work, like that of other dead painters, becomes part of
the very walls surrounding us, giving time a special defiance by
stubbornly taking up space. "Taking up space": that is suggestive!
As a living being, Florine Stettheimer occasionally impressed her
friends as feeling that *she* took up *too much* space in the physical
world of men and things.

For she was fragile of person, retiring as an afternoon sun-
beam, remote as anyone who—saint or artist or philosopher—ever
fixed his gaze on a world beyond the commonplace. As an inveterate
elegante, she lived an existence that most would call precious, and
yet, though usually surrounded by people, she seemed to wait for
Eternity's more flexible clock, Infinity's larger room, in which to
be, and do, and have, all she wanted. If she *could* be called a crea-
ture of luxury, she was not luxurious; if she *could* be called rich,
she was not ostentatious. And if she *was* precious, she managed to
be an American, too. Here was a tantalizingly elusive combination
for a biographer: a unique person, a unique creator, a unique
American.

With the lightest heart in the world, I can say that all my
difficulties melted under the glow of inspiration communicated to
me by what I learned of Florine Stettheimer. I knew much of her
work although personally I had met her but a few times; then, however, it had been to marvel at the triumphant and valiant unity of
a life seemingly spun from gossamer threaded with sunshine—and
waning at that. In 1946, two years following her death, she was
honored with a memorial show at the Museum of Modern Art. I
well remember—and so do others—what a startlingly authoritative
suite her vivid paintings made on walls where they had scarcely
been noticed before. To certain *cognoscenti,* they now seemed to
belong there naturally and permanently. Not everyone, however,
agreed on this point. Today, when certain schools of extreme Modernism seem to have grabbed aesthetic taste by the throat, Florine
Stettheimer's lyric style may seem an oddity of American painting:
a "quirk" of that mercurial period between two world wars when
Modernism had to win its own world victory.

Florine Stettheimer had her opinion of certain victorious Mod-
ernists; she never presumed, by word or act, to interfere "officially" with their victories. Values in painting, after all, are ultimately determined by unbiased looking, if by biased buying. Since
Modernism, as an historic movement, did win its victory, so Florine

Stettheimer, I hazard, is destined to win hers. Yet even the trickle of fame she acquired during her life must be now renewed and she has to be reclaimed like a lost art. In one great sense, then, the prospect before a biographer was clear enough: Show Florine Stettheimer in her habit as she lived. But in doing so, I told myself, do not adopt the usual chronological round of life from birth to death—growth, revelations of maturity, career, uphill climb, the doldrums and so on, in the order named; instead, seize Florine Stettheimer as a living soul who was a person and a personality; make all these pages a single portrait, so that at any moment the reader, as it were, might stretch out his hand and touch Florine Stettheimer as though she were present, sitting for her portrait; and moreover, treat her works in the same way: as though (for she would appreciate this!) they too were sitting for their portraits.

I hope Florine Stettheimer's spirit likes this portrait of her and her works. If she were alive in the flesh, I know it would be a thing to offer her with the utmost trepidation. For, in her salon, she was as guarded by unwritten law, by tacit etiquette, as temple sibyls used to be. Though by common definition an "art hostess," that dubious term covers but meagrely what she was to the people whom she entertained so constantly: artists or those intimately concerned with the arts. More exactly, she was a tutelary deity that presided over a table loaded with delicacies for the spiritual and physical palates, the high priestess of a religion whose objects of worship (the shrouded canvases with her work-in-progress on their surfaces) could be ignored, and were never to be seen, even fleetingly, till their creator had placed on them the final touch.

No hot, lethal debates on artistic issues ever took place in this consecrated, serene atmosphere. Polite hubbub did, even a loud, disloyally loud, word, but never open warfare, never pitched battles! The New York artists who participated in the Stettheimer rites knew that such issues had to be settled elsewhere. Men such as Gaston Lachaise, Elie Nadelman, Marcel Duchamp and Alfred Stieglitz, all of them her friends, had become, and would become, much better known than their hostess as the years of deflation and inflation waxed and grew fretful. The struggles and victories of these artists remained moot matters within the confines of the Stettheimer studio-salon, where the lucky artists discovered, magically enough, that they could relax. The hostess's own paintings, even when shown in a gallery, were hardly a commercial commodity because of numerous taboos laid upon her publicity by this shyest and most casual of "exhibiting artists." The surfaces of her works never decked themselves with that hustle for fame which obviously professional, obviously modish paintings, today, carry with them like medals and old levis, tousled hair and plumed hats. The official *éclat,* at Florine Stettheimer's gatherings, was seen on the visible guests, not on the visible art.

Readers may be half prepared for the fact that all her life Florine Stettheimer remained unmarried. All the same, and partly because of this, she painted the features of love and beauty on both sexes with the simple fervor and forthrightness of a saint enjoying a beatitude earned by prayer. This became paradoxical when, concerning herself with a great adventure of the modern theatre, the Stein-Thomson opera, *Four Saints in Three Acts,* Florine Stettheimer emerged transiently as that very thing from which her linked little circle of admirers had seemed to protect her from being: a "celebrity." The event virtually caused, at least among her mother and sisters, a family scandal. Yet ironically and profoundly, her success as a stage designer made her aware of the importance of the function no true artist escapes: all his works are made *in* the world, *about* the world and *for* the world.

Was Florine Stettheimer's painting intensively private in its processes and even its appreciation? Well, her subjects were often public buildings and public people. Did her fellow artists love her as a painterly spirit, as the muse of her home-made "cathedrals" of paint? Well, they let go by the question of whether her works were only piquant and amusing—or memorable and important, works of true scale; *not* doll houses *imagining themselves* as cathedrals. All her life, Florine Stettheimer possessed a few sincere admirers, some even taking up her cause in print, but in any case their persuasions had little or no effect on the public's attitude. Her critic friends—less than could be counted on four-fifths of a hand—included the formidable Henry McBride, yet even when all they did was manoeuvred and said, her art, during and after her life, was basically a "family affair."

Now, it becomes much more than that: her best friends, such as Carl Van Vechten, Virgil Thomson, Marcel Duchamp, the late Henry McBride and the late Pavel Tchelitchew, when I approached them about this book, agreed that (no member of Florine's immediate family being left) there was no point in keeping up the unjust silence about this artist, no reason to observe the inviolability of the web of exclusiveness she wove about herself during her lifetime. To the gentlemen just named or to their spirits, inevitably, goes the preponderance of my thanks in helping to reconstruct the obscure but fascinating life and times of this memorable artist, whose career, concentrated in the hectic twenties and thirties, was like a Roman candle showering its brilliance only for a few chosen guests on a private estate. From these, I verified that Florine Stettheimer was a person with a large gift of intimacy, in that she accurately measured how much of it she wanted from individuals and how much these individuals wished to give, while assuming that her friends made the same careful measurement of her own desire for intimacy and theirs.

All those to whom I talked confirmed this—and more. For vital information, insights and documentation about my subject, I am also much indebted to Mr. R. Kirk Askew, Jr., the late A. Everett Austin, Jr., Mr. Cecil Beaton, Mr. Adolfo Best-Maugard, Mr. Louis Bouché, the late Philip Moeller, Mr. Carl Sprinchorn, and Mrs. Marguerite Zorach: I thank them all. From the closest surviving relatives of Florine Stettheimer, Mrs. Julius Ochs Adler and Mr. Henry Wanger, I received much-appreciated courtesies and advice on biographic matters. To Mr. Joseph Solomon, trustee to the Estate of Ettie Stettheimer, I gratefully owe the commission of this book, as to which Messrs. Askew and Van Vechten were his advisors. Additional thanks are due the directors and staffs of the outstanding institutions where I was enabled to see the works of Florine Stettheimer (listed in crediting those works here), and especially to Mr. Donald C. Gallup, Curator of the American Literature Collection at the Yale University Library, where most of the Stettheimerana reposes. To Mr. Charles Boultenhouse—last but not least—must go my gratitude for rewards reaped from crucial conversations with him during the early stages of this book's composition.

I *In the Beginning*

 DISTINGUISHED ARTIST draws to his name, in posthumous retrospect, every conceivable question asked by human beings about one of their kind. Since Florine Stettheimer died nineteen years ago, a cloud of vagueness inevitably settled about her origins. Everyone knew she was an American with her family roots in Germany. And, of course, as was clear during her lifetime, her drawing-room, held with her two surviving sisters for most of her maturity, created a resonant if limited legend in the

godhead
parent
palette

varied life of America's great center of culture, New York City. Various writers, of whom I shall speak in these pages, have paid tribute to the utterly unique features of this legend; few—perhaps, basically, none—have felt it necessary to inquire into the biography of the mistress of the legend. Certain very original, virtually "ageless," personalities give the impression of being self-created. This impression, above all, is the aspect of the Stettheimer legend that will come naturally to the fore as Florine's story is unfolded.

Many biographers have known their subjects personally, and some of them intimately. In this respect, I was scarcely acquainted with Florine Stettheimer. Yet, talking to her family and friends who survive and cherish her, and reading her diaries, I have found it natural to begin saying "Florine" and never "Miss Stettheimer." So "Florine" my subject will constantly be called hereafter, just as her sisters must constantly appear as "Ettie" and "Carrie." However intimate and exclusive the Stettheimer home, a great formality—I was told—always reigned and touched the commonest intercourse with "outsiders." Even when Florine was "Florine" to her friends, there was often a hint of a "Miss" when she was thus addressed.

To be sure, that unspoken intonation seems to have signified more than a personage; it also hinted the withdrawn, the remote-in-privacy: the *cloistral* as much as the *regal*. If, at some hypothetic reunion of Florine's closest friends, the question should be asked if there was not something "cloistral" about the Stettheimers, and especially about Florine, I am sure there would be unanimous and emphatic assent. Yet no great person, least of all one whose greatness is art, is able to hide his inmost truth—however subtly secretive he be. When the moment came for Florine to slough this mortal coil, she doubtless had such things as "personal secrets," things that were never discussed socially, things perhaps implicit but never in the open. On the other hand, the very fact that certain lacunae existed in the visible social front made by the family inevitably told a great deal. Much is newly brought to light by Florine's diaries, which it is a pleasure to read, but not all that might be expected in the way of "facts." Shortly before her own death in 1955, Ettie Stettheimer (then her only surviving sister), carefully edited Florine's diaries and cut out everything that pertained—as she noted on their flyleaves—to "family matters."

In this, there was a certain impartial logic. Ettie believed she was scrupulously carrying out Florine's own, most personal wishes. But posterity is permitted its own insight, its own ultimate vision. Florine, doubtless, would not have desired many things she did desire, had she not felt instinctively and changelessly that she was a definite kind of person. In fact, strange as it may seem, considering her inveterate worldliness, she possessed certain qualities in common with St. Theresa, the heroine of the Stein-Thomson opera, *Four Saints in Three Acts,* to whose fame she herself contributed. Chiefly this was a cloistral—indeed, a regal—quality even if, as in St. Theresa's case, it had its confessions and its plainly legible symbols. When Marcel Duchamp, one of Florine's oldest painter friends, casually spoke to me of her as a "bachelor," he meant it as a tribute contained in a serious play on the sex implied in the doctoral degree in art: Florine lived and died a spinster. About every artist's creative self, there is something purely formal and beyond the sexes. Of all Florine's friends, Duchamp is ideal to have sounded this keynote because he had given his own "Bride" her "bachelorhood" in his magnificent visual metaphor that is now in the Philadelphia Museum of Art: *La Mariéc mise à Nu par ses Célibataires, Même.** How curiously—though no special attention seems yet to have been called to this fact—Florine felt herself a kind of "bride" and even painted herself as one . . .

BORN IN 1871, Florine Stettheimer lived a life of extraordinary and continuous youthfulness till very close to the end. On May 11th, 1944, she died iu The New York Hospital after two operations, nearly a year apart, failed to revive what she had brought so vividly and generously into the world. At that moment, many of her friends must have reflected that she had never married, and presumably neither would her then-living sisters, Ettie and Carrie. During college days, three of the Stettheimer daughters seem to have enjoyed the usual harmless diversions supplied by the opposite sex also in the process of growing up while being educated. But these diversions tended to become "ancient history" as time wore on and only Stella, the eldest of the four, eventually accepted a marriage proposal.

It is remembered well that the family atmosphere among the remaining three daughters, Carrie, Florine and Ettie, was strictly matrilinear—a matter of much significance, as will be more and

* The Bride Denuded by Her Own Bachelors.

more evident, to Florine's artistic themes. At the apex of the family group in her painting, *Heat,* sits the sweet-faced, white-haired Rosetta Walter Stettheimer, their mother. The simple genealogical fact behind the ritual atmosphere of the matriarchy was that Florine's father, Joseph Stettheimer, had come of a Jewish banking family of German origin, but that, when his five children (including a boy, Walter) were still extremely young, he had disappeared from the immediate life of his family. In the extant body of Florine's diaries, he remains unchronicled.

LIKE ALL STORIES of mysterious human origin, Florine's has left its peculiarly unmistakable clues, some of them prodigal of suggestion. It is not known at what date she wrote a certain poem in the collection of her verse, *Crystal Flowers,* issued for Florine posthumously by Ettie in 1949. This poem is certainly a reminiscence of childhood or early youth, and so undoubtedly the incident it relates took place in the last century. But the title evidences a postpaternal judgment in which God the Father is placed strictly, significantly, in a purely aesthetic order of being. The Maggie of this poem was her Irish nurse:

FIRST PLASTIC ART—HERR GOTT

Sh—sh—shushed Maggie
Sprinkling holy water in my face
On entering the little chapel
From the sunny village street

In the light of the tall window
An enormous statue stood
A man in a purple gown
With a high golden crown

He had very pink cheeks
And a long white beard
And his hand was raised in blessing

Maggie knelt and pulled me down
Crossing herself as she loudly whispered
"That is the Lord God
With the high golden crown"

As most probably Florine and Maggie spoke English (although the scene may have been Germany), "Herr Gott" was an expression once quite natural but now really alien. The statue represented an alien God to Florine, perhaps, as much because he was a "Mister" as because he was a "god."

OWING TO ABSOLUTE lack of evidence that the Stettheimers practiced any sort of traditional religion, at least formally, it must be supposed that Florine was present on this occasion only because of Maggie's devotions. According to a casual but ironic remark in her diaries, the artist entertained no expectation whatever of a life to come. She had a vision of other worlds, but these were strictly contemporary with this one and indicate, like the subjects of saintly vision, spatial rather than temporal distinctness. If she visualized life after death, it was the life of her art works, which would have an eternal power to invoke her.

But Florine, when Maggie was her unofficial preceptor, was still a girl. Herr Gott must have been one of the first plastic images or sculptures of which she became aware. She was destined at that moment to receive a full art education, an even fuller one than she may have dared to anticipate as the fond Maggie was prompted to "throw holy water" in her face. Perhaps the gratuitous act turned out to be strangely, fatally initiatory. At all events, in retrospect, it was the statue's colors she was distinctly to remember: purple, pink, and white.

The tone and style in which she speaks of this early experience remain strikingly constant in those poems (such as the versified notes to friends) dealing with her mature life in New York, which she found so new to her on her return here in the midst of the first world war. Usually in vers-libre rhythms and easily assuming a nursery-rhyme idiom, these verses show the simplicity and directness of a witty mind as unafraid as Gertrude Stein's was of seeming "childish." However, the question with Gertrude Stein was literary style; with Florine, it was perduring youth and its ageless discoveries of fresh pleasures and displeasures. Just because her poems are so diary-like, they are as acceptable for personal testimony as are her diaries themselves.

One of the artist's oldest and best friends, Carl Van Vechten, gave tongue to the legendary aspect of Florine's supposed dislike of purple by telling me that the lavender socks she bestowed on him in his portrait signified one of the few times she used the purple palette. But purple as purple, deeply saturated, appears oftener in her paintings than Van Vechten seems to remember. In fact, it seems to have appeared whenever Florine wished to do justice to the broad, bright palette of which she was so fond. After all, it might be insisted that purple is essential to the declension of the spectrum. An artist can use any color he wants, and frequently does. Florine, who was a sort of permanent Fauve once she really got started, took a ceaselessly naïve delight in color. Not that she imagined herself attached to a school or a movement; she would have been shocked to be included in one.

"Things mean their colors," she blandly pronounces in one of her poems. So far as purple itself was concerned, her distaste for it seemed to depend on what object bore it. It is curious, and I think meaningful, that one poem in her book is directed against a flower, the aster, though she loved flowers in general and particular. The title boldly declares she is thinking precisely of one species of flower—and how typical that in this poem she introduces a foreign word as though it were a mere colloquialism!

ASTERS

You degoute me
You tame
Purple
Pink
White
Asters—
Black beetles
Crawl
All over you—
When I step on one of your Shiny Bugs
And burst it open
It is full of you
You tame
Purple
Pink
White
Asters—

Color communicates itself and may even be parasitical: so the beetles are full of the aster series of colors. This identical series, we may notice, characterizes Herr Gott—Florine's first image of "plastic art." He has a *purple* gown, *pink* cheeks, a *white* beard:

a compromising triple combination from which, apparently, his golden crown could not rescue him. Perhaps God's essence became, for Florine, translatable into a color combination. Why not, indeed, just as *Mary's* color is *blue?*

A brilliant lavender suit is given Marcel Duchamp in Florine's painting, *Picnic at Bedford Hills* (1918). Florine was fond of Duchamp; it could not be that she gave him a purple hue because, like asters, he "disgusted" her; perhaps she gave it to him because he was a male and perhaps without realizing that this was why she did so. It is also true that when she was asked by the Theatre Guild to design sets for a play, she is said to have declined because she would have been required to include lilacs. Lilacs are purplish, pink-purple, or white. Florine loved white but preferred it, above all, with gold or red. Herr Gott had had a white beard and a golden crown. But he had also had, fatally, a purple gown and pink cheeks. Likes and dislikes work as much by dissociation as association. The "thing," the color-possessing object, could vanish in Florine's eyes and retain only a color-association, such as the purple-pink-white series.

THE ARTIST'S MOTHER, whom she loved and revered, is associated in a poem titled *And Things I Loved* with Veronese green and modulated tones of it as well as with lace flounces, shawls, and fichus, lace being typically black or white or in the natural yellow gamut. The sky in *Heat* (1919), which celebrates Mrs. Stettheimer's birthday, is a Veronese-like green, and the rest of the painting full of yellow and red. *Family Portrait No. 2* (1933), one of the artist's most important works, has a green fern and a huge, deep pink rose, but the primaries, with black and white, dominate it in force, purple being the only secondary absent. I suggest that purple is absent because the ultimately indissoluble family of the mother and three daughters—Carrie, Ettie, and Florine—represented a self-sufficient cult of females and so tended to exile purple, the particular secondary created by combining red and blue; that is, pink and blue being colors reserved to genders: "male" and "female." Hence, symbolically involved with red and blue was a "duality" (the two sexes) and a "oneness" (marriage), so that their fusion in purple made that color, in one sense, the color of marriage and, in the other, the androgynous color.

In the beginning were red, blue, and yellow—as "mystically"

irreducible as the individual himself! Playfully, Duchamp suggested to me that Florine liked the American flag because it has the red and white stripes of peppermint candy, but perhaps she grew fond of it because it was, like the Stettheimer sisters themselves, tripartite, being red, white, and blue. In reverse, Florine could have liked red, white, and blue because these are the colors of her country's flag. Ettie once remarked that the three sisters, in regard to their artistic labors, always worked "in single strictness," that is, without each other's help or advice.* Thus used, it was a peculiar phrase because customarily it applied to the state of being unmarried. If a Stettheimer could imply sex where it was not involved, she might fail to imply it where it was . . . Florine could have disliked the plastic image of Herr Gott (possibly serving as a pun for the English "Her God") because he wore purple, or she could have disliked purple because it was worn by Herr Gott. Florine's own god, to speak in the aesthetic idiom, was Apollo, and in a secondary sense Eros, beings strictly associated with Classical white and gold.

Another Mister in her poems is "Meister," explicitly her art teacher who, whether or not his beard was white, came "at noon . . . in white tie and tails" to look at her work and told her, "red vill last foreffer," something he said with more than the authority of a "Herr." Because red had this peculiar historic authority, it may have seemed to Florine the true, or anyway the acceptable, "male color." It is associated with Eros because of the heart and with life because of blood. Florine's painting reminiscent of youthful romances, *Love Flight of a Pink Candy Heart* (1930), held a benign red because the pink was on the orange rather than the lavender side. Red is certainly "royal" and signifies, according to the Meister's dictum above, a kind of immortality. In the same poem, Florine chooses it as the color with which to "paint the walls / for tout New York / on my return." She speaks in her poems of having had "art student days in New York" and it was there she returned to make her debut in the professional art world. Why to New York? Florine *was* an American and liked *being* an American.

However, when she wrote the poem last quoted, she was evi-

---

* *The Stettheimer Doll's House.* Introductory Foreword by Ettie Stettheimer. (Privately printed pamphlet, undated, on the occasion of presentation to the Museum of the City of New York.)

dently on one of the many visits she paid Europe, usually as an art tourist. Born in Rochester, New York, she lived in Berlin, Stuttgart, and Munich, and travelled abroad with her mother and sisters up to World War I because, as the legend has it, it was more economical for the family to have a home-base in Europe during the days of their reduced fortune after they had found themselves fatherless and husbandless. One is tempted to think that Florine, at some undisclosed date, chose George Washington, the Father of His Country, as a hero because she felt the need of a substitute male parent. She honored Washington with a white bust of his image, which reposed in a conspicuous corner of her studio, and dressed its vicinity in red and white, with touches of blue: red and blue, the pure, *primary* colors. Washington's statue in the Wall Street district appears all of metallic gold in her painting, *Cathedrals of Wall Street* (1939), where he is much the largest figure, and where the artist shows herself presenting him with a large bouquet. She never hesitated to spread red and gold as wide as she liked on her canvases. Red was a palette favorite, doubtless, partly owing to family tradition, one feature of which was, says an early diary, "our red parlor. . . ."

In the apotheosis of the family pictures, *Family Portrait No. 2,* the palette shown in Florine's hand holds spots of red and blue at one end, yellow at the other. The blue of sea and sky and of the outside margin of the rug, in this fantasy design, is probably a more or less deliberate recollection of what a poem about her Berlin schooldays terms "our parlor of tufted Nattier blue." The pattern of the rug is not obviously taken from any in her home at the time of the painting. Florine's procedure in coloring was naïvely whimsical, and in this same work she follows a logic of color rather than of image by allowing the blue-and-white design of the rug's outer margin to encroach, on the left side, onto the logical arc of its inner design of red and gold. In all probability, she had for this a consciously technical reason, but we may be allowed to comment that, while *blue* thus might push *red* aside, it was forbidden to fuse with it into *purple*.

A letter of the artist's to her then lawyer, Benjamin Tulka, dated September 22nd, 1914, and sent to the United States from Berne, Switzerland, reveals that the family was marooned there because the artist had "chosen a bad moment to become ill." She was ill enough to have consulted a will made two years before. On finding it "too fantastic," she had speedily changed it, leaving everything to her mother and her sisters, Carrie and Ettie, in a brief, handwritten statement which she enclosed (not having forgotten to have two persons witness it) and which she begged Tulka to make legal. As to what had impressed her as so "fantastic" in the previous will, it may have been (as will become dramatically clear) her desire to have all her pictures placed with her corpse in a mausoleum.

HAVING COME BACK home as soon as Florine recovered, the family of four found themselves pleased "to be riding for the first time in our own car in our own country." On the United States' entry into the war, their patriotism was duly stirred and soon thereafter Florine, with her two sisters and her mother, visited West Point to witness the Pershing Review, which proved so thrilling to the artist that she proceeded to commemorate it in a painting called by the name of that great military academy.

This work occasioned one of Florine's first uses of the palette in the service of family symbolism, of which much more was to come. The four Stettheimers, appearing several times as a party in this "narrative" picture, are individualized by each being dressed entirely in a different color. The mother is all in black while the three daughters are respectively in red-and-white, yellow, and blue. Cleverly, Florine preserved within this group—making a row in the nearest image on the ferryboat's deck—the patriotic series of colors and indicated as well the family capacity to exhaust the primary palette without help; keeping them distinct from one another was likewise an ingenious way of keeping them together. The "family frieze" was to become traditional in Florine's imagination and only the individual portrait and the large Conversation Piece would be able to compete with it. Florine's relation to the family was somewhat slackened when her brother, Walter, and her sister, Stella, both entered married life; Stella, the eldest daughter, had married in 1890 and settled in California.

Maybe Florine believed that George Washington was so extraordinary a man because he avoided the Imperial Purple, the sign of a tyrant, by fathering a democracy, whose national colors kept the palette cleanly, squarely "individual" by being primaries. Politically, Florine was always a liberal Democrat and consistently voted as one for Franklin D. Roosevelt. Lest, because of what

Portrait of My Teacher, Fraulein von Prieser, Stuttgart, painted in 1929,
oil on canvas.

Portrait of My Teacher, Fraulein von Prieser (detail), Florine Stettheimer as a child. With her brilliantly spare impressionism, the artist paints a mirror image of herself with a wide-eyed though composed and knowing look.

Florine Stettheimer in a costume she is seen wearing in her painting, *La Fête à Duchamp,* 1917. The setting may be Europe, more probably the United States, *circa* World War I.

Opposite: Portrait of Carrie Stettheimer. Photographer unidentified. She volunteered as a nurse in this country during World War I.

Left to right: Florine, Carrie and Ettie Stettheimer, circa World War I, photographic collage. The background is a commercial postcard of a view of landscape in Berne, Switzerland, where the Stettheimer sisters were staying when war broke out.

Coll. R. Kirk Askew, Jr.

future pages reveal, she be considered a snob, I must quote a straightforward passage from the diary she kept while visiting California with Ettie in 1936. It was not primarily to visit Stella or her family—Stella herself was then dead—but for the sake of Ettie's asthma that the two sisters made the trip. The fact was that immediately after Mrs. Stettheimer's death, Ettie, the youngest child, had become the "family invalid." This did not daunt Ettie's spirit, however, but seemed to quicken it.

Disappointed in Hollywood glamor despite the late Philip Moeller's efforts to make it interesting for them, the sisters soon removed to Palm Springs, the luxurious desert "oasis" where Ettie's health was expected to improve, and of course they stayed at "the best place": "Miller shoe salesman lunched here today," Florine wrote of it, "Ultra-violet ray assistant was playing kino in the lounge. Chauffeur who drives us [they had a private car for touring the vicinity] sits in the lounge. It's all the way it should be in a democracy."

Florine was as infinitely sensitive to the figurative "spectrum" of society as she was to the actual spectrum. Of course, like all artists, she knew that every painting contains its own spectrum and that the most deeply saturated of primaries is necessarily altered by contiguity with another color. Herself saturated with a certain social wit and irony, she knew how to be pure, and hence her personality-palette, so to speak, was never put off or greyed by contact with other hues of the social "spectrum." And yet she was not one for mixing actual colors; what came straight from the tube seemed to her quite good enough—as she said once: "the best you could buy."

THROUGHOUT FLORINE STETTHEIMER's life ran a pattern of primitiveness that is characteristic of people who decide to be themselves by resorting to immediateness: to cutting off much that has been acquired and in a sense "beginning over." Deprived of a father, Florine and her sisters might have looked logically to their brother Walter to be a substitute parent, but though he became successful in business on the West Coast, he had grown distant from the three "Eastern" Stettheimers, who represented the family's unmarrying branch. By astute advice from the legal firm of Alfred A. Cook, the fortune of the three sisters and their mother, though imperilled

Opposite: Portrait of Ettie Stettheimer by Arnold Genthe. The penetrating, pensive gaze, with hair drawn close to the brows, was characteristic of Ettie.

by the 1929 crash, survived and steadily increased through investments.

For Florine, personally, losing a father was a sign of destiny such as appears to saints in the sky, to kings in dreams, and to artists in their visions of the world—and perhaps locally in their palettes. Indelibly, it was a sign telling her that the artist's individuality is the same as self-creation. She did not need to be "told": she knew. After being trained in art according to school formulas, Florine cast much of it off, intuitively combining the rest of it with her own sense of invention, even with her own perversity. Maybe it was a "perversity" that prevented her resorting to medium in oil painting. Yet all so-called perversities have their origin in valid wishes.

If, for the distance beyond the green tree in *Picnic at Bedford Hills,* she used a full-sunlight Impressionist palette of prismatic pink-blue-lavender to show harvesters at work, she so far ignored this application of stylistic principle as to make the shadows of the tree, whose foliage is rendered in two tones of green, the same as the light green tone of the leaves. Though these "shadows" seem more transparent than the foliage itself, they are far from having the transparency of prismatic shadows falling on green grass. What happened was that, for the incident of the picnic in the foreground, she abandoned the prismatic as such and colored it much like a self-instructed school child. The grass is entirely a saturated yellow on the lemon side, and flat in tone except for slight modulations in rhythmic curves of dots and dashes. Despite strong local reds, the deep purple of Ettie's sunshade, faintly prismatic whites, and a black rug, the yellow grass occupies most of the painting, though it is challenged every inch of the way (or every foot of the true scale) by the figures set in its path around the quadrangle of the picnic cloth on the ground. Who would have dared such contrasts but Florine—or a school child? One recoils from the glare of the yellow grass, which isolates the varied colors and figures about it while it seems to imbed them non-atmospherically into a single substance.

Florine's art has eventually won a double reputation: she is a mere naïf whose interest is primarily as a social documentarist and she is an original of great charm, sophistication, and virtuosity: the present writer, as might be supposed, champions the latter view without stint. To the mystery of color vibrations, one's sensory and emotional response to them, Florine added the mystery of her personality, of whose projection her palette, of course, forms only a part and (in artistic terms) the less significant part. Her palette's daring, its challenge, its unexpected beauties and odd triumphs, are, so to speak, in being essential to the artist, minor to her art. So densely iconographic an art as hers has to be even more "primary" in imagery than in color, however much of primaries the latter may be composed. Remember that the fate of one secondary, purple, is bound up with a definite memory of Florine's; in fact, were it not for the "antithesis" that was purple, we would lack an important clue to the "synthesis" that was Florine.

art
amusement
rebirth

AN ARTIST LEAVES behind him various legends of unequal importance, one legend being Florine's aversion to purple, considered important enough by *The New Yorker* to mention anecdotally in a brief review of her posthumous one-man show at the Museum of Modern Art. It is, above all, the biographer's duty to assess all legends about his subject, great ones and small ones, and if I have begun with the purple-disliking one, it is because it is so closely related to the matter of ultimate parenthood and selfhood: a matter bearing on Florine's identity as individual and artist. Till now, no one has seriously attempted to evaluate her art as a whole or in any sense as a radical thing. This, in consequence, is another reason that origins are so important in discussing that art.

Ideally, Florine Stettheimer dealt with the whole palette as such, the sometime exclusion of purple being made on a "democratic" or liberal, rather than an "imperialistic" or inhibitive, basis. Yet no one can be an individual without prejudices, without those antitheses that reveal the eventual ideality of the synthesis. The red spectrum itself is full of shades, and as a henna or a burnt orange (such as that in the carpet of *Family Portrait No. 2*), red is not very far from the flame-red that frequently appears in Florine's work. The insidious thing about her palette was her fondness for whitening colors, as the grass in *Picnic at Bedford Hills* is a whitened, rather than a greened or greyed, yellow. The white was either an over-all base (as in Oriental painting) or a way (as in *Spring Sale* and the white dresses in *Picnic*) of turning red into almost pink. Where most artists using a wide palette would employ medium or mix colors to give total variety, Florine increasingly used white to key up her colors. A saturated purple, without white, is dark, as in the almost black pansy in Virgil Thomson's portrait, while a lavender, as in Van Vechten's socks and Duchamp's suit, is a whitened purple; a mauve, as in a male floorwalker's suit in *Spring Sale,* is a greyed purple while a fuchsia, as in the piano in *Music,* is a reddened purple. Her way of contrasting light grounds with figures, evident in *Spring Sale, Picnic, Music* and other works, recalls the obsessiveness of Oriental artists with playing rhythmic outlines against white or very light grounds. On the other hand, she had a startling way of blending figures *into* their grounds. See the high diver, poised for action, in *Lake Placid.*

What easily springs to mind, therefore, is that this artist thought not indirectly but directly of *color* as *light,* at first according to a medium-light Impressionistic prism (as in the front and rear views of the Stettheimers' André Brook residence) and then as color appears in fire, which under certain conditions exhibits the primary palette. Although the flesh-shading in the recumbent nude, *A Model* (circa 1915-16), is bluish, her hair is a pure nasturtium red, indeed the same color as the artist gave herself in her self-portrait with a palette, done about the same time as *A Model.* In the later flower pieces, Florine would return to the cool or bluish-white spectrum, but after *Family Portrait No. 1* (1915), flesh consistently appeared as a hot pink developing a gradual white highlight. White heat, as we know, is the intensest degree of heat and white light the intensest aspect of light: what is encountered by the eyes looking directly at an unclouded sun. Such a sun is seen in the artist's recumbent self-portrait (1923), where her eyes appear heavily lashed in bright red as though hair were an intensification of flesh-color and body-heat. Variations on a henna-red seem to have preoccupied Florine during her mature period in a way constantly to suggest flames. As we shall see, however, fire itself had its peculiar danger for her: a painter's colors indicate his relations with life in the way that a mirror shows a face.

In the mythological sense of the artist as fame-seeker, he is one who dares to give the sun look for look and to dwell in its ultimate blaze while always running the same risk as did Phaëton. It is the same blaze as that identified by Henry McBride in the most worldly legend about Florine. The Stettheimers, he said, were "unbothered by the white light of publicity that used to beat on kings but now beats only on newspaper personalities," and went on:

"They took no precaution to avoid public notice and on the other hand never courted it, and by not courting it, escaped it." *

Everyone who testified to me on this point confirmed Mc-Bride's view; indeed, opened his eyes and raised his voice a bit to proclaim Florine's indifference to publicity. The basis for this impression is without doubt genuine although partly, too, the result of writings about Florine, themselves influenced by the gradual determination on the artist's part to compensate for an early, severe shock of a professional nature. This was specifically her failure—when she became so bold, in 1916, as to make a bid for public success—to substantiate her belief that she had become an artist in her own right. She *had* become such an artist: she had *found,* that is, *created* herself . . . But the evidence had not had long enough to accumulate; or, to put it better, the world's response to the evidence was behindhand.

FLORINE STETTHEIMER WAS known to her friends as a maiden lady who painted as she pleased, and who wished to surround herself intimately with an elite from the world of culture. Socially, she enjoyed nothing better than entertaining artists and made no secret of her scheme of values or that she was morally and aesthetically dedicated to it. Yet there was another side to her attitude, a more strictly private one, and it was well developed by 1934 as something held in natural community with other artists. On April 7th of that year, "Virgil,** Maurice,*** and I," says her diary, "stopped at Salons of America being hung in the Rockefeller Forum to deposit Virgil's portrait and arrange for acceptance of Maurice's portrait of Virgil (publicity we hope)." Parentheses, one might remark, often shield the peacocks of one's pride. Six years following her first one-man show in 1916, she was enough acclimated to the milieu of publicity not to protest (at least to her diary, where it was noted as a matter of course) that Carl Van Vechten should have had her portrait of him placed in Brentano's window to advertise his current novel, *The Blind Bow-Boy* (1922), a fact of which the novelist duly apprised her by postcard.

Long before 1934, Florine had discovered that she was an

---

* Artists in the Drawing Room, by Henry McBride, *Town and Country:* December 1946.
** Virgil Thomson.
*** Maurice Grosser.

original, and that she would never compromise at being anything else. With characteristic consistency, the intimation that there were people who rated her pictures as less in value than she did became increasingly distasteful to her; thus, those who knew that she abhorred the idea of commercializing her art by getting a dealer and having him "push" her, also learned automatically the reason: her paintings were materially precious to her and she shuddered at the idea of their being in strange houses where they might languish for admirers. Hence a parasitic legend is attached to that of Florine's alleged coldness to publicity's white light: that of the technically morbid esteem in which she held her own works. But the time has come when "morbidness" cannot be too carefully inspected for signs of health—not to say, also, of genius.

Some of Florine's poems, read isolatedly or superficially, might give a false impression of standoffishness, bolstered by such a true enough legend as that she declined to have a show at the Galerie Charpentier in Paris (to which Henry McBride had made relevant overtures) because she would not entrust her paintings to anything so dangerous as an ocean voyage or endure so long a separation from them as a foreign show would entail. In this light, one cannot deny the genuineness of the moral note sounded by the following versified sentiment, replete as it is with well-known obsessions of Florine's:

THE UNLOVED PAINTING

I was pure white
You made a painted show-thing of me
You called me the real-thing
Your creation
No setting was too good for me
Silver—even gold
I needed gorgeous surroundings
You then sold me to another man

That she meant by the last line not "another man," but rather "a man," is indicated by Carl Van Vechten's story that she dreaded the idea of one of her paintings entering a strange house. "Suppose," she once told this friend with very genuine horror, "it were to hang in the bedroom of some man!" In the above poem is an explicit identification of the work with the self, as though a picture were an artist's bodily extension. To Florine, the self was virginal, and white was therefore its symbol. The setting of gold, symbolic of royalty and preciousness, was typical because of many gold decorations in her home and studio and the gold-leafed or -painted frames she was fond of designing for her paintings in alternation with white ones.

However, when we read the following frivolous bit of doggerel (like another visionary, Blake, she was not above writing doggerel), we hear a cynical laughter whose current may or may not seem, at sight, to run deep in the author:

ART IS SPELLED WITH A CAPITAL A

And capital also backs it
Ignorance also makes it sway
The chief thing is to make it pay
In a quite dizzy way
Hurrah—hurrah—

To stop and reflect on this, even out of context with Florine's life and works, is to be sure that she knew what it meant to grow "dizzy" about making art pay and what occurs in an artist's heart when his "Hurrah—hurrah—" greets a painting sold or a favorable review by an influential critic.

MANY FACTS INDICATE that Florine Stettheimer was far from reluctant to allow her paintings to be seen but that, as though out of pique, she would decline to sell them owing to the abiding fear that they would be undervalued. Finally, in responding to inquiries about prices, she assumed the practice of naming a sum so high that a would-be buyer was rebuffed. This type of subjective pride goes by the name of vanity, but in essence it may partake, as it did in Florine, of an impervious aristocracy of sentiment. As she was known to have money, it struck people as extraordinary that she spent nothing on self-promotion, neglecting through the years to hold regular one-man shows or to engage a dealer.

Consequently, there came into being the legend that she was a gilded (if undeniably gifted) amateur and that she cared for nothing but the amiably implicit admiration of fellow artists, whose affinity was as much with her, personally, as with her creative work. This social image of Florine was the anti-professional *persona,*

wrought by fatal circumstances in reflex-action to the more ordinary professional she had actually gestured toward being. Well,
destiny may be as impervious as some of its victims! But an artist
uses the imperviousness of destiny for his own ends, turning the
tables by victimizing destiny: Florine's rebuff by the art public was
to be dialectically absorbed by her into a leitmotif for her paintings.

The truth is that after coming back to the United States—an
event which caused Marcel Duchamp, who met her shortly afterwards, to say that she "discovered America" at this point of her
life—she was prevailed on to hold a one-man show through the
encouragement and suggestions of friends, among them Marie
Sterner (Albert Sterner's wife), who then worked for Knoedler's.
However, naturally timid and hypersensitive, she had placed a
technical obstacle in the way of her debut by stipulating that the
gallery holding her show would have to be redecorated according to
her ideas. While the artist would gladly finance this undertaking, a
gallery had to be found to welcome it. Wildenstein's was one gallery to refuse—a fact that could not have endeared the art world
to Florine. Appropriately, because Mrs. Sterner was a personal
friend of the artist's, the choice fell on Knoedler's, and so the stage
seemed set for Florine Stettheimer's successful debut.

The incidental theatrical metaphor is not, after all, by chance.
Florine planned a setting that would provide as little dislocative
violence as possible for objects (her pictures) which might have
been construed to have human feelings. In this, she resembled
Picasso, who said that to him his paintings are human beings. As
an instinctive primitive, Florine was a thoroughgoing animist and
would have pooh-poohed anything so coarse as the Pathetic Fal-
lacy. Whether or not it was known only to her friends, she was
planning her career not by halves, but a whole, and her first one-
man show would be such as to distinguish it from all others which
she, or anyone else, had ever seen. Her home was already known as
a consciously devised setting of luminously transparent white and
gold for paintings of flowers, figures, and flowers with figures; its
exquisiteness of effect was to suffer as little loss as might be
through transference to a commercial gallery. The walls would be
disguised to suggest the perspective *chez elle,* and in the midst of
white draped muslin the pictures, like actors, would take their
places as though they had not stirred from home. But Florine, a
wraithlike lady who seemed a bit shy even to very good friends, had

Heat, 1918, oil on canvas. Florine Stettheimer's icon for the family tradition of celebrating her mother's birthday, July 22nd; reading clockwise from bottom left: her sisters Ettie and Stella, Mrs. Stettheimer, her sister Carrie and herself. The pyramidal arrangement of the figures was both calculated and instinctive with this artist of many rare devices. *The Brooklyn Museum*

decided not to rely on the transformed walls alone. She would also effect a magical transference of Florinesque atmosphere by reproducing in the gallery the canopy over her bed, thus presenting her works in the atmosphere to which they were accustomed and in which they had been created: that of the boudoir!

Marie Sterner must have warned her gallery that the artist was very sensitive and idiosyncratic. They could have assumed as much when they had been informed of her plans. Even so, Florine Stettheimer entered Knoedler's shortly before the opening of her show, which had its *vernissage* on October 14th, 1916, without having become personally acquainted with the Knoedlers. Perhaps she herself had held back, allowing Mrs. Sterner to be her intermediary; in any case, she apparently stole in without previous announcement, for she reports in her diary getting so near Roland Knoedler (still unknown to her) that she overheard him pronounce her name while yet unaware of her presence.

One can imagine the trepidation of this artist on ground where her art was to be tested by the barbarously intent gaze of a public with which she was not at all acquainted, and of which she nurtured reasons to be suspicious! She found herself at Mr. Knoedler's elbow. She heard her own name! Her presence was discovered! She was introduced by a cousin, Professor Edwin Seligman, thanks to whom, she recorded that night in her diary, "at last the Knoedlers know who I am." She may have prolonged her strangeness to them deliberately. All the more, then, did it seem dramatic that Roland Knoedler should have her name on his lips at the moment she appeared. The dealer hastened to assure her that he had been saying her work was especially welcome to Knoedler's because the art world needed "more modern painting." This was the song Ulysses heard and bound himself hand and foot to escape answering!

Nevertheless, Florine was already committed. She was on the point of—as she prophetically wrote in her diary—"rehearsing," with the assistance of four men, the shaft of light to occupy the interior of the "transparent gilt-fringed canopy" that was a duplicate of the one over her bed. Her verse tells us that she loved "all tinsel things." As to fringe, she was a miracle-worker with it, gilt or beaded, using it even as a picture frame for her painting, *Music*, which for a while hung above her boudoir table.

Henry McBride's annals of the Stettheimers mention the care and ingenuity Florine spent on her studio and home-settings by remarking that interior decorators alone could appreciate the work and imagination that had gone into them. She was a true architect of atmosphere, if not at all an orthodox one, for she mixed styles in furniture and walls as she did styles in painting: at will. Correctly feeling that her own personal formula held everything together, she wished to avoid showing her pictures in too "public" and ordinary a setting. Hence, to Florine Stettheimer, the "first one-man show" meant a visual kind of chamber-opera in which a phantom monologist appeared in a fantasy bed surrounded by her paintings. The sheer truth was that the future designer of *Four Saints in Three Acts* had been practicing for it most of her life. . . .

Yet the present occasion, her "X," as Florine glibly termed it in her diary, had quite the opposite public reception from the phenomenal acclaim to be given *Four Saints* by the *cognoscenti*. The "rehearsal" had been—the gallery's deference was a fact—the paintings, although in darkness, were "hanging at Knoedler's" on the night before the *vernissage* . . . A shaft of light, like one from Heaven, now awaited only the pressure of a button to deliver them to the infinite mercy of art connoisseurs *en masse* . . . Florine felt something in her bones which her diary mysteriously, accurately expressed this way: "I am very unhappy and I don't think I deserve to be. I thought I might feel better after dinner but I have had dinner." It was a very personal way of admitting to herself that she had the "first night" jitters known to every actor after the last dress-rehearsal.

This state of feeling was sad and quiet, obstinately inward and private—like Florine whenever she was unjoyous. Instinctively, she grasped the seriousness of the occasion: Florine Stettheimer was showing the world the fruits of private labor and asking it to judge not the creator's love that had gone into them, but the naked fruits (or rather, flowers) as they might look in a museum. It had been out of fear of the public that the artist, so to speak, had stacked the museum, redecorated the gallery in a "private" style. The grandeur of the Borghese Gallery in Rome had once seemed to her part of the glamor of the art works it held. She would be another superbly half-recumbent Pauline Borghese: chaste as marble amidst marble—but diaphanous and warm where marble was dense and cold. Florine eminently succeeded in that much, but alas! it was *not* the point in New York's art world of 1916. Today, it might well prove a timely revelation . . .

THE STETTHEIMERS WERE family aristocrats and Florine was their chief in concentrating that aristocracy into artistic terms. Like titled nobility, aristocracy is assumed to carry its mark by real signs as well as by personal miens and acknowledged identities. Yet, at this moment, Florine must have felt all too much democratic community with that same artistic individual she termed in one of her nursery rhymes "young artist rat," who

> In a garret sat
> Caught in a trap . . .

Actually, she satirized in this nursery rhyme a sort of Modernism she disliked. But a great advantage which such a "rat" had over her (it must have occurred to her subconscious at this time) was his complete poverty of fame: he had nothing to lose. Florine—at least so she imagined—had her drawing room reputation to lose; not to "lose," really, she could hardly have imagined that, but to be tested in wider, really *universal* terms. In her home, the slightest, most nuanced of compliments were the informal currency of fame. In a commercial gallery, however transmuted, there was only one currency: selling—the satisfied desire to acquire through purchase that was to become a bogeyman in Florine's proud, self-possessive world.

Her diary says nothing of how the *vernissage* went off or who was there. Of course, her friends were there—possibly much the same group that appears in her picture, *Studio Party*—and some of the critics, but the latter she considered a threat rather than a reassurance. She was indulging herself in some first-class self-deception: she was pretending to be "at home" while displaying her wares in order to sell them. . . . Instantly, in terms of the legend, her friends surviving her today will protest: "But it didn't matter to her! Florine never *wished* to sell her paintings!" According to the above-mentioned will of 1914 and what her diary reveals, this was true only after 1916 and the commercial failure of her one-man show. For the will states that, while all the paintings and drawings are left to her family, "They may sell them if they wish, but I request them not to give any of them away." In simple fact, this was the reverse of the artist's final attitude toward the posthumous destiny of her works.

Carl Van Vechten, who says he constantly disagreed with all

the Stettheimers though it made no difference to their friendship for him, was one of Florine's confidants and he believes that she had a "grievance complex." One is tempted to furnish its origin through the following statement by the artist, of whose authority there can be no question. Nothing about her show, incidentally, nothing of what the reviewers said, or anyone said, appears in her diary. But an undated entry, apparently made soon after the *vernissage,* relates: "Only one person asked to see the price list."

She must have waited a few days, then, without inquiring about prospective purchasers. Was she lying in wait just in order to foil them? She probably visited the gallery every day to assure herself that her paintings looked as always, did not seem inconsolably out-of-place. The following entry looks like a magical way of tempting fate at a time when, to her certain knowledge, she had still sold nothing: "I am not selling much to my amazement." Then, before one knows it, the diary has been taken to the 30th of October, when the show had closed. With that blunt truthfulness and curtness possible only to diary-writing, she now recorded: "Sold nothing." Emotionally, this abrupt and minimal language is susceptible to our interpretation. But a certain dramatic rhythm is established by every diarist worthy of the name. . . . Those two unattractive words had come like the echo of the thud made by a curtain descending on a palpable flop.

THE STRANGEST PART about all this was that a potent defense-mechanism seems to have grown daily in Florine's breast from her deepest sensibility. A diary, of all literary forms, has a prejudiced viewpoint. It tells far from everything. Indeed, it is treacherous to both diarist and diary-reader: the latter especially should be on the alert. Florine's defense-mechanism was the very "leitmotif" which later found her consanguineous with the heroine of *Four Saints in Three Acts,* Theresa, and which can be described only as absolute joy: the "joy of temperament" rather than the "giddiness of fortune." It was the other aspect of every one-man show, the inevitable reaction behind the scenes of the artist's own nature. Florine confided to her diary that she was "amused" to have her "name up on Fifth Avenue," where Knoedler's was then located. This response, independent of any public reception, connotes an emotion without which it would be impossible to focus on the artist's view of her own genius, which was celebrated once and for all in her last work, *Cathedrals of Art*. In fact, where she wrote, with a seeming note of alarm, "I am not selling much to my amazement," it would not surprise anyone familiar with her life and ideas to read, as though by a slip, "amusement" rather than "amazement." That would be "so Florine"!

Years later, she was to consider it equally amusing that Julien Levy, a dealer eager to persuade her to have a second one-man show, should attribute to her a superiority-complex in just that term. At least, Levy identifies himself as the "J.S." to whom the poem recording the incident is dedicated on page 57 of her book, *Crystal Flowers;* he accounts for the error by assuming that Florine's handwritten "L" was transcribed as an "S." A grievance-complex is first cousin to a superiority-complex; grievance, indeed, is the form taken by those inferiority feelings successfully repressed by a superiority-complex. Florine was pleased by every simple, outward sign (such as having her name up before the public) that was an indirect acknowledgment of this fact. Ah! If only the coin of life could have had but one side! If only business were pleasure, if only fame could thrive without finance! *But it couldn't* . . . If only one could really have been, for instance, a Medici or a Sforza! But *that* was history . . . The objective failure of a superior-minded person naturally results in a superiority-complex, or cements one if it is already nascent. In failure, as in success, Florine temperamentally found humor rather than despair. Her professional's despair, worsted by her amateur's joy, became a mere grievance. After all, lack of recognition only emboldens a creative purpose, it never stunts it.

The sense in which, for Florine, *recreation* was identical with *creation* is exactly the sense in which her amusement was identical with her amazement. The universal element in so private an art as hers is expressed vividly by a poem in *Crystal Flowers*, quoted in the late Henry McBride's book on her and appropriately concluding her book of poems:

OUR PARTIES

Our Picnics
Our Banquets
Our Friends
Have at last a raison-d'être
Seen in color and design

It amuses me
To recreate them
To paint them

Florine's language, whether in diary, verse, or conversation, was so simple that it is always to be scrutinized for very particular inflections of meaning. The last two lines are apparently in apposition, but the noun-form, recreation, is almost identical with the noun-form, amusement, of the verb in the previous line; hence, *paint, amuse,* and *recreate* are in a series uniting them as benignly as *purple, pink,* and *white* are malignly united in *their* series. This almost ostentatiously versified statement posited form ("color and design") as the "raison-d'être" for life. Parties had come to be organized in Florine's life as subjects in the natural way that, on the stage, human situations immemorially have become theatre. In this respect, she was a highly professional artist like the novelists who cultivate society, as did Henry James, with the object of harvesting themes.

Whatever happened "on stage," Florine had a terrific "behind the scenes" confidence; at the same time, according to Ettie Stettheimer in a letter to Carl Sprinchorn, Florine found "the commercial and professional business behind-the-scenes abhorrent." Her confidence had been strengthened during the very weeks of the Knoedler show by her friendship with the dancer, Adolph Bolm, and his wife. Bolm (whose image she put in two of her pictures) had come to New York with the Russian Ballet, and was in the habit of asking Florine backstage to his dressing room, where she took it upon her zeal for art to advise him about his make-up in the ballet, *Sadko,* choreographed from a scene in Rimsky-Korsakov's opera of that name. To her great pleasure, she found, from a theatre seat one evening, that Bolm had altered his make-up according to her suggestion, and that as a result he "looked much handsomer."

Universally, it is in the theatre where one finds amusement, if nothing more. Florine staged herself; she was stage-minded. "Tout New York," whose walls she had planned to paint red while still economizing on living standards in Europe, wore, according to one of her poems, "make-up." New York was also where "sky towers had begun to grow," where "people sprouted like common weeds / And seemed unaware of accepted things / And did all sorts of unheard of things.'' The climax of the last three lines defines her encyclopaedic motif of amusement:

> And out of it grew an amusing thing
> Which I think is America having its fling
> And what I should like to do is to paint this thing.

She *painted* it.

UNFORTUNATELY, FLORINE'S LITTLE poems are not dated. Found stuck in odd places or hiding among correspondence, they were collected all at once by her sister, Ettie, and edited by Carl Van Vechten, who titled the book and its sections. Yet most of them clearly point to a cohesive phase of experience bridging the war years (1914-1918) and introducing Florine to her maturity. The blurred line between the bedroom-studio and the commercial gallery which had been ominously drawn at Knoedler's was already, when the above poem was written, establishing itself as both more and less than the line over which a vain lady painter, with ambiguous timidity, had proffered the public her flower pieces. Flower pieces there were and continued to be, and first-rate ones, too. But in the years immediately following her first one-man show, the tenor of *Family Portrait No. 1* (a beautifully arranged Conversation Piece) would expand into epic Conversation Pieces of both commercial and public-ritual character; into, in brief, the world as Florine's circus, theatre, and church, as well as her art salon and private fête.

The self-consciously frivolous surface of many of the little poems was probably meant less to beguile readers into will-o'-the-wisp fancy—in case the verse should ever find so remote a thing as a ''public''—than to so beguile the artist herself. Their key-emotion of amusement was an outgrowth of her introduction to a wartime and post-wartime America; it was part and parcel of that euphoria of the twenties which created the popular philosophies of speakeasies, flappers, jazz, and speed. These same customs of the time were celebrated by the artist in verse-lines as glib as any that might have appeared as a contemporary columnist's idle daydream; for example, these, rather redundantly titled *New York*:

At last grown young
with noise
and color
and light
and jazz
dance marathons and poultry shows
soulsavings and rodeos
gabfeasts and beauty contests
skytowers and bridal bowers
speakeasy bars and motor cars
columnists and movie stars

Considering a drawing-room as fastidious as Florine's, such a forthright verbal response to vulgar amusements was an exceedingly trivial aspect of her life even when it became articulate. She looked upon such things, and shared them, only as Marie Antoinette looked upon, and shared, the life of an actual milkmaid. As earnest about herself and her calling as any artist, Florine Stettheimer overlooked not the faintest irony of living in a society that was nothing if not multileveled, multifaceted, and multiindividualed. Her portraits, most of which came close together in the early twenties, show her loyal admiration for the Individual, revealed as supreme in his private domain above and beyond the "crowd."

ALL ART IS at once the most intimate self-confession and the most objective possible commentary on the world. But by no means is it valued at all times for just what it is: the organization of a whole and indivisible sensibility. Many frequenters of Florine Stettheimer's drawing-room were tempted to take their hostess as a talented woman whose chief talent, apparently, was "staging" herself; many friends who were really amused by her work doubtless avoided gauging its place in modern art and fell back on its sheer originality, just when its originality should have been the incentive for measuring it by universal standards. How little the artists and other celebrities who came to Florine's house suspected that, long before she induced herself to give her one-man show, she had been a close and critical observer of the commercial art world and its standard of value.

Proof of this is found in her diary of 1912 when she was in Paris. Assuredly, it is not easy to believe that the lady who would deliberately prevent the sale of her works by asking too much for

Studio Party (or *Soirée*), oil on canvas, painted by Florine after 1915, when the Stettheimer ladies were back in this country. It is the first Conversation Piece, an intimate Tribuna, of the élite company Florine Stettheimer gathered about her from New York City's art world. The grouped figures (reading from left to right) are as follows: Top left: Ettie Stettheimer, Maurice Sterne, Isabelle Lachaise; bottom left: Gaston Lachaise and Albert Gleizes; seated, center: Avery Hopwood and Leo Stein; above them: an uncertainly identified Hindu poet; far right, reading down, Mme. Albert Gleizes, Florine Stettheimer, and part of an unidentified figure. The visible paintings are by Florine; top left: the lower right of *Family Portrait No. 1;* top right: *A Model.*

Sunday Afternoon in the Country (detail). Preoccupied with painting, the artist seems to ignore the rose being offered her by the oddly self-involved Faun, who at close range is more a mischievous, flirting, very boyish young man than like Nijinsky, the dancer whom Florine so much admired when she saw him, in Paris in 1912, perform *The Afternoon of a Faun* and *The Spectre of the Rose*.

Opposite: *Sunday Afternoon in the Country,* 1917, oil on canvas. The setting is the estate occupied for many years by the Stettheimers as a summer residence, André Brook; the stream is seen running through the picture's center. The persons as groups are, reading down, top left: the dancer-poet Paul Thévénaz, doing a handstand for Marie Sterner; Ratan Devi playing a musical instrument while Adolph Bolm balances a parasol; Ettie Stettheimer supervising as Edward Steichen photographs Marcel Duchamp; center: Arnold Genthe and Mme. Adolph Bolm; Baroness de Meyer (under parasol) converses with Paul Reimers; seated (seen from the back) Baron de Meyer; top right: the artist, painting, an apparitional Faun seated by her; Paul Chalfin picking flowers; the Marquis de Buenavista (B. Alvarez) leaning against a tree; Alfred Seligsberg (arms crossed) and Carrie Stettheimer (back turned); Albert Sterner with an arm of the sculptor, Jo Davidson, across his shoulders; the artist's mother, playing Patience.

West Point, 1917, oil on canvas. The artist's tribute to her country's military youth.
The three Stettheimer sisters, with their mother, Mrs. Rosetta Walter Stettheimer,
are portrayed on the foredeck of the ferry taking them to the great military academy. As a story picture, it traces their progress by automobile and then on foot.

Sun, 1931, appeared in Florine Stettheimer's round of picture painting as a ritual tribute to family heraldry : a gesture toward a coat-of-arms. It is the painting whose sun was seen by the late Pavel Tchelitchew in a prophetic dream before meeting the artist (see main text).

Picnic at Bedford Hills, 1918, oil on canvas. A more intimate and romantic pleasure excursion of the Stettheimer sisters, taking place on the farm of the novelist, Rupert Hughes. Beginning left and reading clockwise: the artist, Ettie Stettheimer, Elie Nadelman, Carrie Stettheimer, Marcel Duchamp.

Lake Placid, 1919, oil on canvas. The family sought "vacations" even from
André Brook. Here Mrs. Stettheimer stands on the veranda; Florine
walks down the steps; the Marquis de Buenavista poses on the raft and Elie
Nadelman clings to it.

them could have written in cold black and white: "Cézanne's the kind that are swamping the market." It could not have been detachment, whatever it might have been, that she expressed in the fall of that year by this down-to-earth entry: "The picture market is crazier than ever. Knoedler [of all dealers!] bought a painting by a Regnault called *Salomé* and paid 500,000 francs for it. He bid against Les Amis du Louvre. I saw it at Knoedler's today. It is an abomination . . . They must be mad." This is to be called, so far as professionalism is concerned, hitting on all cylinders.

From the elevation and relative detachment of later experience, Florine would have disdained those very words as naïve, although she might have found it "amusing," when time had healed the wound dealt her by the Knoedler show, to reread them. She had secretly nurtured an illusion and then publicly exposed it; whereupon, it had been demolished. *That was that!* So she might have been moved to put it in her diary's curt colloquialism. But *what* was it? If the critics had been kind (only McBride of the *Sun* was), she might have borne not selling anything; if she had sold a lot, she might have compensated for the critical coolness. Actually, the experience was essential to the tragic clarity with which every true artist, however joyous, views the depths of life (which cannot be concealed from him) and endures the sight even as the saint endures the lowest image of his despair.

SOMETHING TELLS ME that Florine Stettheimer knew this as soon as the experience was old enough to assume distinct objectivity. The ensuing years could only make her cultivate its tragic pathos and its opportunities for lyric flights of illusion. Such things are like the hidden grandeurs of those diseases that carry, along with suddenly recurrent pains, suddenly recurrent ecstasies. Obscurely, behind the scenes of her one-man show, in the true boudoir where she was not only at home but could be deeply alone with herself, she had lain under the spotlight of self-revelation: the invisible white light which appears only in the darkness, after the light has been switched off, and falls straight on the soul, already opening to receive it. Long after 1916, the artist was inspired to write in her diary: "I am alone in my studio. I am lying between perfumed sheets. It is raining warm rain in Bryant Park." This has the tranquil, simple pathos of Japanese poetry. It is the exaltation of a sequestered being and yet is "perfumed" by inexpressible yearn-

Opposite: *New York 1918,* oil on canvas. While the artist's works were often reminiscences of persons and places, this painting was prompted by an immediate contemporary event: President Wilson's visit to the Peace Conference.   *Coll. Virgil Thomson*

ing. With nothing of the dramatic or sensational about it, the human situation it connotes is still one in which any thought or vision may burst upon the defenselessly supine consciousness.

The setting of this fleeting little passage is reminiscent of ritual and encloses the magic calm before the lightning of revelation. Surely, revelation did come to Florine like this: a revelation about which she was silent in direct terms except in her paintings, but these, like the works of all artists, would be a continual revelation. The message she received was extremely simple: her artistic destiny entailed a sacred marriage to Apollo. Several surrogates for the god of the arts (a hero in white and gold) would appear in her pictures. After all, had not her canopy at Knoedler's and the one over her bed, falling down from a peak, suggested the white veil worn alike by nuns and brides of the world? Canopies have an historic iconology; invariably, white canopies denote purity.

To Florine there came, we can speculate with reasonable certainty, a less overt conception of love that may have determined her whole attitude shortly after 1920. This was her friendship with Adolfo Best-Maugard, of whom she painted a portrait whose singular ingredients will be discussed later. This Mexican artist, the author of several books on design,* was the final influence on Florine's style, coming along as he did during its most crucial period. He was distinctly a method-teacher of art: one of the many to heed the pictorial postulate of Cubism by turning to the scientific method of drawing human—and indeed all—figures according to basic geometric, or at least analytical, means. He said that his books were intended for both very young and adult students, and their contents fully justified his claim. To all appearances, he had been influenced by the articulate mystical aspect of the new art (for example, Kandinsky's theories) and, like others, saw everywhere in nature the cosmic design that appears in the spiral universes of vast outer space.

What may have appealed to Florine about Best-Maugard's ideas, of which he talked to her when he visited New York, was their insidiously plain way of attaching grandiose spiritual ideas to simple pictorial ideas. Of movement, he said, ". . . instinctive and intuitive action . . . acts by itself and thus disturbs the great organic rhythms unless it be conditioned, controlled, harmonized

---

* The two most important are: *A Method of Creative Design,* Knopf, 1927, and *The Simplified Human Figure,* Knopf, 1936.

in its action by its 'divine spouse' which is LOVE.'' It is by no means irrelevant, in this regard, to notice the anticipation of that Divine Spouse that was to be part of Florine's future: St. Theresa's. It is a truism that the deepest artistic quest is imbued with saintly fervor. With so much mere studio experience behind her, the eloquent marriage between spirituality and technique as proclaimed by Best-Maugard must have carried great appeal for Florine's essentially simple, though highly susceptible, mind.

This was the mind which would think of George Washington not at all as would an historian but as an image of ideal paternal dignity, whose heraldic colors belonged to the primary palette, and whose white or gold, as well as painted, images represented a masculine kind of chastity corresponding to her own. It was also the mind that must have been influenced, from the beginning, by her friend Duchamp's growing contempt for professionalism in art. Later, we shall see how very attentive Florine was to Best-Maugard's technical postulates.

In 1916, her vital plastic imagination had not yet found the right formula for its flowering. But the very image of her bed-canopy, untenanted at Knoedler's, certainly suggested to Florine its status as an abstraction and the faculty of its interior light (joined to the whole palette) to create a kind of marriage which in essence, according to the classical heritage, was no other than an artist's marriage to his muse. The extent to which we can think of all this as a ''mystical'' experience may be a matter of doubt. The question could arise solely from a piece of evidence from Carl Sprinchorn, who recalls an ''explosive'' occasion on which Florine, tête-à-tête at dinner with him, attacked the so-called ''mystical'' attributes of art.

Now, how could she be opposed to those attributes and constantly indulge, in her work, in so fantastic a symbolism: one expressing so positive a spiritual insight? Just because I am about to forward this story by an evaluation of the element of white light in Florine Stettheimer's consciousness, her ''anti-mysticism'' must be dealt with once and for all. Though a rationalist, and even a hedonist, she never hesitated to accept the imagination and its works as the prime reality; otherwise, she could hardly have been an artist. But she had the hard sense of a craftsman who knows that artistic accomplishment depends on an imitation of tangible visions. It was as an artisan of the visionary, I take it, that Florine protested to Sprinchorn against the facile custom of praising and labelling an artist for "mysticism." It was a sure token of her sound technical training and sound creative outlook that she rose up to protest on this point.

True, as we shall see, Apollo was one of her favorite "men." But pagan gods were adapted to the mystical tradition: the sort of tradition that survives in painting and poetry as intuitions of ancient ritual and magic. In a way, this is the longest and deepest tradition. While Florine may secretly, and with good sense, have cavilled at mystical verbiage that was beside the point of painting, she could not have failed to connect its basic idealism with the basic idealism of spirit: with the magic that was "white light." As we shall also see, she was to be deeply involved with the undeniably mystical persons of *Four Saints in Three Acts* and she would freely use the conventions of supernaturalist painting.

For these reasons, the tremendous importance of white light in Florine's art reasserts itself in her biography as though she were pushing the button that illuminated the Knoedler show. If Best-Maugard's method and other factors, reviving in her memory, were to help her mould her mature style, still it was white light which would provide the luminous cocoons of her future vision. Following an artist's ritual rebirth, the necessary discoveries and rediscoveries are made because they are implicit in his ritual death, which merely initiated the whole process. Florine's return to the United States was a classical peripety: she would lose no time in *refinding* her artistic self after its shocking annihilation—that first one-man show—among the "sky towers and bridal bowers" of the Manhattan which she epitomized in her verse.

II *White Light in the Crucible*

UMAN BABY AND kitten are born with an amnion, the may-fly emerges from the nymph with its pellicle, the artist appears with his invisible caul: an aura that will visibilize
mayfly
follies beauty
flutterby
itself in many ways. If I have conceived Florine Stettheimer's life as beginning with a birth by trauma, a birth into the blinding white light of "publicity," it was to mark the ritual breaking of this caul. It was an act of violence in its way, but so is the severance of the navel cord an act of violence. By an act of violence, the gentle

amateur Florine had become the gentle professional. A *rite de passage* had been conceived by the inventor of a "transparent gilt-fringed canopy" resembling one given the Madonna by Fra Bartolommeo but coming closer in image to the frail, scalloped sort that typically adorned Victorian dressing tables.

Covering the eyes, Florine's caul acted as a medium, and thus in her recumbent self-portrait (1923), we find her eyes made up as for the stage, the lashes weighted with red mascara: eyes *to be seen* rather than *to see with*. Yet beneath this pair of eyes, faint but articulate, issues the illusion of a second pair: eyes still under a caul, eyes fixed simultaneously on all inward and outward things and penetrating to their secrets. Let us pause to fix our own eyes on two contingent factors: the curious resemblance between these echo-eyes and the way Marcel Duchamp painted, à la Cubiste, the eyes of the central figure in his *La Sonate* (1911) and those in several heads painted by Adolfo Best-Maugard to illustrate one of his books.

FLORINE STETTHEIMER WAS an art-trained student who decided at a certain point to be an original artist. This peculiar form of naïveté —an automatic borrowing that is paradoxically a phase of the student's when striking out on his own—has been placed by this artist unconsciously, yet perhaps more consciously than we know, as a symbol in her recumbent self-portrait. Duchamp and Best-Maugard, being painters, were spiritual surrogates for Apollo, and she had known both several years before her self-portrait's composition. Like Apollo, these men served as instructors whom Florine could heed without their being really aware of it.

Best-Maugard, in a section on eyes in his book on the human figure, included several heads, showing little talent for painting but illustrating the power of the human eyes to convey mutual understanding. "Anyone who has known the look of pure love," he wrote, "cannot fail to recognize it in the eyes of anyone attuned to that order of loving, the vibration of love being a super-personal vibration, transformed and sublimated, so that those who experience the vibration of super-personal love are exalted by it, are bound together by it: all feel the same love, the archetypal love, the only love."

Florine, of course, listened to the same ideas, conversationally expressed, long before they appeared in book form, and thus was moved to give her self-portrait its extraordinarily large and fixed eyes, eyes of a type she did not paint before 1920, but which she proceeded to give to Ettie and her mother as well as to other subjects of her portraits. Her own eyes were actually rather small, and this may be the reason not merely for the heavily mascara'd lashes of the portrait but also for the delineation of the eyeball through the flesh below the eye that was a Cubist device, and that conveys the illusion of another—or at least an *extended*—eye: which is only the "beauty" purpose of accenting the lashes themselves. Florine's conception of another "dimension" was apt to be naïvely additive, as in the third hand she put on the "cosmic clock" in the center of Duchamp's portrait, a device which the subject attributes to something he probably said to her about time as a "third dimension." Or is she referring to the stop-watch used in match chess? As a player, Duchamp would push the limit in deciding his next move. . . .

IN THE RECUMBENT self-portrait, Florine's eyes seem to stare at the beholder in a trance of "super-personal love." Yet this is but one dimension of her long, arabesque figure afloat in space on a couch. Above her hovers the image of a mayfly, the same as the insect mentioned in one of her poems:

> I broke the glistening spider web
> That held a lovely ephemere
> I freed its delicate legs and wings
> Of all the sticky untidy strings
> It stayed with me a whole summer's day
> Then it simply flew away——

The late Pavel Tchelitchew, who became a close friend of the artist, said that Florine considered herself an éphémère, "the transparent insect"—in his own words—"that is so translucent one can hardly see it. Art is ephemeral—all illusion—world is too." The mayfly was Florine's private *persona*, her *anima*,* which she projected

---

* I use Jung's concept of the *anima-persona* psychic dimension somewhat unorthodoxly here. Jung's idea of the *persona* is the individual's social mask, the side of him seen by the world, and his idea of the *anima*, and *animus*, the vague figure of opposite sex that haunts dreams and is identified with oneself. I have preferred to consider Florine's *animus* (orthodoxly her George Washington ideal) an *anima*, and her *persona* as essentially the self-image designed for the world's sight.

all the artist's figures. Yet, indelibly if illusively, it is both *Florine* and *Florine's* . . .

TO BE FOUND among her pictures, occasionally, is a more fantastic version of the mayfly, identifiable as such because of the long filament-like double tail, which is usually triple in the order of Ephemeridae. Florine sometimes called this mixture of butterfly and mayfly a dragonfly, such as the one designated as such in *Three Flowers and a Dragonfly* (1928). Zoölogically, it is least of all a dragonfly, for while it has a moth's or butterfly's wings, neither moth, butterfly, nor dragonfly has the mayfly's tails, which we see in this picture and on Florine's versions of it elsewhere. Possibly the double tail was her own translation of the tapering, baroque extremities of the lower wings of certain butterflies and moths, while the "dragonfly" was chosen as a name because of the glistening transparency of its wings.

In her poems, she tells of a frightening experience that may have had something to do with her naming her wingèd *anima* a "dragon":

THE 13TH OF OCTOBER

A black butterfly
with a long black shadow
was there
in my room
when I switched on the light
in the very middle
planted on my copper-colored carpet . . .
It was motionless
it looked permanent
it thrilled me
with horror . . .
In my chill terror I make a vow:
I shall do my room
in white and gold
and paint gay flowers
on the walls
and honey bees
and white butterflies
and the song of birds
and the sun's bright rays!

Is it possible that this poem was written on the eve of her one-man show in 1916, which opened on October 14th? But I fancy that it was written earlier and that Florine may have attached its significant title later. Here in any case, the mayfly, Florine, experienced an intimation of her mortality: an intimation that was prophetic in a sense as literal as these very words.

It was symmetrical with this that the dancer, Adolph Bolm, should ask the artist, on one of her visits to his dressing room, to "create a butterfly" for him, a request agreeable enough for her to record, yet apparently without consequence for the dancer himself. For Florine, it was otherwise; at some time, she invented her own name for her legendary insect: "flutterby." After the black butterfly incident, she had reason to celebrate the mournful implication of her nickname for éphémères. With strange fatality, the incident emerged in the very environment which she had invented to frustrate the baleful omen of the previous poem:

> I saw a flutterby die . . .
> It was on Easter Sunday morning
> in my white-and-gold bedroom
> overlooking the Tuileries gardens.
> It must have hidden away
> in a bunch of lilies
> out of which it limply fluttered
> to the high sunny balcony window
> and then swooned . . .
> I tried to revive it
> I sent Jeanne for the honey jar
> I sent Jeanne for the sugar bowl
> but the flutterby crawled
> over my sky-blue satin couvre-lit
> spread its yellow wings
> and did an unbeautiful act
> . . . It died . . .

The mythical implication of Easter Sunday and lilies, of course, is resurrection. Both black and yellow butterfly poems could have been written during the year Florine spent with Ettie in a Paris studio in 1912, when she followed the art market and discovered the dance art of Nijinsky and Bolm; that is, before everything had crystallized, in the United States, into paint. At times, such "mythical" happenings as in these two poems are invented; then again, they may have more than the pure validity of symbolism, which doubtless they have. The "sky-blue satin couvre-lit" was to be utilized in Virgil Thomson's portrait as a prelude to the devices for the sets in *Four Saints in Three Acts,* where one saw an elaborately, in fact literally, "draped" sky.

At all points in Florine's life there is the viable continuity of artifice, as though the world itself were an *objet d'art* and any reflection of it in a picture were a documentation of reality. The world, for her, was a "little theatre" in the way that a "still life" is the reduced image of an interior. Every solution of the painterly problem of space meant, for her, the building of an individual world. Not that nature suffered, or was meant to suffer, through such artifice. Florine had a Far Eastern view of nature, especially in the Japanese sense. Nature is with us not so much to be "improved" as to provide, by means of deliberate variation and refinement, a constant reflection of mankind.

FEW ARTISTS IN history have been so self-fixated as Florine, yet if we consider the number of people (and things) visible in her canvases, she tends only to be one of the crowd, or at best a prominent figure in a long Conversation Piece. According to Freud and others, the strict biological facts of birth have an importance never to be overlooked in the serious scrutiny of a life. But what if the parent be an artist, the child his art? We can then discern the facts only in terms of the art: the imagery of the self and the world projected by the artist. In *Cathedrals of Art,* Florine's last picture—left unfinished though she worked on it till six weeks before her death —we find the celebration of a communal birth: that of the new century's art portrayed in unassuming nakedness.

I say "the new century" as a matter of course, though this picture's date, 1942, is much closer to mid-century than to 1900. Presumably, there is a subtlety to the presence of Art as an infant aside from the mere chronological incidence. The object of intense spotlights directed by two shirt-sleeved photographers (one of them the late George Platt Lynes), Art lies on his stomach, engaged in work, at the foot of the grand staircase of the Metropolitan Museum, and appears again beyond the head of the staircase, and beribboned with a prize, being led inside by the Metropolitan's former director, Francis Henry Taylor. One day, just a decade after Florine's death, Robert Hale, Curator of American Painting, was to lead inside the very work containing this symbol.

Like all the *Cathedral* series, the *Art* is a combined inside and outside rather in the manner of an open-air theatre, for the candelabra on the outside staircase of the Metropolitan are most prominent. Representing Classic Art, high and central in the place of honor, is the image of a painting by Franz Hals, *Portrait of a Woman,* which I hazard somewhat resembles Mrs. Stettheimer, Florine's mother, when middle-aged. *Cathedrals of Art* is not Florine's chef-d'oeuvre, but it is of great interest because traceable in its elements and composition is the whole history of her life in art. It might never have been painted, however, had not Virgil Thomson met the artist at the right moment in 1929, when he had just completed his score of *Four Saints in Three Acts,* and told her that, should fate be so kind as to see the realization of his opera, *she* must do its sets and costumes.

Directly under the Hals portrait, old musical instruments are ranged beyond the dense column of light filtering down from one of the candelabra which hang in each of the three domed sections of the Metropolitan's main hall. This invocation of music, besides sounding an Apollonian note, seems a reminiscence of her own art's connection with Virgil Thomson's. If Florine had not had the actual technical problem of projecting her ideas in terms of the theatre, and beheld them living in the concrete three dimensions of the theatre, it seems possible that she would not have done some of her best pictures in the grand climax of the *Cathedrals*. The date of her audition of Thomson's score was March 27th, 1929; by then, it is unlikely that she had completed her first *Cathedral* subject, the *Broadway,* which commemorated America's, and her own, habit of going to the movies, and is dated 1929.

FOR MANY REASONS, the creative apotheosis of Florine Stettheimer's theatre sense seems predicated directly on Thomson's "annunciation." At both her studio and her home, the composer was enchanted with the atmosphere which Florine had engendered so objectively, not only with her paintings, but also with shining décors of crystalline and opaque whites, enlivened with original accents such as flowers of cellophane and metallic gold—all of which bespoke a fantastic and playfully naïve invention.

Having come to New York for some musical engagements,

Thomson had brought along the vocal and piano score of his opera. Carl Van Vechten then arranged an evening party at which he was to perform parts of the work and preceded the larger affair with a dinner, where, besides himself and his wife, Fania Marinoff, there were only Ettie Stettheimer and Virgil Thomson. The former quickly became interested in her dinner partner and also in his subsequent display of talent; hence, she lost no time in inviting him to a party at her home to meet her sisters and render his opera there. Florine, in turn, was impressed, and arranged for the composer to visit her again so that she might hear his work in seclusion and at length. Her diary contains a perfect account of how their spontaneous artistic accord ripened without delay: "Virgil Thomson played his whole opera, *Four Saints in Three Acts,* for me today. He sang the whole. He makes the words by Gertrude Stein come alive and flutter and in sound have a meaning. He wants me to do the visual part of the opera."

While diaries may or may not be written for posterity (as I strongly suspect they are), they certainly are as much *a posteriori* as any other account of past events. They are supposed, it is true, to come always on the heels of time and to still have the tenor of the present; to be ever young and growing. But in substance, a written version of anything, however unpretentiously embarked on, is a reflective matter just as art itself is. One therefore detects in the last sentence of the passage just quoted an inevitable understatement—a deliberate underplaying of an already "historic" emotion. After all, to Florine, the composer's professional invitation was like something too good to be true. Yet it was something that subjectively had already come true, for even at the moment she wrote, "He wants me to do the visual part," she must have seen in the back of her mind the canopy she had put into her one-man show ...

Ettie Stettheimer, in her introduction to *Crystal Flowers,* writes: "Florine was one of those fortunate beings who live in the present because they love the present. And she loved the present because she was always preoccupied with painting and she loved to paint." Florine understood the carry-over value, the wavelike rhythm, of every separate division of life. While she listened to Thomson sing, something in her "came alive" and "fluttered," and continued to flutter. Before it would flutter by, it would certainly (for genius was Florine's butterfly-net) be captured. The composer himself resembled one of the *putti* she later placed on either side of her canopied bed. He had a childlike freshness and at that very moment, in the interior life which Florine symbolized so prodigally in her pictures, he was a somewhat disguised surrogate for both Apollo and Eros. It is interesting that once, where the word "guises" was to be expected in connection with the costumes for her saints, Florine wrote "disguises."

stage-designer portraitist elegist

ABOUT THIS TIME, the artist confided to her diary worrisome periods of sterility when she was too exhausted or disturbed by daily affairs to paint. The following passage is from the 1928 diary, and the last part of its lament refers to the fact that, while Mrs. Stettheimer in these days had a nurse, the sisters arranged their time away from home so that at least one daughter was always with their mother: "This winter has worn me out very much. I look haggard and feel prostrated. I have had to watch time slip by while I sat in enforced idleness, when I could have painted, because of the equal division of time to be home with mother." It must have been the last of the year and so only about three months before *Four Saints* came into her life. Thus the opera announced itself as a major salvation for Florine—salvation being, for any artist, *inspiration.*

The project of doing something for the stage fitted exactly with her conception of art as necessarily a theatre of publicity, saturated *(like it or not!)* with an equally necessary white light. She loved white light for its own sake and, as her black butterfly poem could prove, she had conceived for it a sacred utility. The gold and white dominating the walls of the new studio home she took at the Beaux Arts, following her mother's death in 1935, formed a concrete metaphor for sun and air: they shut "in" as well as "out." At last, she actually lived where she worked, and could think of her life in that ultimate primitive way the artist has of establishing a real symbolic continuity between himself and the world.

Each of the sisters' bedrooms at the old mutual residence, the Alwyn Court, had expressed her own individuality, while the general living quarters there—though Florine's ideas tended to prevail—had had to express compromises of taste. Exchanging a typical one-room studio at the Beaux Arts (with tiny balcony) for a grand studio with two floors, Florine had space not only for a dining room and kitchen, but also for a boudoir as well as a bed-room. By means of festoons of lace, including drapes at its arched windows that overlooked the main salon downstairs, she induced the boudoir to carry out that universal transparency which seemed a law of its tenant's survival. Writing to her sisters on July 4th of 1938 (the tendency then was to write rather than phone) to let them know the state of her health, Florine said, "The air in my lace bedroom is much better for me. The sun helps."

Apparently, she slept in the boudoir across the hall from the salon-bedroom, where now the Alwyn Court bed was canopyless, and the spiral standards beside it wore plumes echoing the pink tarleton and cocoanut-fibre leaves of the palm trees she had conceived for *Four Saints in Three Acts*. As for the boudoir's all-white intimacy, its source was historic. White was a version of the fresco she had learned to admire in Italy and of the white underpainting —similar to Japanese *gofun* and the gouache grounds of Persian illumination—on which she founded her own pictures. Casein delighted her because it looks like fresco and is a chemical compound of milk, first becoming curd and then powder. "And now," she wrote in a poem, "it is pictures." That is: a conversion of nature into the artificiality she dearly loved in so many forms. For this conversion, her refrain—mimicking the "How vonterfool" of her Meister in white tie and tails—was "How wonderful . . . How wonderful . . ."

On the malign side, the recumbent self-portrait serves to betray its subject's consciousness of white light as also the flame fatally magnetizing the éphémère. Malignly, if not fatally, a white light had done just this when she had used it in her Knoedler show —"fame," she might have said in another poem, was almost the same as "flame," but she was to express the really serious aspects of herself, as always, in painting. Just what had happened in her one-man show? She had innocently transported technical effects that were poetic and pure in her home and studio, where they delighted her friends, into public terms that exposed their limitation only too painfully. The event had introduced a real twilight mood into her psychic life: a black mood that fluttered in and out of the white and gold.

CARRIE AND ETTIE Stettheimer could never be called, in any way, disloyal to their sister. But after the shadow cast on Florine's art by her public rebuff at the time of her one-man show, the artist's sisters were conscious of a vulnerable point in the family's worldly fame; Florine's impending collaboration, therefore, stimulated the critical spirit attested by Ettie's unrelenting gaze. When discussing the distant glamor, Ettie harped upon the "risk" it would entail. Implicitly, if Florine's décors for the opera were not a raving success, the family self-esteem would be considerably shaken up. Ettie hinted—we may suppose—that this collaboration would be seeking a rather leonine, if not vulgar, share of the world's glory . . . Was it not, in short, a rather too rash tempting of fate?

In all seriousness, Florine's family temperament could not remain wholly immune to these arguments, officially sanctioned as they were by Carrie. Not that this was the source of ambiguity in Florine's temptation. Ambiguity was rooted in her life by her dread of the myth that "white light" marked a fatal boundary-line between the art salon and the art gallery: between boudoir privacy and drawing-room publicity. Even as she discussed the question of collaboration with her sisters, she must have divined that Thomson and his opera were the precise magical formula required by white light to burst out of its old impasse . . . The simple moral motivation of Florine's professional reticence seems never to have been concretely identified.

As a woman of means, she wished not to seem to buy her way into the fame that was notoriety. Things are not, to be sure, put like this in articles for society magazines. But Florine's hard core of confidence in herself was not rendered justice by McBride's appellation of drawing-room artist. Florine knew *who* she was by 1916; thus, she also knew who she was while painting the Conversation Pieces—the town-and-country festivals—and when Virgil Thomson first sat down at her "Baroque" piano to perform *Four Saints;* for, by then, the early portraits were behind her . . . Still, the *world* did not know. And between the world and the artist there should exist a real, even if mystical, communication. Her pulse beat hard; she took sudden, nervous inhalations.

Then she must have called to the aid of her imagination the small triumphs and the large ambitions. Had she not, in a way, assumed the responsibility of her own prophetic visions? Such a trivial thing as her successful advice to Bolm about his makeup had helped sustain her faith in her gift for "theatre." And had she not vowed, in the casein poem, to paint the town red "for tout New

A corner of Florine's Alwyn Court bedroom; the Belvedere Apollo, seen on
the mantelpiece, is impersonated by a friend in her work, *Cathedrals of Art*.

Corner of the drawing-room with view of the foyer at Alwyn Court, town
apartment of the Stettheimers and their principal residence (after returning to this country) till Mrs. Stettheimer's death in 1935. On adjoining
walls: left, the artist's *Portrait of Our Nurse, Margaret Burgess;* right,
her portrait of her sister, Carrie.

Florine's bed at the Alwyn Court apartment: model for the one gracing
her show at Knoedler's; its gilt fringe was to supply a motif for her sets
for *Four Saints in Three Acts*.

Another view of the Stettheimers' drawing room at their Alwyn Court
apartment. It illustrates the life-scale of her paintings; from left to right:
*Portrait of Ettie; Family Portrait No. 1; Portrait of My Aunt, Caroline
Walter Stettheimer; Portrait of My Teacher, Fraulein von Prieser.*

York''? She could not rush recklessly ahead but neither could she leave everything suspended. The fact remained that ''publicity,'' in 1916, had more or less permanently invalided her. However, Thomson had no sooner departed for Europe in April, 1929, than Florine, feeling her fund of fantasy perfectly intact, embarked on a portrait of him. As if miraculously—in resuming her portrait manner of including printed names—there appeared on her canvas a ''St. Virgil,'' a ''St. Gertrude,'' and a most suggestively abbreviated ''Florine St.''

THIS SMALL VERTICAL work, an ecstasy of light and images associated with the opera and its authors, features the composer as its symbolic maestro and original performer. Finished during 1930, it was a new portrait in her already established style. But it had to wait till 1932 to be greeted by its subject on his return to the United States. At his first glimpse, Thomson urged the artist to begin without delay on the sets for *Four Saints* inasmuch as its production, then, was a virtual certainty. Florine's heart gave a great leap! How plain everything was ... Literally curtained with white light, draped with illuminated clouds, the horizons of her art were *opening out ...*

Beyond doubt, the *world might get to know.* And yet, aristocratic as she was, she was leisurely by instinct. Perhaps a little incredulous still, and in fear of Ettie's sibylline skepticism, she procrastinated by objecting to Thomson that her ideas on the subject had been exhausted. The composer, having a nature giving short shrift to procrastinators, amiably threw back at her the irresistible words: ''Then get some new ones!'' Before very long, Florine had made model sets and costumes for all three acts, including doll performers wearing just what she wanted, in material and cut, for the actual production; because, moreover, she held that painting as such was inadmissible to the theatre, everything in the models carried out the program of real textures she had invented: lace, feathers, gilt, gloss, transparency. Living textures suggested to Florine very particular forms. For her unproduced ballet, *Pocahontas,* she conceived projecting the desert as pink velvet.

WHILE VERY CHARMING, Thomson's portrait is probably not Florine's best. Yet its importance is paramount since it expresses, along with the ideas in the stage models, the leitmotif of the artist's maturity, which was to appear under various guises in the *Cathedral* series and to reach its apotheosis in *Cathedrals of Art*. It is a vision amid the clouds and conceives the theme of religious ecstasy as a sunburst of inner and outer light. As directly related to a saint's vision as was Gertrude Stein's original text, it shared Miss Stein's uniquely naïve-sophisticated sense of the material. But more than that, it utilized the convention of the concentrated burst of supernatural light which originally could have been suggested to Florine only by the religious painting with which she had been saturated in Europe, and features of which she had already made into personal symbols. Like the sudden but recurrent fragmentariness of a saint's insight, an artist's imagination flowers, as it were, in pieces of intuition. It operates all at once in works spaced years apart, and has an invisible organic life in space as well as eventuation in time. This essential process was tightening up in Florine.

Whenever she thought of Virgil Thomson, as she frequently did during this period, she automatically thought of an instrument of revelation. Carl Van Vechten's words concerning Florine's portraits are to the point here: "She was more interested in the atmosphere of feeling of the character (which she often reproduced with deadly accuracy and a kind of mystic acumen) than she was in actual physical values, although often her physical likenesses were striking." I would amend this to say that when, as often, her physical likenesses were striking, she had used the most economic possible means to define face and figure, and that this economy was a part of the "mystic acumen." Partly, too, Florine painted people according to a more or less consciously determined "type" derived sometimes from literal associations; the fact was that, less than a year before she met Thomson, she had painted the portrait of a priest, Father Hoff, her only portrait of a religious person. However, all Florine's portraits share the religious faculty directly rendered in the composer's portrait and known as divination: the grasp of the unseen in terms of the seen.

NO ONE, LEAST of all Thomson himself, discerns any resemblance of physical feature between the portrait and the subject. Though practically all Florine's subjects expressed forthright pleasure in what she reproduced of them, a number—among these Carl Van Vechten—have found in their portraits an emotion perhaps best to be described by converting a stock phrase: "Any physical resemblance between me and my portrait is delightfully coincidental." According to the artist's diary, Alfred Stieglitz (in whom she caught a highly expressive demeanor) and Joseph Hergesheimer (who offered her $500 for his) were distinctly charmed with theirs.

Some uncertainty exists as to whether any of Florine's subjects ever really "sat" for his portrait. If an early portrait of Marie Sterner (arranged somewhat like Degas' *Woman with Chrysanthemums*) looks as if the subject might have posed, the also early one of Avery Hopwood looks as though literally derived from a photograph. Florine asked her nephew, Walter Wanger, to pose for her on the eve of his leaving to serve in the Air Force during World War I, and her 1916 diary notes that Bolm had consented to pose; perhaps the result is in *Music,* where that dancer is seen as the Moor in *Petrouchka.* Again, she recorded an ambiguous incident in regard to Father Hoff, whom she asked to don his "vestments" prior to her visiting him with the object of doing his portrait. Later, she admitted, she worked from a photograph and some "data" about him, though one can only speculate as to what the data were.

Her rule was, or became, that the subject did not even know his portrait was being done. Henry McBride is the sole subject, to my knowledge, able to testify that he actually caught the artist jotting down his characteristics—in this instance, from an obscure corner of a room. Florine seems increasingly to have preferred studying her subjects, without their knowledge, as they looked and moved in life. This was probably part of the "unprofessional" atmosphere she had long decided to cultivate in her art. As we have seen, there were subtler reasons for the threatened absence of "professionalism" than might have been supposed.

Van Vechten, being jocular when remarking how Florine believed models were invented by men painters, implied her maidenly shyness of nudity between the sexes. But a little verse in *Crystal Flowers* hints that the desire to create a style of her own had as much to do with this view of "models" as did the sexual element:

MUST ONE HAVE MODELS

must one have models forever
nude ones
draped ones

costumed ones
"The Blue Hat"
"The Yellow Shawl"
"The Patent Leather Slippers"
Possibly men painters really
need them—they created them

Certainly, here, *female* models are assumed. But Florine's verse is like a breeze on which apocalyptic odors are borne. Men painters no more "created" women models than Adam did Eve or Pygmalion, Galatea, for it was Aphrodite who turned Galatea into a woman. But if we are to assume that somehow Florine meant a "play" on the legend of creation and that of the female model, she succeeded by using the word "need" in apposition to "create": Adam *needed* Eve; therefore the original human being was split to *create* her. The Pygmalion act of artificial creation only rehearsed this primordial "need," of which Florine, being a woman artist, was free . . .

A basic fact remains: Florine's portrait method was not dependent, ostensibly, on how closely she had wished, or been able, to observe her subject's physiognomy. A latent meaning resided in her indifference to literal features when it would please her to ignore or approximate them. This was nothing but the radical truth of ideality: the fact that an image may exist pictorially in terms of the emotion it creates as much as in terms of its literal physique. First of all, the visual center of personality, the head, had attracted in Florine's mind a halo of reverence some years before *Four Saints* presented itself. She had done a painting of Marcel Duchamp's head which vibrated with radiant light as though it were Christ's on Veronica's Veil, and even her subject's classical features seem idealized there as they do not in the artist's other— much more interesting—portrait of him. Since a sunburst-halo is found in *Music* about the whole body of Nijinsky (whose dancing had entranced Florine in Paris in 1912) a certain theatricality seems always to have inhered in her consciousness of this device. The point is especially pertinent if we think metaphorically of theatrical fame as a spotlight.

THE PORTRAITS AS such imply, therefore, what I may term a widened concept of the halo, which compasses a number of transfigured objects: things rendered symbolic or particularly meaningful. The visual mechanism common to saintly ecstasy and theatrical illusion was then merely crystallized in Florine's awareness by *Four Saints in Three Acts*. The opera furnished a most happy synthesis with a deep and lasting effect, cementing her art's instinctively religious tendency, its reverence for that light in which mystically every person may be presumed to live and carry about with him. Virgil Thomson, in his portrait, exists in a "Spain" which obviously is a dreamland or a saint's vision, and whose literal sign is a sunburst through clouds. For Florine, things could exist purely in terms of color, and she knew how much light enhances color. If objects such as the moon may have a recurrent nimbus (as suggested by the clock-face in the Duchamp portrait of 1923, which has a very large one) why not human beings also? Florine was intensely personal about people because she had a very particular vision of them related to their immediate surroundings. She made this discovery of method—by no means an original idea in painting—through her dramatically maturing response to everyday images. Life and all it contains becomes sacred by devotion to the things with which a person surrounds himself as her own paintings were rendered sacred by her devotion in keeping them near her.

Consequently the person—or better, the *persona*—was composed of décor as much as of himself. The *persona* was his second skin, like the pellicle which comprises the mayfly's sheer transparent coating when it emerges from the nymph. As the past, in the shape of memory, enters the *persona*'s scheme, part of the individual's halo is his thoughts, especially his memories. Hence it is exactly right, in Florine's method of painting portraits of her mother and her nurse, to have placed their memories of the small Stettheimers halo-like above their heads, varying the effect to suit the special subject's viewpoint.

Virgil Thomson's portrait, accordingly, furnished a vehicle for translating ideas in his opera into terms with which Florine was already familiar, and yet which now appeared fraught with new significance. The religious heart of her worship of white light stood, once and for all, revealed. Mundanely speaking, white light dazzles the eyes, creating a "veil" or obstacle on which, as it were, objects are transfigured into illusions or mere images. At the same time, such bright light has always meant a divine manifestation. As a mere optical experience, where the values of depth and solidity tend to be lost, it holds a possible rationale of painting: the art of two-dimensional representation. So, in this respect, Florine's artistic inspiration was dual: both technical and literary-mystical. These two elements were inevitably to pace each other in her work like partners in a duet.

THE 1923 PORTRAIT of "Duche" (as the sisters affectionately used to call Duchamp) is where the artist literally illustrates the mechanism of her portraiture as the projection of the *persona*. In its way a kind of Narcissus image, the *persona* is really not private but quite public since it is, as a supposed projection or extension, invisible. In the simplest terms, it is what one wishes to be: one's social *imago*. As the Stein-Thomson opera suggested to Florine a way of expanding to a larger dimension the theatre of life in which she was interested as a painter, so six years earlier, Marcel's own fantasy-self, Rrose Sélavy,* had suggested to her the individual-istic essence of the social world in which she was interested as a human being. Marcel is portrayed seated, one hand surreptitiously turning a crank elevating Rrose Sélavy (i.e., the rose that is life—"c'est la vie"), independently conceived by Florine as a kind of Harlequin, a pretty dancer-like young man, his tight garment all rose-color, sitting on a spiral spring that rises from a flower on the floor, and making an affected gesture as though explaining some-thing. That the Harlequin, as a handsome youth, has an erotic con-notation seems clear from a little poem called *Duche* in *Crystal Flowers,* identifiable with the portrait because of its first line: "A silver-tin spiral." For this image, the artist was indebted some-what, I imagine, to the "corkscrew arm" of Duchamp's own work, *Tu M'* (1918), and to the characteristic conceptions of his *Chocolate Grinder* and *Water Mill.* In any case, Florine's brief, mysteriously "surreal" verse concludes, "And ended the spinning spiral's / Love flight—"

Henry McBride believed that Florine could get any painterly effect she wanted, and in Duchamp's portrait she evidently wanted, because she got, an excellent and economic version of her subject's refined, dry classicality of feature. On the other hand, the *persona,* Rrose Sélavy, while bearing a family resemblance to Duchamp, is a member of that clan of pretty youths to which both Van Vechten and Thomson were indiscriminately made to belong. Perhaps the

* *View:* Marcel Duchamp Number (Series V, No. 1): p. 17.

former's face is not altogether "indiscriminately" so depicted. When Van Vechten sent Ronald Firbank (who had been delighted by the other novelist's praise of his books) a reproduction of his portrait, Firbank immediately cabled back: "You look like the Prince of Wales." I think this comparison, however justified, was merely the chance result of Florine's deliberate laxness in effecting a physical resemblance between her portrait and its subject. In the portrait, Van Vechten's face is very pink and suggests a flame. He is surrounded, like a saint in a Renaissance or Medieval painting, by things which symbolize his immediate interests in life (books, a cat, a typewriter). His seated posture, crossed arms with cigarette held in one dangling hand and legs crossed the opposite way, is much the same self-involved pose which Géricault gave his *Artist in His Studio,* and the latter pose, as Meyer Schapiro has pointed out, signified the new consciousness of individualism which matured in the nineteenth century.

Van Vechten says that some of the portrait's décors, such as the prominent, fringed black curtains, were never in his house but were contributed by the artist. Herein lies a layer of constant truth in portrait-painting: the artist's own subjective element. Such a method as Florine's partly has its roots in this layer. No painter ever signed his works more conspicuously—or more ingeniously—than did Florine Stettheimer. Her initials or name, whole or abbreviated, could be as large, if not as insistent, as a poster. In Van Vechten's portrait, her possessiveness toward the images of her creation is amusingly emphasized on the keys of the typewriter, which spell her whole name. One can think of her signature as a calling card, left as a matter of form . . . Florine, in fact, was always more sensitive to the rôle of décor than were her subjects, who were not in the habit of thinking of people in the same consistent way as she did; hence, when they came within her aura, they acquired a little of it, like chameleons, and appeared thus transformed in her portraits of them.

FLORINE STETTHEIMER, for more than one reason, may not be considered an orthodox mystic. Yet her fantasy-method invites such an interpretation. Thomson's portrait follows this principle much more than does Van Vechten's. Here is the composer at the transfigured moment of interpreting Gertrude Stein's text in Florine's own home, with its décor of luminous drapes. The sky is formalized

tachings, so, for the production of the opera, the artificial images of two chained lions appeared on either side of the arch representing the Cathedral. These were in no sense meant to look like their sculptured originals but looked like—indeed *were*—stuffed, toy lions; in other words, scaled-up models of those Florine had made for the model sets.

THOUGH THERE SEEMS to be no written or oral evidence to this effect, Florine's conception of the *Cathedral* series must have arisen from *Four Saints in Three Acts,* for it was there, in the implicit contrast between timeless ecstasy and limited dailiness, the "theatre" of the artist and the "world" of ordinary men, that she precisely isolated the area of tension between her art and the implicit size of its audience. What was the Cathedral at Avila but a material tribute to the virtuosity, as to the virtue, of a great saint? Well, such was the Metropolitan Museum in New York, whose lights everywhere could initiate all eyes into the high, imperishable values of Classic Art. Florine regarded the Commère in *Four Saints* as a perfectly legitimate medium between the audience and the operatic spectacle; in her sight, as I have said, Thomson himself was the opera's original Compère, since he had illuminated its text and basically interpreted it to her and the public alike. Ultimately, Florine felt that she could be to the Metropolitan, and indeed to the whole New York art world, what the composer had been to the esoteric twentieth-century text of Gertrude Stein, dedicated as that text was to celebrating phases of "classic" religious inspiration.

In her last work, standing in the foreground at the left, a figure emphatically greater than anyone else in the painting except her partner opposite, Florine depicts herself as the Commère of the art world. In one way so "artful," she had a saint's naïve directness and simplicity in what basically mattered to her. Only in part is Florine here the society woman who sat in a box on the stage in *Four Saints* and reacted amusingly to the performance. Now she is a sublimated Commère, this same woman but with a vision as inspired as a saint's, and the art world we see is only her vision. She is like the donors in the great altarpieces, giving that rôle an intrinsic value by being also the executive, the artist, as well as like the nobility once privileged to share the stage-space with the actors. This was a conception that Florine took the last decade of her life to achieve, but that she did achieve it would be perfectly clear even had we only the white-and-gold canopy about her to tell us how she imagines herself in her last painting. This is the same "transparent gilt-fringed canopy" described in her own words as having been installed at a "rehearsal" at Knoedler's twenty-six years before! It was also the same as the one she had assigned about twelve years before to the two Theresas as an emblem of their sacred distinction and royal privacy. Indeed, as Gertrude Stein literally put it: "Saint Therese has been a queen . . ."

This canopy is only consistent with Florine's portrait theory of the widened, metaphoric halo, surmounted here with two wittily gilded, lily-like flowers as the known insignia of supreme chastity. If there is comic greatness in Gertrude Stein's words and Virgil Thomson's music—as I think no connoisseur doubts—there is comic greatness too in this vaporous image, a masterpiece of Impressionism, which Florine created of herself in *Cathedrals of Art*. Her phantomlike little hands raised in wonder charged with mockery, she stands feather-poised in the white-pink magic light inside the canopy, a bouquet of flowers not in her arms, but magnetized to her side, hanging from which are three bleeding hearts representing herself and her sisters. On her face, lighter than light, is a look somewhere between philosophic amusement and naïve ecstasy . . .

Throughout the history of *Four Saints in Three Acts,* as unique an event in the American theatre as it has ever had, Florine was perpetually hesitant yet deeply engrossed—hesitant, because still afraid of the guardians of worldly success; engrossed, because she felt the insuperableness of will dwelling in every artist, and had found at last a unique instrument for it. What at once encouraged and dismayed her was the coöperativeness involved in this very instrument; she was at work on it with other artists, and therefore was testing herself as part of a larger world rather than as a little world in herself: that drawing-room world in which people such as Henry McBride viewed her. McBride, in his invaluable little book on Florine Stettheimer (issued for her retrospective show)* gives us the most vivid impression of the sort of social-artistic event the première of *Four Saints* was. But he lacked the advantage of having the artist's private angle on this heroic incident. Moreover, he falls into error, on page 3 of his book, by saying that Florine was not in the least "difficult" as a collaborator; no

* *Florine Stettheimer,* by Henry McBride. The Museum of Modern Art, 1946.

doubt, she was a lady through it all, but she was not, through it all, agreeable.

VIRGIL THOMSON ASSERTS that Florine, pursuing her part in the opera, taught the theatre professionals a revolutionary lesson in lighting. The experienced Feder, who undertook the lighting end, held the usual view that "white light" is attained in the theatre by combining colored lights, but Florine believed that this formula produced a "*greyish*-white" light. Her opinion prevailed only by her own insistence, with the result that Feder used actually white lights everywhere, even for the "foots." As it turned out, the brilliance of inundating the theatre-dark with a "white" vision of the stage (the curtains already having been opened) contributed much to the universal success earned by the opera with elite theatre-goers. Even the Broadway critics found more to praise in the sets and the colorful costumes than in the opera as such, which they found uncommunicative. As a publicity-success, however, *Four Saints* can be rated as a record-breaker. The late A. Everett Austin, Jr., was able to compile two tremendous scrapbooks of its *succès-d'estime*, scrapbooks whose contents connoted not so much the *estime* as the *succès*.

To anyone looking for the record in Florine's diary, the première in Hartford at the Wadsworth Atheneum on February 7th, 1934, would seem a flat anti-climax. Her relevant entry, dated weeks after the event, explains that she had forgotten in the fever of the occasion to take along her diary, and like every good diarist, she declined to try to reconstruct her spontaneous impressions. All she would note was: "It was frightfully cold and my radiator made a noise." One suspects, however, psychological forgetfulness, and perhaps a reluctance, even weeks later, to consciously put down thoughts that must still have been fluid and dazed by so overwhelming, authentic a dose of publicity. Indeed, her diary was not all that she forgot that night!

Caught in an all too physical white light of fame was the true crisis of the artist's worldly career. At the most hectic moment, Florine could have made no mistake about that. Taking her inevitable stage bow—from which she shrank even as it was dictated to her feet—only that crisis and its outcome could have been in her mind; she was not, at all events, thinking of the long white gloves which she had brought with her, but somehow forgotten to wear

. . . The little family scandal created by this defection of apparel at her theatrical debut was a repercussion of the great critical interest which Carrie and Ettie had taken in their sister's audacious project. At home, it had been decided that gloves were *de rigueur* since, of course, the intense glamor of that moment of public recognition had been meditated far in advance by all three. Yet, for reasons that must be the subject of speculation, neither sister had accompanied Florine on her epic journey to Hartford.

The weather—as the artist recorded—was most inclement; moreover, it was the custom of at least one daughter to remain home with their mother regardless of the occasion's urgency. Perhaps, in mutual modesty, both Carrie and Ettie had wished to withdraw, and hence it fell out that neither of them would be so selfish as to go. The Stettheimers were given to notable personal independence as well as to inviolable clan feeling. In any case, Florine appeared alone for the Hartford première as if in symbolic assertion of her debut as a professional artist. In fact, her foray into professionalism had injured the devout "amateurism" of both Carrie and Ettie although, some years previously, the latter had published two commercially distributed novels. A novelist, Ettie could reason, did not thrust her person before the public—at least not according to Ettie's private code—whereas Florine, as a "theatre artist," was not only risking drastic failure with this opera, but also encountering her dubious fate before an immediate and visible public: the audience.

Perhaps Carrie and Ettie remembered only too well Florine's reaction to the humiliating fate of her one-man show at Knoedler's, a reaction which the artist doubtless had striven to conceal but which two such attuned sisters may well have guessed correctly. Ettie's novels had been reviewed in warm and superlative terms by a couple of critic friends,* but in their general reception there had been no hint of the acclaim—or the abuse—which a *theatrical* venture might earn. Was there a modicum of human, all too human, jealousy in the bosom of even an adoring sister? If so, it may explain why some people believe Ettie failed even to attend the first night of *Four Saints* on Broadway. Henry McBride recalled sitting in a box at that première with Florine and Carrie, but not with Ettie. Frank Crowninshield, McBride said, visited Florine's box, when the first act closed, to present her with his fervid compliments

* See *The Memorial Volume of and by Ettie Stettheimer.*

and never returned to his own, adjoining, box. As the curtain came down on the last act, when the opera's triumph was assured, Mc-Bride recollected that Carl Van Vechten, who sat in the first row of the orchestra, arose and joined the plaudits by shouting: "Hurray for Florine!"

It was a curiously significant bravo. At that moment, Florine herself—no longer afraid of being "young artist rat"—knew what it was to make art "pay," as her jingle had put it, "in a quite dizzy way." The fact was that her dizziness in forgetting to wear gloves at Hartford had cost her Ettie's dogmatic rebuke. At the postmortem in New York, despite Florine's confession and contrition, Ettie could not refrain from emphasizing her horror of those gloveless arms as her sister had bowed: "It was inelegant . . . It was *inelegant*!" Carrie's emotion, less aroused, permitted her only a gentle echo of the ineluctible word, which in Ettie's mouth had a bite to it. But Florine, standing before the family tribunal, was in secret so infinitely pleased that she had to urge her perverse conscience to quail a little . . . Not to have worn gloves: it *was* inelegant! . . .

IN REBOUND, TOO, she must have been very tired on her return from Hartford: *her* part in the whole affair was over. The theatre's physical eventfulness, as valiantly as she had stood up under it, had taken more out of her spiritually than physically. Notoriously the theatre is a cruel place, a place like a railroad station, where schedules have the aura, however exaggerated, of fate. Curtains and cues may be tyrannical; they are less so than the constant pressure of overtime rehearsals. It is true that Florine was not intimately involved with the staging, yet the peripheral matters of sets and costumes, radical to the production's final state, may entail just as much gnashing of teeth and tearful aftermaths. To tried theatre artists, so much was only the order of the day; to Florine, all this was fraught with a unique fate.

About this production, sponsored by so esoteric a musical organization as the Friends and Enemies of Modern Music, there was naturally a special esprit-de-corps. But human amity, and the mutual respect in which superior artists hold one another, may not be enough to prevent the strain that alienates and destroys. The late A. Everett Austin, Jr., who appears in the costume of Hamlet in *Cathedrals of Art* and who headed the sponsoring musical organization, would have spared Florine her personal trials if he possibly could have. But following the conclusion of arrangements in 1932 to produce the opera at the opening of the Avery Memorial Theatre in the Wadsworth Atheneum (of which Austin was then director), a whole production corps had been organized by the opera's director, John Houseman. This included, of course, some-one to execute the sets and costumes: Florine's surrogate on the life-sized stage. This was the experienced Kate Drain Lawson.

With the traditional bitterness of balked artists, Florine, when all was done, complained of the inadequate realization of her ideas. In his own defense, Houseman responded that her ideas had been 90 per cent realized, a statement which, if true, stands for a high average in such theatrical fortunes. Though she may not have told anyone so, this mathematical judgment must have seemed to Florine only an impertinence. Art implies perfection, the lack of which, for an artist in work by his own hand, may be a source of endless torment and self-accusation. One by one, Florine made zero-hour discoveries of minor or major changes of materials or properties that had been taken for granted as settled. Things slipped by her, furthermore, because she had witnessed none of the final rehearsals in Hartford. She had had to struggle all along, and had convinced the technical staff by some of her arguments as other arguments had failed to alter their professional ex-cathedras.

WHEN SHE GOT to Hartford, the first disaster noticed by the scenic artist, during the performance, was that the male companions of the angels had their trains "wrapped around their bodies instead of hanging" and thus had "no style"; the second, that the novices' trains, in the Second Act, had been "snipped." Florine had arrived in time to avert the major disgrace of "flowers from the five-and-ten in Act 4"*—she must have walked in during the latter half of the final rehearsal. Later, she made a list of her grievances about *Four Saints* and wrote of that floral crisis in the Fourth Act: "I had to make them myself of cellophane." In fact, she had to speed to the same "five-and-ten," probably, to procure the means of making flowers of the kind with which her own home was decorated

---

* As auditors should recall, the opera contains many more saints than the four in the title; also it has more than three acts. Act IV, a brief epilogue, takes place in Heaven and is attached to Act III by an *intermezzo.*

and even someone's car or a taxi could not wholly have protected her, in those circumstances, from the "frightful cold."

Some of the tragic omissions which spotted the Hartford production were rectified in subsequent performances, but Florine elected to list them as though they were instances of Original Sin: i.e., wrist-length gloves for the St. Theresas; the sun and the star-fence in Act II; the chorus in the sky; and a "red velvet runner up the steps of the throne." She could hardly have forgiven this omission of the royal color. It had been tried, but because it was in the form of a carpet, the actors tripped over it and it had been withdrawn. In this concern with perfection of detail and surface, of course, Florine was exercising only an artist's normal care.

It is said that Kate Drain Lawson, her surrogate on stage, labored heroically and with inexhaustible cheer to satisfy all the designer's requirements. But Mrs. Lawson's viewpoint, admittedly, found no sympathetic echo in Florine's possessed mind—at least not in the heat of the worst moments of revelation. To the artist's horror, she also discovered on the Atheneum stage "nasty dirty green leaves" in a flower garland and—worst of all!—a "silvered purplish fan" in the hand of a saint. Those knowing the inward history of her reasons for resenting purple (at least where she thought it did not belong) will be relieved to hear that she got rid of the purplish fan by substituting a white one.

Florine had been pleased with the scenarist Maurice Grosser's idea of mounting the opera as a parody of Sunday School entertainments and yet her criticism of his devices ultimately gave them a less mechanical function. In advance, she had been reconciled to only one defeat in her original plans, which she naïvely imagined had been crystallized once and for all in her model sets. Feder's professional wisdom had convinced her that the globes of glass meant to compose the great double arch would not light properly, and therefore balls of compressed cellophane had been substituted for them. The vigilant wraith that haunted the outskirts of the stage ruled over by Houseman and Feder, for once, was placated. The word "cellophane" in another's mouth must have produced immediate calm in this wraith and paved the way for the substitution of Feder's fact for her fancy. Anyway, her eyes had rested with contentment on the beaded-glass chairs in which the two dusky St. Theresas regally sat.

To set off the one major defeat, there had been a more than

major victory: the great cellophane cyclorama. Here Florine's strategic triumph virtually decided the fate of the production. It had been argued that cellophane would dazzle the audience and it would be impossible for them to see the singers' expressions. But Florine instinctively knew better about both human and saintly vision: "dazzle" can be relative and its after-images all the more potent and significant. Only because she insisted on the cellophane cyclorama, there it was, and remained, in all its halcyon glory. As Philip Moeller (who should, indeed, have known) said of the opera: "The most beautiful thing I ever saw in the theatre."

The sky-blue cyclorama had been only one of the original ideas on which Florine, the "undifficult," had had to insist. For the list is not even yet exhausted. . . . Someone had wanted to paint rather than drape the seats for the chorus. "I had to insist," Florine noted in the list of grievances. Someone had obstinately opposed the pyramid formations of the chorus. "I had to insist," she wrote for the fourth or fifth time. Maybe she had not had to insist, during the New York preparations, on the curtain supposed to hang inside the arch in one scene, but at the Wadsworth Atheneum, the arch nevertheless appeared without it. To be sure, she won back this round when the production came to New York, as the photographs taken there prove of this and other points of her account. The only photographs of the Hartford première were candid shots of the performance. Some of these were taken by Harry Bull (who was to become editor of the magazine for which he then worked, *Town and Country*) and a group was reproduced in McBride's previously mentioned article on the Stettheimers: *Artists in the Drawing Room.*

Florine's personal record was continued in another place, where it appears as evanescent as the flick of a dove's wing: the face of the Commère in *Cathedrals of Art*. There, in the simple cuneiform of which she was mistress, we see the inner expression of the dismayed stage-designer present in the Avery Memorial Theatre for the opera's première. Behind the mask of suppressed annoyance, even then, lived the joyful certainty, the serene irony, and the immaculate triumph that later were to be a *painted* rather than a *statistical* truth. Granted: she was overjoyed at the first high flush of that success in Hartford. Who wouldn't have been at all those waves of applause? *But that was it!* A success of that kind was so spasmodic; it duly disappeared into warehouses with the

Knoedler's Art Gallery, pre-World War I, then on Fifth Ave. and in festive garb. Florine Stettheimer's first one-man show took place here. *Courtesy M. Knoedler and Co.*

Portrait of Henry McBride, by Carl Van Vechten, 1933. McBride could recall being the first connoisseur to salute the value of Florine Stettheimer's art; he wrote up the Knoedler show as critic of the New York *Sun*. Cupids and fleurs-de-lys adorned the façade of the Alwyn Court apartments at Seventh Ave. and 58th Street, where Florine entertained the Mexican artist, Adolfo Best-Maugard, whose portrait she painted. Shown opposite, he holds, as though a flower, Florine's fanciful conception of the seven basic forms which, according to his teaching, govern pictorial art. Her work was influenced by his concepts and her portrait of him shows him tethered to his native land as Aubrey Beardsley tethered himself to Pan in his well-known self-portrait, below.

To Adolfo Best-Maugard

Portrait of Florine Stettheimer, around 1925, charcoal. Originally un-
signed by Marcel Duchamp, it bore only Florine's inscription (seen faintly
in pencil and quoted in the main text) till acquired by Virgil Thomson in
1952, when Duchamp signed and inscribed it.

breathlessly. "It was nothing like the original production . . . The cyclorama was there, but you are right—it wasn't cellophane. There was the singing, of course, but . . . but especially the ballet! Frederick Ashton, a very great choreographer, created the original ballet for very young dancers, who were charming. They kept getting under foot, you know—like children . . . delightful! . . . But the dancers in this new ballet!" The critic—who then looked remarkably like Florine's conventional image of him in his portrait—lifted eyes veritably expressing the despair of a fifth saint, and suddenly dropped his voice. . . .

TIME IS A FLASHBACK. Florine still had a great deal to paint. It was only 1934, and at the very moment, *Four Saints* was creating a tiny, if quite original, chapter in the history of the Broadway theatre. But the theatre as such, though the artist may not have known it, was behind her. Only *Cathedrals of Broadway* and *Cathedrals of Fifth Avenue* had been achieved; *Cathedrals of Wall Street* and *Cathedrals of Art* were still to come. Theatre, Fashion, Money, Art—that was the social cycle of *mondain* New York, eminently urban, eminently recognizable, and also it was the last phase of a major artist, as yet herself unrecognized save by the fortunate few . . . The mayfly: the *anima*? It was still fluttering in the unseen private dimension that infused all Florine's life. With her ultimate *persona,* the Commère, light and buoyancy was about all the Mayfly could ever have in common. The mayfly-*anima* referred only to the primordial sensibility of the totem, which Florine, like other artists, nourished inside her as the reality of the air's magic mirror (where she even totemized her mother and sisters). It did not at all refer to the real social world, the statistical world of men, women, and things. It was this other world where the Commère-*persona,* for her part, had long before found a home. As for the Follies Beauty, she was part of the totemizing: a flutterby-woman.

A study of Florine's recumbent self-portrait reveals her conception of the basic difference between the *anima* and the *persona,* so that in her halo-technique we must scrutinize internal gradations of the personality-spectrum as though it were the color spectrum. In the chemistry of the individual's personality, the *anima* and the *persona* may be confused with each other because so intimately juxtaposed; narcissistically, they may even seem to imitate one another. The *persona* in Florine's self-portrait is of course her

scenery and the costumes,
Austin's scrapbooks—a va
was to be the elegist.

ABOUT FIVE YEARS after its B
given as an oratorio in Tow
Alexander Smallens. Consic
could have been only a sort
vising the production, applied
though there were to be no se
been dressed in "cardinal" go
acts, but now, probably to hon
Florine put them in trailing bla
In addition, she "settled the cu
as the present costume progran
realization. Florine accompani
Spanish bakery to procure the r
expensive." There were repeated
detail. Should the costumes be al
fore the single performance on Ma
Nevertheless, the Negro singers–
cast—appeared in costumes, "the c
monks' cloth." However, "the jewel
at least not what I wanted." Of thi
event she noted in her diary, with gr
another symbolic "That was that'
thud . . .

A virtual parody of Thomson's p
had taken place in a "so-called rehea
Modern Art auditorium, with the com
only a lukewarm imitation of the whit
son in Florine's home in 1929, when he
her "to do the visual part." In the persp
New York revival of the opera by the A
and Academy in 1952 was more in the n
thing else. For more than one individua
for nostalgic repining. Henry McBride, ac
only surviving sister, Ettie, and the famil
mon, went to a performance to find it full
reminders. "We sat frozen in our seats,"

human image: the Follies Beauty that dwelt deep in her dressing-table mirror. This is the individual in his symbolic aspect, transformed by desire and living self-consciously at its center as though it were the world. It is the same "projection" I have already spoken of as the principle of Florine's portraiture. But since the artist herself, as an objective presence, remains outside this painting, we can consider it only a split phase of the portrait-projection: the Mayfly with the Follies Beauty.

By placing Marcel Duchamp's portrait next to hers, we can discern a variation of structure in the typical projection and note three separate phases of the two portraits taken together. In Duchamp's we have what we do not have in Florine's: the literal individual seen objectively by the world, but surprised in the act of doing for himself what Florine did for all her subjects: he is projecting his *persona,* Rrose Sélavy, into the simple imaginative dimension of all *personas.* In his portrait, besides himself, only that is visible; the *anima* is merely implied . . . and what would his *anima* be? I daresay it is the great glass now in Philadelphia, *The Bride Denuded,* across whom, like the lightning of revelation, a complex break in the glass itself fans out. There would be, then, a strange parallel between Duchamp's *anima* and Florine's *anima-persona:* a much mechanized, though insect-like, woman (Duchamp's *Bride*) and an insect-like woman (Florine's *Florine*), who is to her as the Harlequin is to him.

In frankly naïve affectation, Florine once wrote in her diary, ". . . my confrère, Marcel Duchamp." Elsewhere, this artist earned from her an insidiously displaced description of the same sort, a description revealing the degree to which she thought of the portrait-projection as a species of what is known professionally as "promotion." She was impelled to put on canvas, in 1917, the birthday party which the Stettheimer sisters had given their new artist friend, Duchamp, and thus announced the intention to her diary's pages: "It [the party] seemed very real, French, and classical. In my memory it has become a classic. I am about to paint it and entitle it *La Fête à Duchamp.* One more advertisement for him added to the already long list." "Advertisement!"—a highly charged commonplace! The year previously, she had found her own advertisement as an art personality a rather crushing disappointment; nevertheless, it had lingered in her mind as something that might have been the beginning of a "long list."

The fine eye with which she was disposed to assess the ingredients of this list was indicated by the fact that Duchamp, sustaining an aristocratic temperament like hers, could not be construed as a likely candidate for what Henry McBride termed "the white light of publicity . . . that now beats only on newspaper personalities." Certainly, at the 1913 Armory Show of the Society of Independent Artists in New York, Duchamp had created a furore in the art world with his *Nude Descending a Staircase,* a furore in which the back of the public hand was far more prominent than its gladness. As a Cubist-Dadaist-Surrealist, Duchamp may have held in his *persona* (1917-1923) the future note of the century's art, but his work then, as Florine must have known, was hardly calculated to capture the American market. In 1923, indeed, Duchamp was to renounce the "profession" of artist, an act with which, doubtless, Florine sympathized without being disposed to imitate it.

The truth is that, in the above diary entry, the artist was reasoning as naïvely as she ever reasoned before or afterward. She was calling something by a vulgar name ("advertisement") which was by no means vulgar in itself, the *Fête à Duchamp.* She did this, beyond doubt, out of automatic compensation for her own, quite recent disappointment in which a sarcastic amusement was mixed with the comedy of getting ahead as a professional. In substance, what I have called the trauma of her first one-man show had left her with a conditioned-reflex about all promotion.

The Stettheimers were not hostesses at self-seeking displays, characteristic of a vulgar high society, and inaccurately called "parties." Florine went to the trouble of defining just how "real, French, and classical" the party for Duchamp had been. As a matter of fact, her portrayal in paint was faithful at once to the tradition of the Conversation Piece and the Narrative Picture. Her use of the word "advertisment," thus, must seem wholly gratuitous. But, in truth, it was charged with ironic ambiguity and invested with profound disdain. As offhand as its "amused" use was, it came as the backwash of a flood of dried—or perhaps simply "dry" —tears. Artists, especially theatrical ones, must have great power, expressive or repressive, over their surface emotions. Diaries are by no means informal things. They are simply where the diarist stages himself in the narrowest, rather than the widest, part of his world. (Yet we cannot know if this diarist *really* wept!)

saint
commère
muse

IRONICALLY, FLORINE STETTHEIMER was not a hostess in the regular sense for, prior to 1935, her sister Carrie technically filled this function. Yet the role of "art hostess" unquestionably fitted Florine. Already in 1917, her paintings were part of the Stettheimer "entertainment," and if the admiration for them by friends was a trifle ambiguous, it was substantially genuine. Of course, the fluidity of identity between artist and hostess that made life unusually pleasant for Florine and her guests made it also, to her, an object of fatal suspicion. She had pictured her *anima* as the éphémère, doomed to be singed by the blaze of publicity's sun. As much as the éphémère felt with this sun an ineradicable affinity, Florine was incapable of the social crime of "advertisement" with which, by 1923, she had playfully saddled the posturing, poised Rrose Sélavy: the fascinating Harlequin whom she conceived as Duchamp's *persona*.

She loved the society of the art world, but she could not love it without criticizing it and even rejecting it. Without it, truly enough, she would have reduced to half the stature of her art. Through the art world's innate comedy, the comedy of its outrageous "professional" flaw, she saw the lineaments of all worldly comedies of conspicuous consumption, such as those she portrayed in the busy Conversation Pieces: *Spring Sale, Beauty Contest, Natatorium Undine,* and *Cathedrals of Broadway.* The second was dedicated "To the Memory of P. T. Barnum" and in her diary we find: "Beauty contests are a blot B.L.O.T. on American something —I believe life—or civilization." What was it that made Florine's ambivalent feelings for commercial entertainment into a cohesive, functional thing such as a painting? Not "advertisement," no!— but "amusement" mixed with "amazement."

IN HER CONVERSION to the immaculate calling of Art Hostess (circa 1915) Florine felt an arrow of love pierce her breast as it had pierced St. Theresa's: its point secretly aroused the exquisite thrill of a "sin." That all human relationship, for this artist, was a "light" that could hurt cannot qualify as a mere ingenious hypothesis by a biographer, however much it might otherwise sound like one. She actually felt a light within her offering an invitation to friends who, as she wrote, "Rushed in / Got singed / Got scared / Rushed out / Called fire . . ." On page 42 of *Crystal Flowers,* she says that her friends never enjoyed this light—much too intense for them—and so, "in courtesy," she would "turn on a soft / Pink light / Which is found modest / Even charming / It is a protection / Against wear / And tears . . ." Human and divine love, as Florine and Theresa knew, is a war. To become Florine truly "in love," the "soft pink light" had to reach the intensity of the pink-white interior of the Commère's canopy in *Cathedrals of Art*—where the hearts of three virgins, including herself, are seen gently bleeding themselves away.

Lest there be a vestige of doubt regarding Florine's profound identification of her personality with St. Theresa's, we should turn to her *Family Portrait No. 2,* which she unabashedly came to describe as "My Masterpiece": she does so in a late diary and as reported by Carl Van Vechten from her conversation. Whether her evaluation is correct does not matter: the work is a chef-d'oeuvre. One especially striking feature of it is that against Cleopatra's Needle, visible in the background, is a ribbon in serpentine shape on which are waggishly printed the words, "4 Sts. Seen by Florine," and that on the base is printed "1933," the year of the painting's composition when the realization of *Four Saints in Three Acts* was a certainty.

Were it not for the recumbent self-portrait, where the artist's large handwritten surname ceases after the "St," it would be only after her introduction to *Four Saints* that Florine used this saintly, and of course humorous, inversion of her name. As it was, she must have felt that, in 1923, she had exercised an extraordinary prescience which she was committed to restate seven years later—for restate it she did. In Virgil Thomson's portrait, "Florine St." (printed) is adjacent to the also printed "St. Ignatius," whose personal emblem, interestingly enough, is a bleeding heart.

The moral inference is inescapable. This pseudo-sacred form of the artist's name appeared six times after March 27th, 1929. She had been "rehearsed" for religious themes the previous year when she had painted Father Hoff's portrait in New Jersey, but the printed form of Saint in that picture is "San." Besides Thomson's portrait (1930), these also have the "St," the rest of the signature being covered as if by accidental superposition: *Portrait of Our Nurse, Margaret Burgess* (begun, by the artist's own testimony, in the Summer of 1929); *Sun* (1931), where the "t" of "St" is only partly visible; *Family Portrait No. 2* (1933); *Cathedrals of Wall Street* (1939); and *Cathedrals of Art* (1942), where the letters of her name are hung in the sky. In three of the foregoing, as in the Thomson portrait, the abbreviated name appears on a ribbon. By 1929 and later, a tangible object was required to obliterate the rest of the artist's worldly surname . . .

THIS NEGATIVE VISUAL illusion suggests a positive spiritual illusion: saintly pride and its danger; that is, a danger akin to that of the artist's pride in creation and self-creation. As a dedicated being, possessing an intractable sense of humor and aristocratic pride, Florine could not have failed to grasp this inmost danger even before she grasped her inmost temperament when first, in her signature, she had sainted herself. As for her poems, these embodied the trumpery jewels of her vanity; they were among the "tinsel things" she loved which naturally caught the light from wherever it came. As for martyrdoms, she had found these, during her prewar tours of Italy's museums and churches, "entertaining" by her own verbal evidence. In those years she was learning to take her own future "martyrdom," the Knoedler show, in her stride. Even though the Mayfly was the symbol of her personality as fatally attracted to the blaze of a boundless publicity, she was protected against herself, as she was protected against others, by daily wit, reflective wit. At the same time, such wit could be, and was, tried to its utmost by reality. The Commère Florine (circa 1942) was one to whom this dilemma and its terms had long been familiar incidents. Its solution, the individual's victory, was symbolized by the single word "amusement," whose content may be defined as the Commère's worldly ecstasy: an efflux of pure feeling given restraint, form, and proportion by the subject's personal wit and irony. In Florine's face in *Cathedrals of Art*, this appears at once shadowily sly and decorously childlike: a complex emotion in whose white-pink depths is a clear belief in earthly immortality, in the classic ideal of work and its limitless rewards. Despite all pangs, it is a serene thing. It triumphs consciously over a bleeding heart and justifies every worldly ambition for which a heart may bleed.

THE LAST PAINTING by Florine, however, is not merely another self-portrait. It is a cosmic tribuna in which everything is as simply, crystallinely stated as a fly in amber. While the artist still planned work on it at the time of her death, it is fundamentally a finished picture. It leaves nothing out, not even the public: "the anonymous

artist's oblique satire. On the corresponding side, Everett Austin leans picturesquely against an institutional pillar, casting at the great critic across from him a Hamletian eye of ironically magnetized curiosity. Florine gave Austin this place because of a certain freedom from professional care he had at heart, care from which she felt that McBride—for all his urbane, superlative appreciation of art—could never dissociate himself. Unrecognizable 57th Street dealers include a masked man whose identity may be guessed. Recognizable and to the fore, Julien Levy and Pierre Matisse hold balloons bearing the names of artists they represented. Behind Levy stands Kirk Askew, Jr., whose status as art dealer did not prevent his becoming Florine's personal friend. His balloon has flowers painted on it; a kind of prophecy, for Askew at last gave Florine her third one-man show in 1948: "The Flowers of Florine Stettheimer."

With Olympianly elevated brows, Pavel Tchelitchew is seen directly behind Austin, raising hands at once expostulatory and damning. Alfred H. Barr, Jr., his form following the curve of a modern lounge-chair, relaxes complacently in the security of his lesser institution, surrounded by two Picassos and a Mondrian (on which a third infant Art is playing hopscotch) while, on a lower floor of the Museum, two neo-Classic women by Picasso race past the Douanier Rousseau's fabulously poised lion in *The Sleeping Gypsy*. The Whitney Museum (then in its old home on 8th Street) appears faintly forceful on the other side. Close to McBride's GO sign, Marie Sterner is contentedly absorbed in cradling a bust by Houdon. Florine's miniature transcriptions of well-known modern paintings are remarkably just, and this justice seems well calculated in the context to act as the minimum of tongue-in-cheek irony she desired to exploit. A figure on the roof-terrace of the Museum is setting aloft two streamers, both of which are composed of the vertically arranged letters of Picasso's name. It is hard to gather what the contiguous letters spell but they look like the beginning of Bouguereau: a completely esoteric reference for there was a joke between Florine and Tchelitchew that Matisse was the modern "Bouguereau." From over the roof and seen in reverse (as is only proper) the letters of Florine's name with the "St" abbreviation have also been set vertically aloft (by whom one can only guess!). Carrie and Ettie then lived at the Dorset, which geographically is at exactly this point in the painting.

ONE THING HERE is more than certain: the identities of Florine as the Commère (so marked by a ribbon at her feet) and an old friend of the artist's, the late Robert Locher, as her partner, the Compère, dressed in a white dinner jacket. Not only do these richly equipped figures admirably solidify the two immediately at their inside (Austin and McBride), which in turn are modulated by the two photographers, but also the latter are virtually pinned in place by the hieratic figure of Alfred Stieglitz in profile, placed with dramatic asymmetry on one side of the grand staircase in a black cloak. The Commère and the Compère hold up the sides of the work not only structurally but also with a lucidly effective symbolism. Like her, the Compère is tagged with his title, also on a serpentine ribbon, and enjoys an almost equal seclusion provided by a graceful screen; perhaps unconsciously, the artist made this the type of screen found as mirror-plated in *Spring Sale*. Aside from any private affinity with Locher that may have caused Florine to select him as her all-important partner, the Commère and the Compère have about them identical marks of the Classic and Antique.

The golden arabesque surmounting the Commère's canopy is recognizable as the trisula, universally encountered in ornament, and sometimes regarded as a version of the fleur-de-lys, the version here implied, since one of the pair of white flowers in the center is a calla lily. The trisula has a wide range of symbolism among which is the bifurcate nature of the universe, sometimes referring to the dateless myth of an original androgynous god, whose various names include, of course, Eros. The trisula's implicit importance is the purely symbolic way in which it unites the Compère and Commère, the male and female godparents of the infant Art (or Eros) seen twice more in the rest of the painting. In the Classical perspective, the Commère might seem, because of her flowers, to be Persephone rather than Aphrodite. Yet Eros-Art has a direct relation with Aphrodite and is equivalent to a *putto,* a pair of which stood on either side of Florine's canopied bed. An artist who constructed as associatively as did Florine leaves room for all these symbolic traits, including the moral association of Virgil Thomson's physiognomy with that of the infant Eros: the one who, in the Christian form of an angel, traditionally aims his arrow at St. Theresa's heart.

Withal, Florine Stettheimer remained a pagan and here stamped herself as Classical. The much-fringed white dress she wears brings to mind one she casually mentions in her diary: "a white gown with fringes for dinner—Greekish—." White and gold, one of her favorite combinations (for which she used either metallic paint or gold-leaf) has come down as typically Classic and is here embodied by the canopy and its trisula as well as by a short Classical column, on which the Compère rests an elbow, and at both ends of which the trisula-motif is repeated. The ribbon identifying Florine's partner does not curve merely at his feet but continues, snakelike, to wind itself about the column next to him. This clue is unmistakable: we must recall that the Belvedere Apollo, expressly named in *Crystal Flowers* as the author's "beauty norm," stands by a stump around which a snake climbs. A small porcelain version of the same statue, with the snake climbing about the stump, stood on Florine's bedroom mantelpiece. In several paintings, she used a motif identifiable as snakelike, explicitly calling one such work *Flowers with Snake* (1931). Yet the snake never appears in her work realistically but always heraldically; even the tickertape in *Cathedrals of Wall Street* (making an S-form directly below Roosevelt's portrait) has an outline as much like a stylized snake as like anything else.

Out of private associations and personal, even professional experience, Florine finally presented in *Cathedrals of Art* an amused criticism of art by a Classical Muse. As Apollo was in charge of the Muses, he was, of course, supreme judge of the arts. Florine had an autobiographic reason, moreover, for identifying Robert Locher, the Compère, with Apollo. This was not necessarily his personal beauty, though naturally there was room for this element, but more urgently, because he had shown with her in the early twenties at Louis Bouché's Belmaison, at Wanamaker's Gallery of Decorative Art, and what he had shown may be assumed to have engaged Florine's active sympathy; on one occasion, at least, it was flowers painted on glass. There is still another reason for this association as pictured in the painting. Locher is secluded behind a screen, and it was at the same Belmaison that Florine exhibited a screen on whose panels, with neo-Pompeian effects, she had placed her first individual family portraits: herself, Caroline (Carrie), Walter (their brother), and Henrietta (Ettie); this screen, in fact, was where she first used object-symbolism for personal identification: the tendency that developed into her portraits' halo-technique.

FLORINE CERTAINLY WISHED to make no mystery of all this symbolism. It was merely the artistic form taken by the sublime sort of joke— some heartache but more lyric joy—at which she ultimately valued life; or more specifically, her life in art. Her head in this painting is so archly cocked to one side while her mouth is set in so phantom- like and amiable a grimace! Is the joke not made, at last, behind the hand as love had to be, all along, the formal symbol of a bleed- ing heart? But we are immediately reassured by the image of poise this last "self-portrait" conveys. Florine, it is strange to think, was forty-six when she found her métier in such pictures as *Picnic at Bedford Hills* and *La Fête à Duchamp.* In 1942, therefore, she had been in full and fertile possession of it for a quarter of a cen- tury. She had evolved a style capable of handling the final group of problems she set herself in the four *Cathedrals,* each of which is a literal Theatre of the Profane with a High Altar at its center. Each perspective has the illusory and the real depth of a tremen- dous stage viewed at the exact center, so that one problem was to diversify the strict bisymmetry of the abstract structure.

If one knows all her work, Florine's bisymmetry of layout in the *Cathedrals* suggests an elaborate technical precedent in her oeuvre's own limits. An apparently early flower piece of the "elon- gated" structure of *Delphinium and Columbine* (1923) shows a bouquet and a "dragonfly" floating in the sun's rays. This water- color, on the back of a reproduction of which Ettie wrote "De- stroyed," may have been one of the many destroyed by the artist on her permanent removal to a larger studio in the Fall of 1935. A bouquet of four flowers is tied with a fringed ribbon and looks oddly, in its strict anatomic bisymmetry, like a mannikin, a zinnia being the head, a morning glory a canopy, two fuchsias the arms, the two largest of the stems extending into legs, and the tied ribbon the dress. More significantly for the bisymmetric structure, we may derive from this anthropomorphic image a strange insight into the dragonfly-mayfly-flutterby series. The quadruple-winged insect that floats in the sunlight is apparently an organism composed of two sets of upper parts joined at the middle; that is, what might pos- sibly seem the legs of the mayfly appear to be another set of an- tennae, owing to the palpable presence of an added head where one would expect only the termination of a dragonfly's or butterfly's body.

I believe the solution of all such "symbolic mysteries" in

Florine's art can finally be simplified, regardless of their "reading," to a definitive conception of all aesthetic form. Aesthetic form is the great cocoon, the image of the cosmic web, which an artist spins out of himself for himself—and for the world. Florine came to it by a somewhat indirect route not without its falterings and its failures. Everyone's life turns up blind-alleys where boredom or cynicism or madness becomes the very face of the world—if not the face (as with van Gogh) in one's own mirror. A great sense of humor saved Florine from the sin of cynicism. Sheer moral strength saved her from that of madness as well as of boredom. But before the possible recurrence of such confrontations, each artist must have the patience of a saint and a saint's will to fix his eyes on an ultimate vision.

Nevertheless, an artist's life can be revived in words only if colored all over locally, shaped and reshaped with dailiness; only if one makes oneself go round and round with the clock of his body! This roundness I have set as my own problem in time and space because I am faithfully relating Florine Stettheimer's life in art. So in the poise and total triumph of Florine the Commère, I perforce see also (strangely urgent) the helplessness and pathetic fragility of Florine the Ephémère. Today, Florine Stettheimer is visible on the world stage of art—and yet she is equally visible being dragged out on a real stage by the entrepreneur Austin, on the night of *Four Saints'* première, to take her solo bow.

In both "roles" she is unquestionably stirred to her depths, suffused with white light. But only in one has she succeeded in making a Muse out of Amusement! In the other she trembles, as Austin himself all too truthfully put it, "in an agony of embarrassment." It is this agony, at once human and divine in every artist, that fixes us and toward which all our sympathy is drawn as to a festival. A festival?—a carnival, that is, in the oldest and the newest sense; a dionysian revel (subject to drawing-room rules); a martyrdom (complete with posters, sideshows, and elegant white gloves that are left behind).

III   *In the Eyes of the World*

O THE LATE Philip Moeller, who had known the Stett-heimers since near the start of the century and lived opposite them on West 76th Street in New York, Florine *virgin* was "the 'lady genius' " as well as, for brief messages sent her *lady of fashion* while he travelled in this country and abroad, "Floridia" and *confrère* "Florada": pet names with an apt flavor of the Rococo. In a letter to Carrie and Ettie, dated April 6th, 1934, Moeller speaks of find-ing Florine's mind "increasingly fascinating"—"do you know,"

he wrote, "she wanted to have the Capitol at Washington as the mystical city in the skies?" That is, she had proposed it as a device for harboring the number of windows in the famous passage from *Four Saints:* "How many windows are there in it?" Moeller interpreted her idea as betokening a "quaint new ingenuousness in her unbelievable cerebrations."

Everyone, in preparing *Four Saints in Three Acts,* had perceived the wit of making the Capitol building into the celestial vision that was the subject of Miss Stein's straight query about the number of apertures that opened onto mortal activities . . . But the second thoughts of someone prompted an objection that had weight. At a time of such economic crisis, in the days of Home Relief and the WPA, the recognizable Capitol might function as oblique propaganda for the current Administration rather than as a fantasy in the rapt mind of a saint . . . What, then, to do about it? Mrs. Lawson thought of something making the Stein-Stettheimer vision look harmlessly anonymous: she cut off the Capitol's great dome so that the "mystical city" seemed vaguely classical and remote—a compromise presumably acceptable to the embattled set-designer, who in compensation must have held to other points all the more desperately.

To Moeller, for his part, Florine's "mystical city" had embodied a daring exoticism that had turned out to be *too* daring. Being a theatre professional, Moeller—despite his unstinted enthusiasm on the night of the première—had been one of the skeptics regarding the prospect of the opera's success. Apparently his just-quoted letter was written to communicate an anecdote about a symphony concert at Carnegie Hall, to which he had escorted the artist. A Tchaikovsky work had barely started, he wrote, when Florine began to fidget and then remarked to her companion: "No, that isn't tobacco smoke." A few minutes later, "mysterious fumes" came drifting out over the audience. "Five minutes ago," remarked the lady genius divinatorily, "I knew it was wood burning and now it's combined with wax." This made her companion marvel at her "acute sensibilities."

She also proved herself a woman of decision. As they were sitting in Row Z, they quietly arose and Moeller helped Florine into her black, ermine-trimmed coat and gripped his topper. Even as they moved into the aisle, a lady, who had come up from down front, walked calmly but intently back again; she had acted too

One of Florine's first superlative portraits: *Marcel Duchamp*, dated 1923, oil on canvas. Already a New York-addicted Frenchman, he had become part of Florine's artistic circle many years before; he still lives in New York City. See the main text for this work's interpretation.

People and places, private and public, became Florine's constant preoccupation during the twenties, with aquatic subjects prominent. Above: *Asbury Park South,* 1920-30 (?) Coll. Fisk University; Carl Van Vechten in the reviewing stand, Fania Marinoff and Marcel Duchamp foreground center; the artist near them under a parasol. Opposite: *Natatorium Undine,* 1927, Coll. Vassar College; at upper left: the artist reclining on a couch, Fania Marinoff writing, Ettie Stettheimer dabbling her feet in the water.

suddenly and forgotten her coat. At this moment, half a dozen others started to leave their seats, but now there was a growing clamor of hushed calls that everything was "all right." The conductor, Koussevitzky, paused in his occupation to assure the audience that "it was nothing" and promptly resumed the Tchaikovsky. However, Florine and Moeller left and walked home, only to decide after a bit to return to see if anything was "happening." Nothing was. But they were not sorry about the concert . . . Smoke, after all, is the least attractive aspect of either fire or music.

That the lady genius had not behaved with the cravenness of a mouse did not prevent Moeller, in reminiscing of their friendship, from calling her "a little mouselike . . . she drifted into the room." Drifting isn't scampering or creeping. However, "She was silent a lot," he said. "You felt she was thinking, being critical." Downright moral gestures such as the artist's refusal to do the sets for a play to be produced by the Theatre Guild helped the legend of Florine's self-effacement, her shrinking from the spotlight, and could not have discouraged the concomitant legend that she was, as a "critic," very choosy. Of course! She had been burned; she was afraid of fire. And the color of fire, in regard to the Theatre Guild play, happened to be purplish; the sets required lilacs, and though this flower is also white, the fact that it was in a natural sequence with purple was decisive in making Florine shun the commission.

She could take a very rich pleasure in the negative: a pleasure and a privilege cultivated by aristocrats and independent ladies. To refrain, for Florine, was a moral luxury challenged just when she felt most like a frightened mouse—when, for instance, Austin took her by the hand and dragged her into "the white light that used to beat on Kings but now . . ." Poor mouse? The audience applauding, even cheering, might be ever so elite, it was still full of strangers. Florine's mind was never so acutely personal as when she made the following observation about herself—and others:

> The world is full of strangers.
>   They are very strange.
> I shall never meet them.
>   It is easy to arrange.

To this artist, an "audience" was the namelessly vague public,

Opposite: Florine's prophetic *Portrait of Virgil Thomson*, 1930, oil on canvas, painted while he was in Europe. The preceding year he had asked her to do the sets for *Four Saints in Three Acts*, based on Gertrude Stein's play, but first she did this portrait.

her mythical kingdom of would-be and might-be buyers that still intimidated her. Secret pang and shameful history! Henry Mc-Bride's picture of this anti-climactic theatrical moment is "the shrinking violet Miss Stettheimer taking a solo bow with extreme nonchalance." Yet Austin had just disposed of the "shrinking violet's" shrinking by sheer force; hence the nonchalance may well have been natural dignity hastening to the aid of petrifaction. After all, though indeed she had forgotten those essentials of elegance, her gloves, the artist had all too poignantly foreseen—maybe even *rehearsed*—that supremely taxing moment.

IF THINGS DO "mean their colors," the "violet" of McBride's above-quoted description of Florine was no happy thought saving by inadvertence. It would be interesting to know just when the artist wrote a poem called *The Revolt of the Violet,* which in entirety is as follows:

> This is a vulgar age
> Sighed the violet
> Why must humans drag us
> Into their silly lives
> They treat us
> As attributes
> As symbols
> And make us
> Fade
> Stink

It is the note of anti-publicity and its point here, I think, is a naïvely rational one. Why should violets, being "shy," be forced into notoriety for having a quality foreign to notoriety? If, like other flowers, they are brought forward in bouquets, they too fade and stink. Here is another intimation of mortality: the emotion of the sun-struck Ephémère. At the same time, out on the stage, where a spotlight focusses all eyes on an object, a being is *exposed*. But *who* is?—*what*? Was it the portrait-*persona*: the self-hypnotized Follies Beauty? *She* was something to risk upon a real stage. But Florine could not help but think, no matter what, it meant certain defeat. Actually she knew herself to be a rather nervous, essentially shy lady of sixty-three, though it is certain that no one in the

audience guessed or knew her age except (at the New York première) the artist's own sister, Carrie.

Apart from the ideal Narcissean dimension, there was a point
to the mascara and the timelessly youthful face of the self-portrait
that had nothing to do with a real stage. Superficially, it was a
mask to present to the glare of footlights! In that practical sense,
for a solo bow, it was very suitable, but unfortunately it did not
feel available. The true youthfulness of the Stettheimers lay elsewhere; lay, in fact, in that infinite self-care of which deliberate
repose is one element. "They were preserved," as Virgil Thomson
says of the three sisters, "like royalty." Even before 1934, the
family unit of three daughters and the mother (though, in another
year, the mother would be gone) had come into the paradisial domain of an earthly immortality. As the sisters were never to marry,
neither were they to leave the "marriageable age." However serious in mien, Carrie the eldest, Florine the one-between, and Ettie
the youngest, were equally "girlish" and had that surviving look
peculiar to a certain type of spinster. In fact, the only thing that
might bring the look of careworn time into their faces was age itself as a topic of conversation.

WOMEN, OF COURSE, could not be expected to have inferred from the
persons of the Stettheimers exactly what men did. Such friends of
the family as Georgia O'Keeffe, Isabelle Lachaise, Fania Marinoff,
and Marie Sterner, would think of their hostesses only as well-
dressed ladies of much distinction—indeed, exoticism—who knew
how to entertain. They were such dear things, too, and Florine was
—their "ages"? But after all . . ! A man, however, could argue
that the Stettheimer sisters, as unmarried, were still theoretically
eligible for romantic pursuit and their ages were therefore a point
of consideration. Hence, the men friends of Carrie, Florine, and
Ettie—some of them professionally trained in matters of vision—
might be supposed to have given them an all-around scrutiny.

Not that, in 1917, more than a shadow of romance was actually
present. This shadow, considered by some rather corporeal, was
Ettie's preoccupation with the sculptor, Elie Nadelman, then still
a bachelor. He and Ettie would take long walks by themselves and
discuss life and books. Overtly, it was, as the saying goes, an innocent flirtation. But Duchamp believes it may have been more serious on both sides than either imagined of his partner; that is, it

was somewhat like a movie plot except that, in this plot, nothing happened.

The delicious *Picnic at Bedford Hills* (another *Déjeuner sur l'Herbe*) shows the Byronic-looking Nadelman prone, next to Ettie dreamily prostrate on a rug, while Carrie and "Duche" are busy setting out lunch and the artist sits musingly under a dainty parasol, her gaze fixed, perhaps, on an insect . . . Florine's capacity to be beguiled by the sudden appearance of insects contains an oddly negative, though very funny, inflection. Maybe insects, like the flutterby itself, lived chiefly in her consciousness rather than in the world.

Maurice Grosser, who devised the brilliant scenario for *Four Saints*, tells of being at the Stettheimers' and hearing Florine exclaim, apropos of nothing except that her attention had just been riveted, "Look, sister, a fly!" After a due pause of consternation in all, Florine announced even more unexpectedly, "I've never seen one before!" It was doubtless an ordinary housefly, and probably the utter commonness of it had shocked someone used to looking at mythical insects and fatal butterflies. Florine's vision was individualistically constant. As Marie Antoinette's boudoir was all she had liked in the Palace at Versailles, Lalique's crystal boxes and vases were all she had had eyes for at the Old Salon, in Paris, in 1910.

In the *Picnic,* her mind's eye may well be filled with the image of a Lalique butterfly in jewels, originally seen in a New York shopwindow but now resting on the grass near her. Yet, truth to tell, the Mayfly and the Follies Beauty were as scarce in the social consciousness around Florine as the flutterby, as such, was in nature. Those were timeless, spaceless images while she, the objective individual, lived—a little mouselike!—in time and space. The three portraits most revelatory of Florine's method (those of Ettie, "Duche," and herself) have the fewest props, seem the most spaceless. All the more, then, was the figure in them isolated for its own sake. Looked at by the eyes of male artists and photographers, Florine "had no female body under her clothes" (Duchamp) and "her clothes hung on her" (Cecil Beaton, who also said, however, that she had "a powdery, delicate quality that was delightful").

Carl Sprinchorn's reaction to Florine's person was forever conditioned from the moment when she unexpectedly reproved him for claiming her fingers too ardently in a handshake. The three sisters had originally met Sprinchorn at the opening of his first one-man show and had taken to him. Gently, Florine pointed out the preciousness of an artist's "working" hand, and thereafter was pleased (letting a vagrant twinkle come and go in her eyes) to offer her hand with the assurance that Sprinchorn had been initiated into the delicate dynamic by which her being was governed. By the same token, a wild revulsion must have possessed her when Everett Austin commandeered her hand to pull her onstage in Hartford. For his part, Austin thought that the slight Florine emanated a continuous warmth. "She was crushable," he confided to me with innocent sadism. "You felt like hugging her . . . or pressing her between the pages of a book." How the flutterby-motif would pop up when one least expected it!

Virgil Thomson implicitly warned me against the legend of Florine's fragility by pointing out that she worked alone in her studio and handled her biggest canvases (the *Cathedrals:* 60″ × 50″) without complaining or calling in help. This put me in mind of my own impression of her show at the Museum of Modern Art. Doubtless thinking of *Heat,* which finds the four sisters, including Stella, wilting or prostrate on chairs and chaise-longues—and only their mother upright as usual—I wrote in *View* * of the artist's "two-dimensional world of fancy (as though one looked at everything from above and yet found it full-length) . . . Even the dancers, oddly, may be conceived as supine. Florine Stettheimer is a painter who might have worked lying down." Though my review left much to be desired, I feel that in that spot I came upon something essential. The relaxation I meant is the type carrying a peculiar tension, a nervous tautness, similar to the state of trance —especially sibylline trance; it is a subtle suspension in which movement is more expectation of movement; it is a poised waiting, a moment of magic arrestment in which attention is increased and concentrated, and in which ideally the infinite possibility of movement is secreted. Among its modern functions is that enabling the artist, relaxing, to call all his powers to his eyes and observe while being unobserved. I meant the "lying down while painting" only as a metaphor. At the same time, I was taken aback to read, among the notes of Robert Henri, with whom Florine once studied, some advice that it is hard to believe she ever heeded: "Get the full

* December 1946.

swing of your body into the stroke. / Painting should be done from the floor up, not from the seat of a comfortable chair.'' *

I KNOW OF only five paintings of Florine by others and but three photographs—none of the latter being credited to a photographic portraitist. Two of the pictorial portraits fortunately reveal the artist in an unposed or ''candid'' aspect. Marguerite Zorach was very fond of Florine, thinking of her today as a ''genuine person'' and an ''original artist.'' While having many lively conversational sessions with her and Isabelle Lachaise, Mrs. Zorach duly felt the wish to draw Florine as she did all her friends. Despite the fact that under the other artist's scrutiny, Florine would grow stiff and self-conscious, even fidgety, one result (available from several) is a pencil profile of clarity and authority. Even if Florine was as hard to catch in arrested motion as one of her own flutterbies, Mrs. Zorach's line-drawing remains unique as an image of the artist in her maturity: ''realistic'' because the portrait, given its style, refrains from obvious flattery.

The other ''candid'' portrait is full-length: Carl Sprinchorn's small watercolor done in his broad but refined style of instantaneous impressionism; it seems as if, her person being suddenly confronted, her blackly defined eyes communicate a deeply personal but ''coded'' message even as her hand protectively draws about her throat a scarf the same color as her brilliant salmon-red dress. This is similar to the photographic view of her taken, in all probability, on the grounds of the summer place the family had rented that year. The background looks umbrageous as Florine looks (for her) obligingly informal in plain *cloche* and afternoon dress of the long-skirted thirties, of soft summery material and patterned with huge roses. One is struck by a certain masklike quality of face and the moderation of make-up.

Sprinchorn's portrait of her is undated, and unluckily he does not recall even its probable year. One of the photographs (a collage) portrays the three sisters as separate and immaculate fashion-plates in what seems a pre-World War I period: here is the image of their triple young womanhood, fused in the white of high summer with the Goddess of Fashion. The other photograph— that used as a frontispiece for Henry McBride's book—seems also circa World War I for it was in 1917 that Florine painted *La Fête*

* *The Art Spirit*. By Robert Henri. Page 50.

à Duchamp, where she is seen wearing unmistakably the same costume: a white harem-skirt over which a voluminous, flower-embroidered smock hangs down.

THOUGH FLORINE KNEW, and presumably admired, the leading art photographers of the twenties—Edward Steichen, Arnold Genthe, Alfred Stieglitz and Baron de Meyer, the two latter of whom she did portraits—one may conclude that she was never photographed by them. First meeting Cecil Beaton "in the autumn of her life"— a phrase used by Glenway Wescott in speaking of his own friendship with Florine—she and Beaton did not make much of their liking for one another. He conceived the project of photographing her, never bringing it to pass, he told me, because of the disinterest of *Vogue,* three of whose top editors visited Florine to "case" her. Beaton would have liked to take her picture for his own pleasure, but since he found the light in her rooms too dark of a morning, and to have brought there his lighting equipment, requiring assistants, would have been too expensive, he dropped the idea. It is too bad that such a rare instance of predisposition in the artist was not seized upon.

As close as Carl Van Vechten was to Florine, she declined to let him photograph her although, of course, she knew this novelist's passion for taking photographs of his celebrated friends. "It was because I didn't retouch," Van Vechten informed me with laconic pointedness, quite straightfaced "But," he went on, his eyes emitting a roguish gleam, "she liked the idea of being photographed by Cecil Beaton!" By Beaton's time, the dreamy mist in which subjects were bathed by Genthe and de Meyer had almost cleared up. One is faced by the contradiction, to be sure, that this mist was flattering to its passing denizens and that Florine, consequently, should have been tolerant of it. She must have known, for instance, that Garbo had reached the apex of her still-photographic genius through Genthe's subtle skill. Possibly the artist was never asked to pose by any of her photographer friends; perhaps they were not in the habit of complimenting friends in this way. But probably they exercised a second-sight tactfulness: Florine, after wavering, would have refused them. It was not hard for experts in intuition to gather that, as this artist preferred her own vision of people to nature's less calculated devices in producing them, she also preferred to cling to certain images of herself which, however in-

the extant images of Florine done by others: Thévenaz' portrait, the photograph, and a pencil drawing by Duchamp. Virgil Thomson now owns the last named, which the artist inscribed as follows: "chère Florine / à Virgil / 1952 / (done around 1925)." Florine had written on it: "Portrait of me by Marcel Duchamp." All three images have much the same, almost full facial angle and a semi-sweet, composed expression that conveys no special beauty and yet a distinct refinement. Duchamp's delicate head of her, extraordinarily girlish, has the same innate Cubist style as Thévenaz', though the latter's half-length oil hints of that streamlined dusky academism which became prevalent as a derivative of Cubism.

Florine was the suavest of the three sisters, and in the photograph where she wears the harem skirt, one cannot help detecting, as swift and glancing as a butterfly's wing, a look of complacence conspired in by the mouth and eyes. It is the veiled, perhaps suppressed, image of the lyric joy gradually to be accumulated by Florine, the Commère. But it has nothing of the Follies Beauty or the Mayfly; it is a (not particularly mouselike) lady artist consenting to pose in a costume suggesting her profession: the long smock mostly covers the full harem skirt. It is as though she had been moving and, momentarily, come to rest; so perhaps there is a faint hint of flutterby in it.

It is my own keen regret that I was seldom at Florine's house (the Beaux Arts studio) and that for me she dwells without very concrete features in the midst of the Commère's lucid *ambiance* in *Cathedrals of Art*. I think only of a daintiness and a quietness: a pastel sort of presence, floating amid its own fixedness. The truth is that it took a professional photographer such as Cecil Beaton, whose acumen implies a brutal inquisitiveness of eye, to preserve the only first-hand *physiognomic* memory of Florine's appearance I have encountered: "Eyes too near together . . . nose a bit large."

THE PHOTOGRAPH OF her, full-length, shows one who wears clothes with aristocratic fastidiousness, neither quite carelessly nor quite consciously. There is a poise in the midst of them, which is all that, finally, matters. The sisters were most notable for their clothes, which had their own ways of being fashionable. A small seamstress, one thinks, is to be suspected; indeed, Florine's diary verifies this when she mentions wearing a dinner gown created "with Agnes' help . . . oyster-white with overlifesize shrimpish roses." The legend is that the sisters always "did things" to whatever they bought in a shop. While this may well have been so, they likewise patronized such Paris dressmakers as Callot and Poiret and such a New York house as (by the evidence in *Spring Sale*) Bendel's. Florine records that she bought clothes from Kargère and Lord & Taylor, and that Carrie, back from a solo trip to Paris, presented her and Ettie with Maison Giraud teagowns. In 1916, she spoke of Carrie in a "blue metal dress": formidable enough to be haute couture. All the sisters were dauntless shoppers and Florine would repeat grotesque incidents resulting from such forays into the world of buying. Once she found it impossible to get a certain kind of gold braid she had previously purchased. "We don't have any gold braid," one salesgirl informed her. "This is going to be a big Chinese year!"

The sisters, however, did not wish to buy for the mere sake of buying; whatever was really good stayed good enough for them till it wore out. Themselves fabulously preserved, the Stettheimers tended to preserve what encased them. Carrie's evening gowns of taffeta, satin, and velvet, lace-adorned, continued to trail throughout the years: her portrait (1923) reveals one. Ettie was often seen in red, and it may often have been the same dress restyled. At the beginning of World War II, she complained of being unable to find any red velvet in town costing more than three dollars a yard —"and," she went on, solemnly aggrieved, "you couldn't sit down in that."

Her incidental locution may indicate the truth of the universal impression that at parties the Stettheimers were always sitting. As for languishing, it must be noted, McBride testifies that no ladies, guests or hostesses, "languished" at the Stettheimers', by which he seems to have meant indecorous forms of reclining or relaxing. Marcel Duchamp might once have been construed to cast himself at Fania Marinoff's feet, but McBride declares that he only seated himself there, and then only because no vacant chairs were available. When one became vacant, says the same authority, Duchamp transferred himself to it.

VIRGIL THOMSON TENDS to emphasize the gentility of the Stettheimers, including of course the matriarchal Mrs. Stettheimer: a grande dame from another era. "They were," he communicated without seeming too redundant, "ladies." Little was known of the fourth sister, Stella, by Florine's milieu because she had married Sigmund Wanger (né Feuchtwanger) and left the family circle, to which she would return only for occasional and purely family visits. The matrilinear emphasis, beyond doubt, is largely responsible for the ladylike quintessence that pervaded the Stettheimer drawing-room.

The tone of party conversations followed the rule of beyond-which-not. At the same time, assuming that one of the hostesses initiated or invited an opening, polite ribaldry of a Firbankian complexion might prevail. For instance, at a dinner to which the English journalist, A. R. Orage, had been asked, he had no sooner seen his soup than Ettie applied to him to define the Sin against the Holy Ghost: she had never, she explained, clearly understood it. The gentleman unhesitatingly obliged her, striking suitable awe into the assembly at table, rendered mute by this event. When at last silence fell, Ettie slipped back with a brilliant turn of the conversation by invoking Mae West, whose play, *Sex,* had just been closed by the police and the author-star put in jail.

Florine—less, it may be supposed, out of prudery than distaste—would abruptly change the conversation if an inadmissible topic came up, or, quiet as a mouse, would disappear from the room. Ettie, undoubtedly the most overtly "liberal" of the three, was described by Everett Austin as coming into a room "like a gypsy with a tambourine"; something which, however, I think we may take as picturesqueness of speech. At all events, it was Ettie who defined the sisters' basic moral position on an occasion when she felt the masculine consideration being shown them excessive. It may have been when "Duche" or Van Vechten involuntarily betrayed gentlemanly concern for sparing the ladies too stark a bit of gossip. Ettie decided to put things straight and did so with pontifical, if throbbing, simplicity. "We may be virgins," she succinctly gave forth, "but we know the facts of life."

I have found no criticism of anything that took place at a Stettheimer party. The most scandalous disorder may have been the time Philip Moeller and Helen Westley had to be shushed by the hostesses for chatting through Virgil Thomson's rendition of *Four Saints.* "Fugitives from Greenwich Village" are supposed to have gotten in occasionally but it was most unlikely that they were asked back. The Stettheimers imposed telephoning if an invited guest wished to bring someone along, particularly if a stranger to the house. At parties, liquor was never in the same abundance as food. But, so ascendant was the rule of propriety, this precaution against the hazard of overindulgence was hardly necessary. One had come to enjoy himself in delightful company—a little removed from rough reality, but so what?—while partaking of the world's solider elements of subsistence, superlatively prepared by the Stettheimers' regular cook. (They never frequented a caterer.) That was all, and in high tacitness it was enough. Duchamp started up when I prodded him as to the rumor that, either before or after Prohibition, cocktails had not been served *chez* Stettheimer. He hesitated, stared into space, and then with a charming note of assumed concern exclaimed: "There must have been cocktails!"

As a matter of fact, his historical sense did not mislead him. Cocktails of rum or champagne base are recorded in both Carrie's and Florine's menus as sometimes, if not invariably, having arrived in the regular spot before dinner while Kirk Askew remembers daiquiris as the usual cocktail. The meal itself was served with heavy silver on red damask, with centerpiece of Venetian lace or Italian antique filet lace altar-cloths, and Worcester, Rockingham, or Crown Derby porcelain. Afterward, wine-cup might appear. The food, of course, was noted for *spécialités de la maison,* such as feather soup and oyster salad. The latter (says Van Vechten) was introduced to the Broadway stage by Avery Hopwood in his farce, *The Gold Diggers.* Feather soup made one of its more distinguished appearances, followed by squab, when Boutet de Monvel, Cecil Beaton, and the late Peter Watson came to dine with Florine. The Stettheimer household, perfectly real in itself, naturally tended to produce an *ambiance* of fantasy. The fact that the red damask was Roman had no precise value; one's eyebrows would not have been raised to hear that it came from Baluchistan or Guatemala. Thus, when a playgoer heard of an oyster salad being eaten by actors, it sounded weird or funny only if one had not had it himself at a Stettheimer dinner.

At the Alwyn Court, a chateau-like apartment building at 182 West 58th St., for long the Stettheimer residence, Louis Bouché and his wife Marion remember an evening when they were disconcerted to find no liquor; so, through the legend of a default, evidence exists that some kind of alcoholic drink was often on hand; during Prohibition days, however, the Stettheimers declined, on patriotic grounds, to deal with bootleggers. Of course, there were many tea-parties, especially intimate ones, with rich Viennese or German torte and little sausages, perhaps even a glass of Madeira. Then there were tête-à-tête lunches with Florine at her studio. Bouché recalls lunching with her this way, while other friends, such as Tchelitchew, liked to come alone to tea, or perhaps bring one or two others as Florine's only guests. Once, at Tchelitchew's for tea, Florine met Alfred Frankfurter and was pleased to report, in her diary, that he "loved" her portrait of Ettie. Edgar Wind was one of those whom Tchelitchew introduced to Florine. Inevitably, the eminent art scholar was a candidate for the lists espousing the hostess' cause; since he proved well disposed toward her work, it is to be regretted that nothing came of that fact.

Altogether the most riotous incident known to have taken place at a Stettheimer party concerns a weekend on the Tarrytown estate, André Brook, given up by the family in later years when they started to travel in the United States and to frequent New Jersey summer resorts. Adolph Bolm was a guest, and so pleasant was the time spent that Bolm and his wife, with one or two others, missed the last train back to New York and were invited, consequently, to stay over night. Another consequence was that Bolm was obliged to sleep in one of old Mrs. Stettheimer's frilled cambric nightgowns. Before retiring in it—Van Vechten's version goes—he improvised a dance on the lawn that must have been pyrotechnic if nothing more sensational.

Florine's diary verifies this episode without mentioning the dance, which it would have been odd for her to overlook. In any case, her account, including the nightgown lent to Bolm, skips at once to the next day, when she says her late-staying guests "camped on the lawn all morning." This might have been her description of Bolm's dance, which thus may have been a thank-you for staying over. But Florine seems to have been in a curiously detached mood. "I picked my zinnias," she curtly concludes that day's entry, possibly implying that Bolm looked better by footlights than by the morning sun. Maybe some diaries, however, are written as a post-mortem antidote for the irrecoverable loss of pleasant moments: a strategically premature souring of sweet grapes.

LOUIS BOUCHÉ, IN connection with Florine's portrait of him (1923), contributes to the legend of her obsessive attachment to her pictures. Perhaps this attachment, when in regard to portraits, was a form of having friends with her in *persona* rather than in *person*. Not long after giving Bouché his portrait, Florine borrowed it from him, and after he had it again in his possession, it was not very long before the artist borrowed it once more. It is possible she was worried over a certain lack of appreciation she imagined was perceptible in the subject. This time the loan became, for Bouché, almost a forgotten matter. He liked the portrait despite the fact that he considered it bore almost no resemblance to him, but he may not have guessed that Florine, conceivably, was applying a test of the value subjects put on her portraits of them. However, Bouché was abruptly reminded that Florine had the portrait in her possession when he accidentally encountered Ettie. At once, like a good sister, turning a suspicion-laden eye on him, she demanded, "Don't you want your portrait back?" Bouché did not dream of ignoring a reminder phrased like this, so he lost little time in getting Florine on the phone, suggesting that she was sequestering his property. He was not prepared for the minimal hesitation at the other end of the line or the quavering voice that said, "Do you *really* want it back?"

He did. And so today it hangs on the little balcony of his duplex apartment. Bouché does not rate Florine high as an artist, believing—so he told me—that her life lacked the profundity of experience that it takes to be a true artist. I did not join issue with him but allowed him to go on at his own rate. He immediately qualified his harshness by adding that at the same time Florine and her milieu signified something colorful and interesting whose absence left the world of culture poorer. But he wished to justify his verdict on Florine's temperament. "An artist," he rumbled on solemnly, "has to have gravy on his vest!" I instantly grasped what he meant, but thinking of it now, I am constrained to say that, while accidents will happen, I don't know if Florine's wardrobe contained a vest.

Florine loved clothes, their textures, and the imaginative moods they created. As for vests, she probably found them too "tailored." On herself, she did not consider clothes as anything in which, in the real world, to languish carelessly or with care aforethought. If they hinted of romance, it was a faëry kind, such as that evoked in one of her poems:

Mother asked
What are you making now?
I was sewing silver fringe
onto stiff taffeta
pale blue
shot with gold
the color of the sun-glinted sea
that was breaking
and foaming below our balcony—
I answered
I think a bathing suit
or perhaps
a moonwrap

With the rest of the fashion world, the Stettheimer ladies had fallen under the spell of the harem skirt, which had its prototype in the Diaghileff ballet, *Schéhérazade* (premiered in Paris in 1910), but which seems to have been rendered into the fashion idiom by Poiret only after the play *Kismet* was produced in Paris; in any case, the new skirt was considered an ingenious solution of the problem of walking in the prevailing hobble-skirt. Florine and Ettie, especially the latter, seem to have worn versions of it throughout the twenties and thirties; not surprisingly, then, some friends recall on the three sisters only skirts "curving in toward the ankles." Carrie, in Florine's portrait of her, wears a typical such skirt-and-trailing-scarf arrangement.

Today, certain articulate and confident memories are persuaded that Florine was an exception to the Stettheimer "long skirt" rule and that, whenever Fashion demanded it, as it did in the twenties, Florine obediently showed the requisite amount of leg. Her paintings' testimony readily confirms this. Even if her visible limbs in the recumbent self-portrait are only theatrically symbolic, the fact is that in *Beauty Contest* (1924, where she crosses her legs), *Cathedrals of Broadway* (1929), and *Lake Placid* (1919, where she wears a beach robe), her figure displays much bare leg. Even Ettie, in her portrait, is seen outstretched in a décolleté gown whose length seems hardly induced to cover her knees. The ladies' upper torsoes seem to have been notably and invariably modest; in those days, of course, the fashion silhouette encouraged this flattened effect.

As for trousers, Florine by no means considered them a taboo on the feminine. She might well have reasoned, in an international light, that the prejudice against them was narrowly national in any case. In *Natatorium Undine,* she reclines in fancy knee-breeches, and in *Family Portrait No. 2* she wears an atelier costume of black silk or velvet, the trousers pajama-style. Max Ewing (a budding novelist) once wrote of seeing her in "white satin trousers worn under a flowing overdress of spangled net," and according to her painting, *Love Flight of a Pink Candy Heart,* she seems to have had a fling in them on the floor of a costume ball, although this particular image may be pure fantasy.

Van Vechten writes that Florine would appear à la Longhi and Ettie in diamond-shaped garments of flowered brocade, while Carrie was equipped typically with a golden throatband and a crown. It is very possible Carrie imagined she resembled the Queen Mother, Mary of England, which she actually did. If anyone had or has the impression that Florine and Ettie were "very wild" in their clothes, as someone has said, it was a party impression: the reaction of those who seldom saw the ladies wearing daytime or shopping apparel. Florine wrote of buying a cotton suit at Altman's, and she certainly wore, for she says as much, at least one (red) sweater even though it was combined with a filet lace dress. This combination told of her flair for being original.

I VIVIDLY RECALL my first visit to Florine Stettheimer's studio because the date was also the occasion of a thrilling experience of mine in the theatre. Unhappily, I was not around to see *Four Saints* either in Hartford or on Broadway, but in 1936 I went with Tchelitchew to the première of Balanchine's first choreographic version of Gluck's *Orfeo,* for which the Metropolitan had consented to put the singers in the orchestra pit and only the dancers on stage. Afterwards our party went to Florine's studio, where a reception was being held. Tchelitchew, who at that time had known Florine only a year, had created the costumes and the décors for Balanchine's ballet. He had done so with a grave poetic grace blending neo-Classicism with neo-Romanticism as only he knew how. Feder, who had lit *Four Saints in Three Acts,* had devised the elegant lighting.

Inveigling iridescences, pale or ruddy, bathed the great Met stage while the Balanchine-trained dancers, mostly in white and

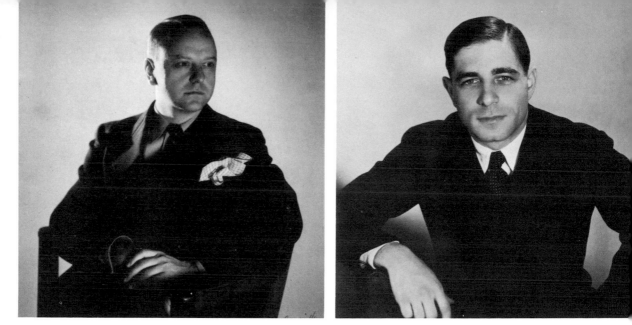

Collaborators in an illustrious cause, *Four Saints in Three Acts,* produced in Hartford, Conn., and New York in 1934. Above left: composer Virgil Thomson; above right: scenarist Maurice Grosser; below: Carl Van Vechten's portrait of himself with Gertrude Stein and Alice B. Toklas, 1935.

Below right: the late A. Everett Austin, Jr., inspired producer of the opera, *Four Saints in Three Acts;* left, the English choreographer, Frederick Ashton, who contributed to it a charming ballet.

Above: the Ashton ballet in the opera as first visualized by Florine Stettheimer's model set and performers; opposite: as seen in the original production of 1934.

Florine's model sets for the opera; below, Act I, St. Theresa in center, the Compère and Commère in front, left and right; above, Act II, the two St. Theresas (Virgil Thomson multiplied her) before the Compère and Commère in a theatre box. Note Florine's perennial canopy to the right.

Opposite: *Four Saints in Three Acts* (original 1934 production); Act I, the two St. Theresas serenaded by St. Ignatius.

Four Saints in Three Acts (original 1934 production); Act I, St. Theresa
being photographed with the Holy Dove.

Four Saints in Three Acts (original 1934 production); the Celestial Mansion, being viewed by telescope.

looking opalescent, moved with a look and a beauty which I preferred, years later, to the Noguchi-designed version Balanchine created, to Stravinsky's music, for the New York City Ballet. Tchelitchew's Eurydice had copious long black hair that streamed untrammeled down her back. When Orpheus persisted in not looking at her on their journey back from the underworld, she suddenly retired a few paces, took a quick, running leap toward him, and planted her knee firmly—I could not tell whether it was love or malice—in the small of his back. And there she stayed, like a bird on his shoulders, for some indefinite, even timeless, time. (Did she tear off his blindfold? I cannot remember.)

It was perfect to go from the theatre to Miss Florine Stettheimer's, where magically my hostess seemed to have acquired some of the opalescence of the stage I had just seen and where I was presented to her for the first time. I remember Ettie, intent and conversational in a harem skirt, and Carrie, mute and regal in a pearl and rhinestone dog-collar. There was a pronounced family resemblance among the sisters, but Carrie, the tallest, had the largest features (a fact distinguishable in *Family Portrait No. 2*), while Ettie was characterized by an intense, level-browed look that one tentatively classed as intellectual. All wore, most of their lives, close-fitting hair with side-puffs, customarily restrained in nets and low on the brow, reddish or brownish in color; Florine alone seems to have left her brow free sometimes, for in *Cathedrals of Art*, as the Commère, she has thin bangs. Maybe it was her last coiffure . . .

A faculty of the domestic setting Florine had created in her great duplex studio was that of hospitality to light and air. All the white and the transparency reflected or admitted light and color, so that the total effect was phantasmal. Above, on the walled balcony perforated with small arched windows, the Nottingham lace curtains of her boudoir were visible. Across the foot of the little red-carpeted staircase leading to it, a wide white satin—or was it cellophane?—ribbon, tied in a gorgeous bow, forbade access to the cocoon of lace upstairs. A large cut-glass punchbowl in the center of the studio kept magnetizing me. In its chartreuse-colored icy depths, immense red strawberries and fantastic chunks of cucumber floated beckoningly. Again and again, I seem to have succumbed to this champagny liquid. Now that I think of it, not water itself ever tasted any better to me.

Four Saints in Three Acts (original 1934 production): Act III, the solemn religious procession with the two St. Theresas under the canopy, the Compère and Commère at left.

THE SMALL PARTY WAS in honor of Tchelitchew, and present among others were Charles Henri Ford and his sister Ruth (now Mrs. Zachary Scott), Kirk and Constance Askew, and Joseph Cornell. Tchelitchew had met Florine the previous year shortly after his one-man show at the Julien Levy Gallery. Florine had seen it and been deeply impressed, so much so that when she read the way one of her critic friends treated it in print, she phoned the critic (she told Tchelitchew later) and gave him a dressing-down for the disrespect he had shown so fine an artist. But they had not yet met when the other artist had his dream.

A light-brown haired woman, in a dress of half-gold and half-silver brocade, appeared suddenly to him and said, "I am Florine Stettheimer. I love your work. I will be your friend to my last days."—"And so," Tchelitchew told me gently some years ago, "it was." An evening or so after the dream, a friend took him to the Alwyn Court, and he met (only a little to his surprise) the lady of his dream. He was hardly amazed, furthermore, to see in the apartment Florine's painting of a sunburst exactly like one that had appeared in his dream of her. This work, *Sun*, was given him by Carrie and Ettie after Florine's death.

THE ARTIST'S GESTURE in *Cathedrals of Art,* similar to Tchelitchew's in the same picture, expresses the sort of united front the two of them privately made against the modern art world. Each intensely individual, each consciously and defiantly "out of the swim," they reacted automatically against prevailing fashions of all kinds—automatically and articulately. Neither supposed, during these years, what eventually would come to both: a retrospective show at the Museum of Modern Art, though Florine's, of course, took place posthumously. Tchelitchew saw in his new friend a real spirit, and he seems to have been unique in drawing from her those "professional secrets"—in his own phrase—which she was so reluctant to communicate to others.

Her reticence in this respect, I think, had been owing to her knowledge that the skill of an artist's hand and the secrets of its movements are precious because essentially induplicable. An artist's tricks are always the things that will be least valuable if they are attempted by other hands. But Tchelitchew, himself a great professional, came to her as a true confrère (rather than a compère) open-handed. It was a matter, not of aesthetic form, but of social form. Other professionals were cavalierly indifferent, politely flattering. These could laugh a little *at* Florine as well as *with* her. She knew this. And she knew that Tchelitchew, on the contrary, sympathized wholly and from within. So she, too, opened her hands . . .

Nobody I know of, artist or critic, has a distinct memory of talking much shop with Florine except Tchelitchew. If Tchelitchew had been as frank about her confidences as Carl Sprinchorn (whose glimpse of a bottle of mastic beside her palette is suggestive), we might know enough not to speculate about such things as the artist's mixing of colors or possible use of medium. Some overt inferences, such as her graffito method of rendering lace that appears in the Bouché portrait, are inevitable from an inquiring look at her surfaces. Yet McBride, while in his book he reports the built-up white subsurface typical of her, has to hazard rather than assert that Florine sometimes wiped her paint with a cloth to smoothe it over.

Virgil Thomson and I, before the work he owns, *New York 1918,* discussed just how much of it was executed with brushes; he claims that virtually everything betokens the palette knife. Some details are so fine (such as the infinitesimal stripes of the American flags on the two small warships) that she certainly had recourse to the brush or possibly to its sharp wooden end. Sprinchorn points out that the deliberate tendency of her paint to make ridges indicates, of course, a knife since brushes would have defeated such a purpose. Mr. and Mrs. Sheldon Keck, who restored some of Florine's paintings after her death, speak of the paint being laid on with a knife like nothing so much as cake-frosting. While nobody ever saw her at work, her diary reveals that she stained-in her late paintings in dry *fresco* after outlining them with charcoal on the white subsurface. For graffito, she undoubtedly made frequent use of a pen.

Some claim that one may read a painter's art in the minutest section of his surface in the way that Goethe discovered the pattern of the whole tree in its leaf; for instance, Vermeer's *Lacemaker,* whose dots presaged Pointillisme, can be read this way. But the form of the snowflake uncovered by the microscope can never be the snowflake that strikes our cheek or the one that multiplies in varying dots like veils shaken out across the world. Florine's frosty whites (seldom unwarmed by red beneath or above) have a strange lack of uniformity, a casualness that is naïve—as naïve as her adaptation of brush stroke to the literal form of a flower petal, whether large or small. But just as she varies her kinds of flower in one bouquet, she varies the shape and quality of the stroke of palette knife or brush in one picture. Actually this is close to an under-formalized calligraphy.

The appearance is not so evident at some times as at others, but a close examination of any single work's surface will make her paint stroke seem whimsical and, like a child's, automatically imitative of the form on which it happens to be engaged. Yet because her intuition is so sensitive, and her practice so genuine and continuous, one finds growing out of some surfaces a rhythm of small strokes such as sparsely appears in *Picnic at Bedford Hills* on the yellow ground's sweeping undulance; possibly, here, a cue was taken from van Gogh. Florine's style is a fusion of strength and delicacy, not uncertain or unstyled in combination so much as susceptible to the uneven inspiration of naïf and primitive artists. Florine, quite sophisticated in her knowledge of this fact, consciously built her life this way. It was a life composed of subtly altering surfaces, snowflakes of mood with girders at their hearts . . . grazes of laughter anchored to grounds of irony.

AS AN ART hostess whose canvases would stand bare to the eyes of her guests, Florine was necessarily sensitive toward being looked at in more than one dimension. Inwardly the artist, one fancies, must have languished in a certain ladylike way even as, alone in her studio, working, she languished out of indifference to the severe modern style that prevailed in so many other studios, and to the universal geometrism that had grown out of Cézanne. One may trace in the architecture of her *Cathedrals,* however, the tendency to incorporate central diamonds with supporting triangles that has an equal, if odd, affinity with the architecture of Cézanne's *Bathers* and the Van Eycks' *Adoration of the Lamb,* no less than with such modern works as Joseph Stella's *Brooklyn Bridge* and Tchelitchew's *Phenomena.*

The farthest Florine would go to bedizening her presence as an artist was to mascara her eyes and wear pants or a beret. Then she was "the lady genius" of high bohemia. In her mind's eye she could not help seeing herself in this rôle among others; as false as it was to any total and true statement of her being, it was real in itself. A "shy violet" from the beginning, she gradually proceeded to the more competent version of her *persona:* the Commère—the Commère who had the "show" graces of the Follies Beauty but with the invaluable qualification of intellect and dignity. More and more, she tacitly assumed that (to her guests) she presented a Veronica's Veil image of Muse to the Art World: one who offered, for good measure, ambrosia and nectar as well as art.

If Florine, as Van Vechten believes and her diary more than hints, had her grievances, she kept them, as a hostess, properly veiled. If imperial fire peeped out, it was no more, on the surface, than a routine rebuke of some slight to protocol. This last category, simple enough, was designed to protect her acute allergy to adverse criticism—a trait to which all who knew her testify. When McBride, for example, ventured to observe that perhaps, in her portrait of Joseph Hergesheimer, the feet were "a little bit small," something he politely put in the form of a don't-you-think, the artist replied with unrepressed annoyance that the subject's wife had assured her that her likeness of the novelist was "uncanny."

Hostessing, however inconspicuous in Florine's case, naturally tended to shed a universally protective gloss on oversensitive surfaces. If Florine had hauteur, it was never by a hostess's warrant. Carrie's function as housekeeper (she invented the elaborate menus) was indispensable, though apparently it was one to which this sister graciously sacrificed her more serious occupations of reading, concert-going, and completing her doll-house. Once, on impulse, Carrie gave herself a holiday by taking a suite at the Plaza, and made no secret of wondering if the Stettheimer habitués would come just to see *her.* Of course, they did. Ettie, for her part, was willing and able to manage the general conversation at large dinner parties, which took place about once a month at the Alwyn Court residence till Mrs. Stettheimer's death, when Florine moved permanently to the Beaux Arts studio and held more intimate dinner parties of her own.

The artist's new independence, with the fresh opportunity given her for painting, entailed increasing isolation from her sisters and the growth of a rather picayune moodiness. If she liked the guests expected at a dinner party given by Carrie and Ettie at the Dorset, where *they* took separate apartments in 1935, she would go; if she felt noncommittal, she was apt to stay away. Artists, owing to their systematic criticism and intellectualization of emotion, feel ambivalences very keenly. In 1935, Florine still had nearly a decade of work to accomplish and was girding herself accordingly. She required, in brief, "aloneness." But creative aloneness is not human loneliness; here, once more, was the inevitable other side of the coin. Whether, as a drawing-room *persona,* she felt herself the Follies Beauty or the Commère, Florine remained a human being—and thus wistful.

A little anecdote given me by Carl Sprinchorn (shared by the sisters as a friend though he came to know Ettie best) reveals Florine's subtle isolation in the midst of people. At a party one night, Sprinchorn became aware only on the point of leaving that, while the society had been lively, he had not exchanged one word with Florine all evening. But suddenly he realized that she had come to his side to escort him to the door. Once at the door, however, she quietly buttonholed him, and it was almost half an hour before he actually crossed the threshold. Florine had been as charming, and as serious, as ever: the "soft pink light" was probably on special duty. Sprinchorn, recalling the incident, was moved to think that her cordiality possessed, in general, a strange contradictory quality. In the same gesture that she asserted it, she seemed to withdraw it; as she came forward, she receded. The same quality is in the photograph which I described above, and accounts for Florine's look of moving while not moving. Essentially, it is the trait of one who consciously studies motion; it is a dancer's as well as, in Florine's case, a painter's art. In fact, as a pure dynamic quality, it is the chief characteristic of the figures of her mature period.

PERHAPS ALL DIARIES, indispensably by their nature, share the paradoxical trait of an abundant reticence; or, it may be, a laconic profuseness. Florine's annual diaries (never kept in the printed "forms") skip whole years and frequently months and weeks as well as days. "I stay home a lot," she wrote after the permanent removal to her big studio, "I like it. I am not to rights making a new home, housekeeping, parties, fatigue, too much to write." The very verbal ellipsis, in so small a space, is indicative. A few sentences may take in an indefinite span of varied or mysterious happenings, especially disappointing along with the gaps finally made by Ettie's scrupulous editing. Yet, individually, Florine's spare entries contain a rich personal economy.

Important facts attest to her hero-worship of George Washington, and as might be expected, she took care to make a diary entry on Feb. 22nd, as she was thus attentive to the family's individual birthdays. On Feb. 22nd, 1939, her diary received this votive memorandum: "Washington's birthday—I put lots of gold on Washington [i.e., on his statue as seen in *Cathedrals of Wall Street*]." Superficially so much like the smooth, embossed-gold surfaces of decorative figures on German postcards of the last century, Florine's also "embossed" gold figures (Liberty and Washington) have the organic surfaces of life. This inversion of artifice is characteristic of her.

Yet what is the entry on Feb. 22nd, 1935? But two words: "I shampooed." And what is to be concluded from them? Something, I think, very affecting: Florine Stettheimer's loyalty was that of a true fetichist, especially one dealing in creative images. Nothing worthy had happened that day, nothing inspired, nothing to add to George Washington's legend—the legend to which her heart was attached as to a bouquet. But the day could not pass without a ritual genuflection to the revered image. At a glance, she could tell —pencil in hand—that only one thing of the least novelty had taken place: she had shampooed. Perhaps it did not happen to be the day for shampooing. But like the saint who feels the intrusion of the dreaded lacuna and prays or tells her beads, Florine had taken an equally adequate measure. Such was her inveterate simplicity.

ONE FACT ABOUT Florine's diaries indicates that she did not write them for posterity; they are for the most part in quite commonplace "frames": ordinary, perishable little notebooks of pocket or school size. According to her own notations, they were all re-read about three years before she died, but they were not in any way "enshrined" then, and no special measures were taken by Ettie, later, to preserve their immediate encasements. Yet a change takes place in their format after Florine began her exclusive residence at the Beaux Arts. They become typewriter-page size and are apparently from tablets whose sheets have been mechanically perforated to be strung together; thus strung, they exist today in the American Literature Collection of the Yale University Library, to which Ettie presented most of the family papers, together with a sheaf of pictorial documents, before she died.

kindness when each of them, knowing how welcome extra cash was to him then, commissioned a piano portrait and sent him a check for $100. Duchamp felt it when he was engaged by Florine to give her French lessons, superfluous because she knew French well. If sometimes Florine and Ettie were frank, even blunt, they never indulged themselves in displays of what is universally held to be artistic temperament, and certainly they were beyond any kind of affectation. With an intimate such as Tchelitchew Florine could be really chummy. Once, tête-à-tête with him, she began to mull over the pretensions of a certain mutual friend whose championship of her was accredited a major virtue. After airing his dark duplicity for a while, Florine exclaimed, "*Why* are we so kind to him?" In reply, Tchelitchew merely shrugged in his expressive way and audibly sighed. "I guess," Florine murmured after a little pause, "it's because we're so kind." At which the two friends exchanged a mysterious smile and broke out in mutual laughter: Florine's a low-keyed pleasant tinkle, the other artist's the merry pantomime of a groan.

VAN VECHTEN CONFESSES that Florine, much to his amazement, brought him to book for not introducing her to people she wanted to meet. "Who, for example?" he countered incredulously, knowing well that the Stettheimers did not hunt lions. "Mrs. Franklin D. Roosevelt," Florine crisply returned. She admired Mrs. Roosevelt and wished to put her in *Cathedrals of Wall Street*. Not knowing Mrs. Roosevelt, Carl had to beg off. "You do know someone I should like to meet," Florine persisted. "And who may that be?" Van Vechten airily wanted to know, not dreaming that the name already being hurled at his head would be Noel Coward's. He had to demur: "Florine, I don't know him well enough. I hardly ever run into him except at Condé Nast's where, you know, about everybody in New York goes . . . So I just can't pick up the phone and ask him to your house."

Florine dropped her eyes and said no more and yet, when she raised them, a cloud of frustration had appeared. She was then on the prowl for what she herself termed her "victims." Unexpectedly, about this time, she was delighted to encounter Grace Moore (another candidate for inclusion in *Cathedrals of Wall Street*) in a beauty shop. Perhaps by then, *circa* 1939, she felt more scrutinizing than scrutinized. But someone absorbed half her life in making pictures of herself, her friends, and certain distant celebrities, always carried the sense of making a picture in her own right. "Monroe Wheeler, Glenway Wescott, and George Platt Lynes," her diary noted in later years, "came to look at me and my paintings." The tandem question of the picture she made, in person or on canvas, had never lapsed.

THERE CAN BE no least doubt that Florine Stettheimer appreciated the refined wit of exposing her dearest "self," her art, to the professional eyes that were constantly around her studio and that waited for the unappointed "birthdays" of her canvases. Four easels stood about the spacious Beaux Arts studio. They were always covered (except at the private exposures) and etiquette forbade any peeking. The highlight of the social milieu the artist had established by 1916, continuing it all her life, was that a different standard prevailed in this exclusive little art world; it was simply that the same yardstick was not used to measure its hostess as was used to measure artists in general; at least, if the same yardstick was used, the marks on it were ignored. Gradually, due to influential people such as McBride himself, Paul Rosenfeld, Marsden Hartley, and finally Tchelitchew, Florine became a muffled cause-célèbre rather than a celebrity. The muffled cause-célèbre was herself capable of measuring the area of fame's spotlight as its trickle extended beyond her studio. That the commotion over the cause was never concerted to any effective degree made this measurement extremely, disconcertingly easy.

A great deal of Florinesque atmosphere is contained in a painting called *Studio Party* (or *Soirée*), which though undated must be earlier than any of the well-known Conversation Pieces since it contains neither McBride nor Duchamp. This work probably commemorated the installment of the birthday-party habit, when a covered easel was shorn of its mystery to bring a new painting to the eyes of Florine's little society. It seems to me that this particular painting possesses an actual moment of time—about three or four minutes, I should guess, after the unveiling, when everybody has looked, offered his initial compliments or pleasantries, then settled back—with the exception of two or three individuals—to steep in the invisible aura created by it. Poetically, one senses in this scene of social relaxation the natural aftermath of those hours of lonely self-immolation that are every artist's glory and slavery. Florine, emerging with difficulty from the creative "trance," had ritualized its aftermath if for no other reason than to relax in sympathetic company.

Studio Party, with the exception of the owner (Duchamp?) of a Harlequin-costumed pair of legs cut off by the margin, is compact of identifiable members of the Stettheimer family and the New York art world of the period. Spread about, besides the three sisters, are Gaston and Isabelle Lachaise, Maurice Sterne, Avery Hopwood, Leo Stein, a supposed Hindu "poet," Albert Gleizes and Juliette Roche (Mme Gleizes). In February, 1954, Ettie suspected that it might have been destroyed, but fortunately it was not. While eliminated from Florine's retrospective show at the Museum of Modern Art by Duchamp, acting in an advisory capacity, the painting has two points of absorbing interest: the large female nude on an easel against the back wall and a canvas on another easel, a part of whose back we see but whose front is visible only to the room, and in particular to two professionals obviously transfixed by it: Gleizes and Lachaise. In the center of the room, the critic Leo Stein, facing it, seems to hold his earphone at an abstracted angle, perhaps in another sort of transfixed response.

It is unlikely that Florine would have made Gleizes' and Lachaise's faces as they are out of mere wishfulness. Their mutual expression of bemused attentiveness is in the artist's best "amused" manner and tells us, I think, just what the canvas of the moment may have been. Florine had just begun her large Conversation Pieces, and hence this very work, an informal tribuna, may signalize the doubly significant current birthday. What could be more plausible, therefore, than the fanciful speculation that Gleizes and Lachaise are studying the very picture we ourselves see? The over-all studio party is therefore a kind of mirror in which the current guests look and in which we, in retrospect, look over their shoulders. It would have been tasteless for Florine ever to have repeated the exact effect seen here. Among her many Conversation Pieces that follow up to the thirties and culminate in the *Cathedrals,* there will be no other tribuna with the artist's home as a setting. The composition here is not so sure or interesting as some she later made of groups even larger, yet her budding faculty for creating an expressive hieroglyph of the single figure is quite apparent and one cannot help thinking of the parallel between Van Dongen's "society figures" and hers. The work's date is certainly post-1915, or latterly of that year, since a bit of *Family Portrait No. 1* (1915) is visible in the upper left-hand corner.

Clearly, in *Studio Party,* we have Florine's summary judgment of the abstract *persona* embodied by her works of art. This *persona* was as apt to be an object of "admiration" in the more radical, ambiguous sense of that emotion as to be one of "admiration" to art specialists in the purely favorable sense. Most of the figures here have the look of not being part of a "tribuna" and this momentary detachment balances the momentary absorption on Gleizes' and Lachaise's faces, which thus become the fountainheads of the work's pervasive comic irony. Florine wished to say that none was quicker to reflect her ambiguous way of admiring the world and its works, including her own, than was she, the artist. She placed her nude (titled *A Model* and a figure evidently too large for her to handle easily) at the back to contrast with the—to us—invisible canvas opposite; the nude, doubtless, had had its ideal moment, in which Florine had put much that was climactic (all her "student" fervor) but this moment was already past: the artist had come upon her new manner, her new ideal, that was to blossom and reblossom till the monumental *Cathedrals.*

She had also been doing flowers with miniature statues of a nude dancer and an Aphrodite, but there is still uncertainty of manner and a hint of strain in the studied Impressionism of these earlier works, perhaps based on memories of Intimism. *Family Portrait No. 1* is the first assurance that, above all and best of all, she was interested in human relations as such; previous oceanside and suburban Conversation Pieces, showing "neighbors," while suggesting her change, had actually been clumsy. The later flower pieces are less straightforwardly Impressionistic à la Monet and Bonnard; increasingly, they suggest heraldry and symbolism and have the kind of transcendent sensibility belonging to Redon, whose flower pieces they more closely resemble than anyone's else. Like Redon, as different as their worlds are, Florine essays a whole universe of symbol. Her blend of objective vision, gay and serenely satirical, with a personal symbolism of intensely private yet communicable kind, has never been properly understood in terms of method. McBride summarily covers it in his book as only thematic: the *histoire de famille* as the background-incentive of the Conversation Pieces.

Carl Sprinchorn's portrait of Florine, as was stated previously, shows her, uniquely, in direct personal contact with the viewer; her gaze is frontally deep and dark with an absolute if intuitive kind of communication ... The same artist friend, Sprinchorn, did a documentary—still unfinished and undated—watercolor of a typical gathering at the Alwyn Court residence when the "family," rather than Florine, entertained in the afternoon. It is as though we see the crowd in a mirror, as Florine might have seen it and herself; for, while she is pictured centrally, she seems just to have entered and perhaps not quite in time for the party, where Carrie and Ettie are to be identified as already in the thick of the fray ... Here is Florine the social observer, hovering with silent wings and unobtrusive, even unobserved, glance: she is small in relation to the unrealistic, non-perspectival vision Sprinchorn has employed for his scene, where an arbitrary scale is given each individual. As a whole, his "scheme" is elusive, but what we have in this spontaneous work is the very flush of that ineffable "party noise": the hum of self-interested, detached, independent, and multiple conversations where everybody is a trifle conscious of the picture she makes—indeed, the *ladies* predominate both numerically and in scale. Beatrice Wanger, stylishly gotten up, is prominent: she was Stella's daughter and therefore the three hostesses' niece; centrally to the fore are Elsa Brill and Mrs. Ernest Wise (Beatrice) Keyser, obviously also cynosures of fashion and personality. Nearby is Mrs. Hilda E. Hellman, Geoffrey Hellman's mother, a relative of the Stettheimers. Carl Van Vechten, done aptly in profile, and Philip Moeller, typically "holding forth," give peripheral but essential accents to Sprinchorn's visual ensemble and shrewdly implied vocal polyphony. Not even in party clothes, but apparently only a quiet shopping suit, Florine's mysteriously suave person is tabulated, among the rest, as one *seeing* rather than *seen*. This is the "long view" of her as the faithful historian of a society she was giving her own, peculiarly subjective, interpretation.

INTO SUCH A gathering, doubtless, Mabel Dodge Luhan was introduced when, as a visitor to New York, she first made the Stettheimers' acquaintance. Mrs. Luhan lost no time before voicing, even above the susurrant tumult, a desire to know "who was who." The very incidence of such a self-conscious note of strangeness in the milieu must have occasioned a certain jar. Yet it could hardly have affected the imperturbably bland stream of the hostesses' tact. Sprinchorn's watercolor portrayed a milieu to which, as pursued in the family groove at Alwyn Court, Florine was shortly to bid goodbye for a more personally elect world. Lurking in her own doorway, the artist probably had fretted for years over not possessing the quietude and self-isolation which she instinctively sought.

Through ordinary ups and downs of mood, Florine was continuing her painter's way, governed by an increasing inner contemplation which, no matter what conventional encouragements or discouragements modified it, issued in an unflagging self-confidence. She became more and more interested in portraits, went along on their wave proliferantly and in Virgil Thomson's did a pivotal one which predicated herself and her family as "4 STS"—and in some sense, then, also "celebrities." That she was casually flirting with fame, she became aware after the acclaim won by her theatre sets. One cannot know exactly how seriously she contemplated being the subject of an American "Meier-Graefe": she might have said she was "amused" by it. Nevertheless, we learn from the following that the experience of *Four Saints,* even as the opera was running, had made her conscious of "star" publicity. "Do you remember the young man who said he was a student at New York University?" she told her sisters in a letter dated March 29th, 1934. "He wrote me that he would like to write his dissertation about my paintings!—à la Meier-Graefe—discover and analyze me. I shall have to keep a secretary like the star members of our cast."

But during the preceding decade, though she had faithfully applied her energies to canvas and shown with various groups, she had earned only sporadic encouragement from the press ("the press" sometimes being represented by personal friends). In spite of the distinction of being asked to exhibit in the Carnegie International of 1924, she could consider herself for the next ten years a largely undiscovered quantity in the art world. While *Four Saints* was in the making, the beam of public notice was esoterically focussed on her when Marsden Hartley and Paul Rosenfeld went "all out" for her in 1931-32. At this time, there was a plausible occasion in the inclusion of *Cathedrals of Broadway* in the Whitney Museum exhibition of the American Society of Painters, Printers, and Gravers, one of several organizations into which Florine had, as it were, "drifted," and then found reason to leave. It is not known whether she reconsidered her resignation from the

A.S.P.P.G. though this organization sent her an urgent request to do so in a letter from the Secretary, H. E. Schakenberg, dated December 10th, 1935. She had also shown steadily at the annual exhibitions of the Independents, which she had joined in 1917 and also from which she eventually resigned.

As the editor of *Creative Art,* Henry McBride made its pages available to Marsden Hartley for an article on Florine in 1931,* an article which the artist duly described in her diary as "delightful —a charming theme—almost a minuet." Hartley's essay was somewhat more resourceful in interpreting Florine's art than her own cursory epithets for his writing. But he was careful to begin by stating that she had never "appeared openly" on the art scene, an historically inaccurate phrase subject to diverse misconstructions. However, he called her art "chamber music meant to be heard by special sympathetic ears," spoke of the eighteenth century, of charm, and of her "ultra-refined experience," and developed a coherent if rather precious atmosphere.

His gallantry was a little too obvious by the time one arrived at two repetitions, in the same phrase, of the hackneyed superlative he had hit upon: Florine's art was the "ultra-lyrical expression of an ultra-feminine spirit." There can be doubt of Hartley's sincere desire to do something for Florine's professional reputation. If only he had not been so self-conscious about her "professional standing." Though he brought in the American element of her work, he kept harping on her feminine nature, placed her in the class of the best European women painters (even, boldly, to the disadvantage of Laurencin), and then, rather anti-climactically, compared her achievement to "the stage art of Mrs. Fiske and Marie Tempest."

Comparing arts is especially risky when attempting to define the specific merits of a little-known oeuvre; it is much riskier when the artist in question is a woman and one repeats how feminine she is so often that any comparison with male artists seems forbidden. Perhaps Hartley had a troubled conscience about Florine's "ultra-feminine spirit." When she had shown him, together, her portraits of Father Hoff and Alfred Stieglitz a few years before, he had found them respectively "very charming" and "very amusing." Then, to Florine's amused surprise, he had been constrained to add, still gazing at them, "Two feminine men . . ."

* *Creative Art:* July 1931.

As a straightforward estimate, Hartley's magazine piece was rhetorically true enough but without finesse or suppleness of judgment; as a promotional strategy, it was weak and ill-advised. The period was the midst of the Depression and a luxurious drawing-room art could hardly be expected to appeal to the strong social-realist, post-Ashcan tendency that had been given an indirect boost by the Wall Street crash. Moreover, this was no way to oppose the international Cubist and Abstract tendencies with American representationalism; in fact, it seems possible to diagnose Hartley's whole critical rationale as not quite ingenuous. Florine was an original (always, as he knew, a frightening thing to announce bluntly) and there was nothing whatever in American art, or Hartley's own work, to justify his essay on her as critical propaganda for a school or tendency, or as a blow struck for anyone but Florine. It was all too right in a private sense, all too wrong in the large public sense. The one material link his subject had with either European or American styles in art was Impressionism but, plainly, Hartley had wished to shun invidious comparisons.

Once Robert Locher (the Compère of *Cathedrals of Art*) prevailed on Charles Demuth, a mutual friend of his and Florine's, to write a favorable opinion of the artist's work. It exists in manuscript in the collection of papers given to the Yale Library, but as it was not very happily composed, Florine seems never to have made any use of it. In an article published in *Accent** after Florine's death, Paul Rosenfeld—who had done an extensive notice of her participation in the Whitney show of 1932—conscientiously if not cavalierly resorted to McBride's authority by quoting him that Florine "had passed as unremarked by the general public as did the poet Emily Dickinson in the 1880's. But when a few years have put the event in perspective, it will be found by the new group of connoisseurs that Miss Stettheimer's place among the artists is just as distinct and just as secure as Emily Dickinson's is among the poets." McBride's tactic was cleverer and more imaginative than those of his confrères, but in 1945, Rosenfeld, while still desirous of praising Florine, wished to correct his 13-year-old collaboration with her art's public progress. So in the above-mentioned article, he proceeded to question McBride's prophecy, just quoted, on the tacit assumption that it had not yet come true:

* The World of Florine Stettheimer. *Accent,* Winter 1945.

Florine Stettheimer's *Cathedrals of Art,* 1942 (detail), oil on canvas; the artist's last self-portrait; as noted by the streamer at her feet, she identified herself with the Commère of *Four Saints in Three Acts.*

Birth and rebirth; opposite: marquee of the 44th Street Theatre, where *Four Saints in Three Acts* had its New York premiére, March 1st, 1934; above: marquee of the Broadway Theatre, New York, where the opera was revived by ANTA in 1952.

Cathedrals of Broadway, 1929, oil on canvas; the artist (seen lower left in dark dress with her sister, Stella Wanger, and the latter's son, Henry) had cultivated a theatrical sensibility before embarking on her theatre sets.

"Extraordinarily," he wrote, "this spinster [Emily Dickinson] possessed the gift of imagination, the power to move the soul in us. Florine Stettheimer's gift was slighter. It was eminently for fancy, for charming or whimsical images, or combinations of them, for daintiness of workmanship and fantasy." Her fancy, it seemed, could reach the state of "fantasy" but not that of "imagination." Unfortunately, this labored and dubious qualification of Florine's gift defaced Rosenfeld's tribute to her memory.

More sensitive and astute than Hartley, Rosenfeld was still an unreliable critic as well as a negligent stylist. He concluded strongly by saying that her art "lends something of that charm, that grace, that etherealness not to any small closed society, but the world." This was at least putting all the cards on the table. Still he had erred in taste and tactic by avouching a wiser mien than McBride's and then attempting to serve Florine's cause by defining the superlative virtue of her limitations. He also walked into the booby-traps of "charm" and "feminine temperament," which he had been foolish enough to precede by pointing to the dubious hypothesis of her work as "anemic, a trifle blasé." Here, too, one senses a deliberate critical compromise.

Rosenfeld's earlier gesture in *The Nation* * had brought out three points of greater importance than all but one of those made in the *Accent* article, where he observed of Florine's works: "The total form rivals the theatre, the opera, even the circus." Thirteen years earlier he had written: ". . . the idea of grandiose documentary caricatures of the land of the free found expression in Miss Stettheimer's art some while before it was popularized in *The American Mercury*." Fine: except that "caricatures" is a false description; "parodies" would be nearer the truth in this sentence. He had initiated even more valuable themes when mentioning "the very Parisian dollishness" of her figures and their resemblance to "archaic popular images," but he had failed to expand or illustrate these fertile characterizations. Worst of all, this earlier article had opened with a statement scuttling its emergent *esprit gallant:* "There are serious people who claim that she's one of the three important women painters of this country, the other two being Georgia O'Keeffe and Peggy Bacon." Every separate aspect of the vocabulary used in this sentence had an un-

* May 4th, 1932.

fortunate implication. A later passage was a good piece of impressionistic criticism, revealing all the sensory means by which a Stettheimer painting affects the viewer.*

Ten years before Rosenfeld's *Nation* article, Carl Van Vechten, comparing Florine's work to Jazz, had written with insight of the special feelings aroused by it.** Yet despite the urbane charm of his writing, he had neglected to evoke the object of her art through his modest paragraph. This was partly attributable, doubtless, to journalistic conventions. On the other hand, a critic on the Pittsburgh *Post,* Penelope Redd, covering the Carnegie International of 1924, where *Russian Bank* (1921) was shown, spoke of a "symbolism as original as the Chinese in this painting" and came close to the mark with this statement, "Miss Stettheimer, more than any painter we know, has developed a symbolic and decorative type of painting that also engages us by its human interest." *** Glowing with (of course) amusement, Florine let her diary know how gratified she was with this reviewer's discerning praise. Miss Redd must have meant that the large bunch of flowers on the table in the foreground, contrasting with the delicacy of the miniature figures in the background, recalls Chinese treatment of landscape and figures readapted to Florine's sensibility.

THE ARTIST DOES not seem to have confided to her inmost self any written tributes to Henry McBride's long, if spasmodic, apostleship of her evolving art. Could this have been because McBride's tone, shrewdly angled and objectively irreproachible, was a wee bit self-conscious: too, too precisely Cavalier? Besides, McBride championed so much else that, after all, Florine Stettheimer could not feel he was her private champion. One's own instinct is brought to bear. Everything about this maiden painter (imprisoned in the Castle of Neglect) seemed to call for a champion to rescue her from those "abhorrent" behind-the-scenes transactions which would have obliged him to "talk" superlatives, as well as prices, in her behalf. At the same time, Florine never lost faith in the capacity of her pictures themselves to "talk" for her. When Dorothy Miller chose the portrait of her nurse, Maggie, for a show at the Museum of Modern Art, the artist confided to her diary: "I hope she [the

* Quoted in McBride's book.
** *The Reviewer,* February 1922.
*** May 11th, 1924.

portrait] will talk for me.'' Florine divulged the very personal way she felt about those on whom the realization or recognition of her art might depend when she wrote of the problem of finding the right music for her ballet, *Orpheus of the Four Arts,* whose text and scenario had been composed in Paris: ''I want a composer all to myself to tell him what to do.'' She flatly turned down, as a musical setting for the ballet, Bolm's recommendation of Swendow's *Carnival,* which the dancer seems to have induced Pierre Monteux to include in a program specifically for Florine's benefit.

Various currents in her diaries and verses indicate that, especially in her youth, men had accorded her such (more or less personal) attentions, including a normal amount of flattery, and had even hinted at the ultimate question a man asks a woman. Being one who seemed as dedicated to the unmarried state as she was to art, Florine must have thought of masculine attentions, as time went on, in terms of sublimation. She left multiple signs that she herself took a Cavalier attitude toward such relations. This aspect of her life was itself a sort of love-game comedy. Briefly, however, Duchamp dismissed the notion that serious romancing was any part of Florine's relations with men while he knew her, and he knew her through all her maturity. Certainly, he added, with noble impersonality, there was no romance between himself and her, though he suspects that the three sisters looked upon him, and others, as typical impecunious artists in typical search of good matrimonial catches. When I asked him what he thought of Florine's portrait of him, he exclaimed, ''I loved it!'' Yet it could not have been in the least a love token, for she never presented it to him and her will did not leave it to him.

Carl Van Vechten solemnly terms the Stettheimer sisters ''virgins by desire.'' One might have said, instead, ''by instinct,'' but perhaps the substitution of the word ''desire'' would indicate the sublimative element. For this reason, I imagine that Florine would have cherished an aesthetic champion who wrote his critical prose chiefly for her—or for her *alone*—because her lack of availability in the flesh, according to the ancient tradition, would have been the very condition of such a champion's fealty. Yet as one living, like everybody else, in the hard quotidian world, Florine probably had too keen a sense of humor, too highly developed an irony, to indulge herself in the mirage of so private, so inwardly vague, a hope.

SUPPOSE, ALL THE same, such a champion had come along! It is true that he would have been in the nature of a miracle. But Florine would have been the last of living artists to have criticized the hypothesis of miracles. Artists and saints are notably alike in welcoming miracles as normal phenomena, and in Florine's secret life she was several personalities, lived in several dimensions. In the more private, non-professional dimension, she must have had a rather flexible choice of knights. If *Cathedrals of Art* be taken, indeed, as definitive evidence, she expressed a preference for Robert Locher as the partner of her Commère. Tchelitchew, though he came into her life rather late, might also have filled such a rôle. Meanwhile, in art's larger domain, there was, first and foremost, Chevalier McBride. As the earliest official Floriniste, McBride could be an object of unusual interest to Florine's family, which beyond its inmost circle was full of relatives.

After the brilliant spotlight of *Four Saints in Three Acts,* it was as though McBride had suddenly hinted he was Florine's "suitor" and the elder members of the family wished to learn if his intentions were honorably serious. There was hardly a need for Carrie and Ettie to be reassured about the genuineness of their sister's artistic gift. Ettie, it is true, bridles embarrassingly in her introduction to Florine's book of verse, expostulating that she has not relied on her "sisterly sympathy" but sought the impartial literary advice of Carl Van Vechten in proposing to publish *Crystal Flowers.* This sister was only too eager to believe that art was something in which the family naturally shared as they shared their income. She was to leave her own artistic legacy in the shape of *The Memorial Volume of and by Ettie Stettheimer,* declaring in her preface to it that, as no one was left to do it for her, she was obliged to do for herself what her own survival had enabled her to do for Carrie's and Florine's artistic remains. The book is composed of Ettie's doctoral thesis on the philosophy of William James, the two novels (praised by reviewers on their original publication) and some short stories. For her part, Carrie spent nearly a quarter century in creating her elaborate doll-house in which hang miniature versions of works by artist friends, usually executed by the artists themselves; among these are Lachaise's and Duchamp's most famous "nudes." Ettie presented the doll-house to the Museum of the City of New York, where it is on permanent exhibition.

The miniature dimensions of these art works, the life-sized originals of which the Stettheimers did not buy, are significant. The sisters collected *objets d'art* but not art, preferring to spend their limited means in entertaining the small artistic world of New York. The whole world, as I have said, was a sort of little-theatre to Florine. The *Cathedrals,* like models of the Baroque Theatre, are outfitted with a set of pseudo-movable actors: the preternatural dolls of a less than life-sized world. Florine, in fact, made dolls; not only those for the model sets of *Four Saints,* but also a large suite of mannikins for an unproduced ballet of her own invention, *Pocahontas,* the synopsis of which she worked on with Virgil Thomson. On view at her posthumous show were larger mannikins (some of them riding animals) for her other ballet mentioned above, *Orpheus of the Four Arts,* which also remains unproduced.

These mannikins are much like her painted figures: simple, graceful, elongate, tapering. When Florine's models for *Four Saints* materialized, nothing could have seemed more natural to the family than that "Florrie" should still be making dolls. Then, when *Four Saints* became life-sized, when it was actually present in the theatre and Florine herself took a bow from the stage, it was all in the nature of things so far as the family distinction went in the eyes of the family. Yet . . . Was it possible that Florine was a—celebrity? that moot, suspect category: a public figure? Henry McBride seemed always to have hinted that she was . . . Now . . . It was a little bewildering to certain family-members.

The white light of publicity had a way of dazzling and revealing, as by a passing flash of lightning, a vast outer world in which the Stettheimers "dwindled" to being like everybody else—street-sized as it were!—at the moment that fame rendered them (or in rich particular, Florine) awesomely monumental: bigger than life. The artist's cousin, Edwin A. R. Seligman, Professor of Economics at Columbia and a famous scholar, was much struck by the fact that Henry McBride, writing in the *Sun* of *Four Saints* as the creative art of its designer, had termed Florine's sets "sublime." To Professor Seligman, it was extraordinary that stage sets should be identified with a quality typically associated with tragic poetry and works of religious art. That Florrie's stage sets, so childish, so "tinselly," should be sublime . . . So he was delighted to find a chance to confront McBride and ask him, "Is Florrie really so

good as that?'' Naturally, the critic was only too pleased to sub-
scribe informally to his printed adjective. The sets were a frame
for the actual representations of saints and therefore it was perfectly logical for them to be ''sublime.'' The anxious cousin was as
satisfied by the critic's reply as he could have been. But, after all,
when celebrities are crowned, *everyone* knows it . . . or *does everyone know it?*

MCBRIDE BELIEVES THAT Florine's portrait of her mother is her best.
I think that of herself and those of Ettie and ''Duche'' are just as
good, if not better, but assuredly the dominating silhouette of Mrs.
Stettheimer and her exquisitely benign face are a complete success.
Everyone found the old lady, in life, delightful though necessarily,
owing to her age and final invalidism, socially inconspicuous. The
portrait shows her physical idiosyncrasy: permanently raised eyebrows that oddly are the reverse of Ettie's permanently lowered
ones. In Mrs. Stettheimer's face, they give a rhetorical emphasis
to the already saturating innocence of a very old, but really ageless,
being. To all appearances, the three daughters were quite sophisticated about the sincerity of Florine's professional supporters.
Tacitly, these gentlemen made a part of the world's absurd weak-
ness for publicity, for vulgar show, the very thing against which
Florine, in celebrating it, directed her most damaging satire.

One would have imagined that, to a family so aristocratic and
ingrown, Florine ''in the eyes of the world'' could be taken for
granted—even with a life-sized grain of salt! Not entirely so. The
tacit sophistication of the sisters, as McBride learned one day, did
not include the less worldly standpoint of the mother. There was,
after all, a generation's difference between mother and daughters,
and perhaps Mrs. Stettheimer could never quite adjust herself,
when called upon, to the subtle laissez-faire which her staunchly
contemporary children had established as the keynote of their
drawing-room. The melodramatic occasion recalled by McBride
took place before the general fame into which Florine so unexpectedly burst as a result of her Broadway ''publicity.'' He found he
had unwittingly trespassed upon the delicate ground of a family
situation regarding Florine's professionalism!

A Seabright houseparty, the critic recalls, was in progress and
we may imagine, that summer day, Mrs. Stettheimer fanning herself in one of those great, oval-backed wicker ''picture chairs'' of

the twenties, and delighted that she had found herself alone with McBride. Perhaps he had just finished a session on the tennis court, so many of which overspread Florine's portrait of him, and was anticipating tea. He was startled by the matriarch's intimate, even conspiratorial air, in engaging his attention; before she could bring herself to speak, her white hair and upturned face, with its round eyes and guileless mouth of a child, solicited him—and then he became aware that to her he was the image of a knight in the lists of journalism, wielding the lance of public opinion, and thus a champion on whose prowess might depend the worldly fame of her daughter, Florine, as a painter . . .

Substantially, the question she put was the same as that eventually put by Florine's cousin, Prof. Seligman, "Do you really think Florine is a good painter?" But it had hardly been formulated when they were interrupted by a patter of footsteps, and McBride had just begun his earnest reassurance on the point, when who but its subject, smiling broadly but plainly agitated, glided between them? McBride gathered at once from the daughter's air and her words of humorous scolding that Mrs. Stettheimer had committed a *faux pas* which she had been expressly forbidden on announcing its intention—yes, the daughters had evidently banded together to suppress the old lady's naïve curiosity: her anxiety about the truth of the rumor (prominently supported by McBride) that Florine was an artist who mattered . . .

The champion felt a bit unfairly compromised, but now it could not be helped. Mrs. Stettheimer had let the cat out of the bag: Florine Stettheimer was mortified to have the critic learn that such a thing as her professional authenticity could become an issue in the bosom of her family. Ever so faint a blush must have mantled the cheeks of the artist as she stood there in the spotlight of critical inquisition, compromised by it even more deeply than either the gallant McBride or her mother . . . For, in the hidden ardor of her heart, it was this very spotlight that was just beginning really to count . . .

IV *The World in Her Eyes*

THE FACTS OF a conversion are one thing; its dates are quite another. We assume that genius is genius—and that's that! But the artist's awareness of genius, while it is in the seed and budding, is often intermittent—punctuated by spates of mental blindness and neglect—and not till it really blooms does it seem as though it was always there. Florine's first periods of art-study under Kenyon Cox took place in the middle nineties and produced highly proficient life-class drawings, probably in-

art

men

things

distinguishable from hundreds like them everywhere in the world. And yet if we look as far back as the first extant record of her pictorial work, a little sketchbook on which Ettie wrote—lest there be any mistake!—"F's schoolgirl production," we find the reason for the standard illusion that genius "is" because it always "was."

This illusion happens to be based on the truth. The first bud *is* first; it is simply that, for a while, it is submerged by the world and its conventional restraints. On the cover of this little sketchbook we find a pencil-drawn heart pierced by an arrow, and inside we find charmingly simple sketches of young people and grown-ups directly observed; observed, that is, in the imagination of a girl. There we find the models for Florine's eventual mannikin physiques and also the "pretty young men," the beau of the moment being, as we gather from the artist's own caption, "Fred." There we find, in brief, the image of feeling that first was transformed into art education and then into the sometime decision to create art . . . that unique moment of Florine Stettheimer's conversion which can be situated no more exactly than *circa* World War I.

At that time, her long period of study in Berlin, Stuttgart, and Munich, and of sketching throughout Germany and Italy, was past. She had produced her official oil painting of a female nude based on a charcoal sketch; she had done, too, her Impressionistic landscape in oil based on a watercolor sketch (as a glimpse of delightfully leafy trees in another sketchbook proves). A sketchbook of 1909 brings to light the original "fashion" figures by Florine that signified her intuition of dress and its elegance. From among some early unstretched canvases, there unrolled a thrilling last-century fantasy like a scroll: one of the artist's first really Florinesque gestures. Two willowy ladies, dressed to the hour of the evening and whitely transparent in the dusk of an outdoor café, gaze, ravished, toward—it might seem—the future.

Nor are the ancestors of the flutterby absent from these earliest pictorial records. They appear as the guides, or perhaps the intended prey, of a boy and a girl in a cockleshell boat, done only in pencil but with the insects carefully if orthodoxly characterized. The "dragonfly" fantasy, with its mayfly-legs, appeared only when genius itself left the nymph stage and took wing. This little drawing was probably made in the late eighties and thus the day of the Ephémère would not dawn till a quarter of a century had passed. "Hard work" is a rather platitudinous *sine qua non* of genius and one inevitably smiles at its evocation. But it is just as true as the ephemeral mistakes of genius. Florine as a student was far too docile in the hands of her teachers in Germany and the United States—but everything she put on paper and canvas was a kind of dancing illusion. Behind it all, and peeping out here and there, were the things she was really learning.

FLORINE STETTHEIMER'S WRITTEN records do not trace her artistic development very literally though her diaries contain decisive information about it. The earliest extant diary is about her trip to Italy in the summer of 1906 with her mother and two sisters. It is labelled "First Berlin Period" since immediately afterward, seemingly, they went to Germany to hibernate in the state of economy which they practiced in those years. As the artist's diaries also show, she worried about subletting her New York studio (probably the one at 5 West 67th St., eventually abandoned for the Beaux Arts) and betrayed other signs of watching how her finances were doing.

The 1906 diary was begun on the boat crossing the ocean, and the diarist (who was thirty-five but probably passed for much less) indicated her emergent Impressionism by seeing Gibraltar one morning "as if Guérin had made it: flat and harmonious." She had long been an art student, of course, and the renewal of her aesthetic emotions was the principal object of this trip to Italy, where in Naples Museum she felt that the *Narcissus,* as she recorded, was looking "as pretty as ever." Those knowing her work should be perplexed by the also announced fact that by then she had not developed her "taste for the Pompeiian wall decorations." Ostensibly, this means that she came to prefer them in their Baroque neo-Classic form, since the screen portraits already mentioned, as well as two other screens by Florine (one a *chinoiserie*) have many affinities with the French arabesques and indeed establish a canon of her portraiture: its symbolic décor.

Florine imitated but did not respond, at least creatively, to a solidly built world of perspective such as Europe evolved, after the Renaissance, in Classical Painting. She admired Michelangelo probably because she had been encouraged to do so by her preceptors in Germany and America. But even at the moment she was admiring Annunciation lilies in Italy in 1906, twentieth-century Modernism was in the bud and growing fast. She was to be weaned away into the manners of American artists who, still alien to Cubism, were nevertheless strongly influenced by the style of its human anatomy; artists, indeed, such as Maurice Sterne, who once frequented her house and is seen in *Studio Party*. Her personification of Spring, a female figure surrounded by animals, appears in a labored, self-conscious work, Spring herself having none of that unique, arrowy suppleness which later gave her human beings their convincing life.

That—Cubism or no Cubism—the modern functional sense of anatomy she finally developed and crystallized was based on academic training is documented by the earliest extant diaries and the earliest extant paintings. It was to anatomy that she customarily applied her knowledge of foreshortening and, without being aware, apparently, that Michelangelo's David had been placed too low in relation to the sculptor's intention, she adjudged his youthful figure "topheavy." Her response to male and female anatomy, especially the former, was alert and critical in spirit; she disapproved of Tintoretto's anatomic drawing and noted in the museums she visited the many "beautiful torsos with ridiculous heads."

One thinks that possibly the wingless angel with a sunburst halo in *Love Flight of a Pink Candy Heart* was the memory of a fourteenth-century angel she called "the embodiment of Spring." The additional fact that her angel's figure there has almost the identical posture of Elie Nadelman in *Picnic at Bedford Hills,* and that he too lies close to a picnic cloth, seems even more suggestive. May not this "retrospective" painting memorialize some profound shift in the artist's attitude of heart—perhaps a farewell to the past; perhaps a farewell to her habit of idealizing real men while she knew them? This work was annotated by Ettie as the artist contemplating "various friends of her youth, whom she has portrayed with a mingling of symbolism and realistic observation." A grown woman, Florine views an imaginary world from a balcony with a delicate wrought-iron railing, where she leans, resting both elbows on a pillow, and through a loop of which she thrusts a leg, as doubtless she did when a small child. The balcony railing is recognizable as the one seen through the open doors in the portrait (1928) of Fraulein von Prieser, her former Stuttgart teacher.

The picnic seems to have been a symbol of flirtation for Florine. About the elegant cloth (like one in a fairy tale) are stretched a variety of young men, two of whom, naked and very dark, seem sunbathing and suggest these verse lines of the artist: "I adore men sunkissed and golden / Like gold gods / Like Pharaoh amber-anointed." The amusing part about the poem that begins thus, *The Golden God,* is that it ends with the image of a male friend who has sought to become "sunkissed" while Florine reclines on her veranda in cool luxury; he returns "Hours later . . . Looking self-conscious and parboiled." Evidently, men had to be careful before seeking to deserve the quasi-divine attribute Florine had taught herself to cherish. That she understood the peril of her own impulses to romanticize her images of men is only too clear from the poem titled *To a Gentleman Friend:*

> You fooled me you little floating worm
> For I looked for the wings
> With which you seemed to fly
> And make you different
> From other worms
> And then I discovered the slender thread
> That fastened you safely to a solid tree
> I touched the thread
> With my fingertip
> And you wiggled
> I snapped the thread and you fell to earth
> And you squirmed
> And wormed
> And only wiggled

Yet Cupid, seen in Victorian dress as a wingless boy with long hair, prevails in *Love Flight's* mellow sentiment and his arrow is evidently destined to pierce the large pink candy heart (suitably trimmed in gold) suspended over the heads of another image of the artist herself, costumed fantastically in trousers, and her dancing partner, a masked Harlequin. Duchamp (considering the presence of the phrase "love flight" in the above-quoted poem, *Duche*) is certainly a candidate for his identity. A cross-referent clue supporting Duchamp's candidacy is the close association of the costumes in this work and the Duchamp portrait as well as the fact, noticed by Virgil Thomson, that the shoulders of Rrose Sélavy are heart-shaped.

TAKING THE LONG perspective on Florine's artistic sensibility, it is surprising that so basically Classical a culture as hers should have turned to a highly stylized type of figure which ignored all the Classical laws. In *Love Flight,* both the Harlequin (who may not be "Duche" at all but a memory of Nijinsky in the ballet *Le Carnaval*) and a formally dressed youth bearing a suitor's token, have the look of animated dolls. It is hard to determine, for example, if Florine's criticism of the Belvedere Apollo's hands and her wish to change his drapery were simply reflections of her masters' informed criticism or whether such feelings may not have presaged her fondness for a theatricalized anatomy such as she saw in Nijinsky, like a Classical statue come to life and yet illusively transformed by a stage costume.

The bodies of gods and angels in Classical art were thoroughly familiar to Florine when she first saw Nijinsky dance in Paris in 1912. In her diary, on June 7th, she wrote: "Nijinsky the faun was marvelous. He seemed to be truly half beast if not two-thirds. He was not a Greek faun for he had not the insouciant smile of a follower of Dionysos. He knew not civilization—he was archaic—so were the nymphs. He danced the Dieu Bleu and the Rose in which he was as graceful as a woman and Scheherazade. He is the most wonderful male dancer I have seen." After her return to America at the beginning of World War I, she paid a tribute to Nijinsky and Bolm in a work already mentioned, *Music,* which also contains an unidentified pianist of comic-romantic aspect.

This work has more empty space than the artist ever used, being even taller than the *Cathedrals* yet figured on a small scale to suggest a stage space, especially the great roominess required for dancing. Nijinsky is centrally poised in one of the famous poses from his Rose part, erect with arms arched closely over his head. However, we do not find in this image what stands out in Florine's impression of him in 1912, the animalism of the "archaic" as in his Faun part, but its very opposite, the womanlike gracefulness of his Rose. How far Florine already had come from practicing a quasi-Classical anatomy is clear from a study of Nijinsky's costume here. While we can conclude she worked from a photograph (as the pose is so familiar) his torso is not costumed as it was in this well-known ballet but wears a "bodice" rounded over the breasts and making him look (with small waist and consequently emphatic hip and thigh muscles) as much like Mae West or a female acrobat by Nadelman as like himself. Yet Florine's image has an authority equally as independent of balletic form as of costume and classic male anatomy. Her lyrically precious Nijinsky's toes are *en pointe,* something foreign to male ballet dancers and a way he never danced this or any other rôle. A good part of the "authority," then, must lie in Florine's deliberate conception of an androgynous being.

Strangely, feet *en pointe* happen to be significant in the iconography of her works as a peculiar property of the male figure, unusually conspicuous since her women, as a rule, wear high heels. Ultimately, Florine never troubled with the sheer nakedness of anatomy, even in respect to the feet, and we consistently find her giving the shoed male foot the look of being in ballet slippers, and at times shaped as conventionally as a doll's. Perhaps she was transmuting the similar pedal conventionality which Marie Laurencin gave her women. Virgil Thomson has such feet in his portrait and so has Joseph Hergesheimer in his. Duchamp's *persona,* Rrose Sélavy, wears a dancer's footgear while Carl Van Vechten's slippered feet are made possibly the most tenuous of all. The slippers on the prone figure of the angel in *Love Flight* have the laces of ballet shoes, suggesting—since this figure is half angelic and half balletic—that the male dancer was a prime source of Florine's romantic symbolism. Of course, ladies at that time used to wear such laced shoes when bathing at beaches, a fact documented by Florine in *Lake Placid.* The pointing of the feet in walking as well as dancing seems a device she exploited for elegance of effect; it imparts a unique buoyancy to both male and female figures and may be studied at large in the crowded pieces, *Spring Sale* and *Asbury Park South* (1920), where the feet may also be found, comically, pointing up. In the latter work, Duchamp appears balletically pointing his toes while promenading with Fania Marinoff, and near them Paul Thévénaz, photographing the segregated Negro beach, points one foot daintily behind him. Florine's democratic spirit, like that of Van Vechten, was offended at the segregation but not at the pictures it made.

One wonders if perhaps Isadora Duncan's bare feet, which were then a part of the milieu, did not appear aggressively "masculine" to Florine, and if this was not part of her reason for snubbing the suggestion of the family friend, Elizabeth Duncan (the incident is related by Van Vechten), that the Stettheimers give a party in honor of the famous Isadora. Perhaps Isadora's reputation for social behavior, on a scale of grandiose individualism quite unlike the Stettheimers', was the only reason for their suave dismissal of Elizabeth Duncan's suggestion. At the same time, it may be wrong to follow the practice of identifying Florine's social prejudices with those of her sisters, who themselves protested, when Florine wished to decorate the common dining room, that "her taste wasn't their taste." It was with equanimity, in 1916, that Florine mentioned seeing, at someone's house, "Troubetzkoy and Isadora Duncan dancing about together." So far as painting went, her style was most ill-adapted to the Duncan school of dancing, and above all to Isadora's uninhibited style, which Florine (since she once spoke out against "nature dancers") might have been tempted to class with the wild exuberance of the dancers in *Natatorium Undine*. Duncan dancing, of course, had a center of dignity.

It was not that the artist was unable to portray, so to speak, the exaltation of limbs. Her figure anatomy, though quite personal in inflection, took on an "activist" curve inspired, I should guess, by Best-Maugard's ideas of figure-drawing. Yet, even when she seemed deliberately to borrow, as where Elie Nadelman's legs in *Picnic at Bedford Hills* are attenuated into simple points as in his own work, *Man in the Open Air* (1914-15), there is no question of imitation: the artist gave him the indispensable Florinesque look.

In all probability, Best-Maugard's "simplified human figure" had a leading role in her revision of classical anatomy, which now omitted the chiaroscuro she had so faithfully copied in her early life-class work. However, only the inward creative process—which can never be read by the microscope of analysis—can account for Florine's extraordinary insight into the integrity of the clothed, as opposed to the nude, figure. While never suggesting armatures, some of the bathing nudes have anatomies ultrasimplified to the point of caricature, such as the radical hieroglyphs in the distance of *Asbury Park South*. But the three dark "ladies of fashion," also in that work, are just as anatomically articulate. The sketchy "hieroglyphs" to which Post-Impressionists such as Monet and Utrillo reduced humanity are, of course, dwarfed for the sake of landscape or cityscape. Yet Florine's figure-technique, while resembling that of a Monet or a Utrillo, kept the stress on humanity by making "crowds" of it.

In terms of physics, the anatomic weight in Florine's figures corresponds to the tenuous fragility found in Bosch's allegoric

Three Flowers and a Dragonfly, 1928, oil on canvas, one of the most interesting and characteristic of the artist's perennial flower pieces.

Portrait of Henry McBride, 1922, oil on canvas, the artist's tribute to the
art critic who was one of her most distinguished supporters.

Music, probably before 1920, oil on canvas; Nijinsky is in the center, Adolph Bolm below, and Florine, couched at left, fantasizes the ballets she loved.

the Country, a synthetic view of typical gatherings at the family's Tarrytown estate, shows the artist in the far background, at the upper right margin, seated before her easel in an eloquently busy posture. The artist painted herself with a palette at least five times: the other image of her at an actual easel is in the front view of André Brook. So close that it seems to touch her crouches a fantastic figure iconographically identified as a faun. Though it may be only a spectator's minor, and delayed, reaction to this work, the whole picture is an anthology of men and beasts. I count there fourteen animals, including birds, besides the man-beast, which it seems positive can be only a reminiscence of Nijinsky.

The way I have read Florine's personality in the preceding pages gives her a triple dimension: Mayfly–Follies Beauty–Commère. But at the time of *Sunday Afternoon in the Country* (1917), the third element—the climactic phase of her personality, the Commère—had not more than hinted its presence, and as yet the other two had not expressly been stated as personality phases. Florine's relation to her social world was still concretely that of the portraitist of the Conversation Piece. Here her detachment and her participation are given at once in an image of herself at work on a painting: she is a social observer. So where does the Faun-Nijinsky, seated at her feet, rightfully enter her imaginative world?

One should note that not everyone in this scenic Conversation Piece is in a specifically social relation. Seen clad in a dressing gown, with head hanging and standing against a tree, the Marquis de Buenavista (then Peruvian Ambassador to the United States) holds in one hand what looks like a manuscript. Is he studying a rôle in a play or is he steeping himself in poetry? It is impossible to say. But it seems clear that he believes himself, or wishes to be, alone. This is the kind of weekend party that culminated in an episode already given, with Adolph Bolm staying overnight in Mrs. Stettheimer's nightgown and dancing on the lawn. It is also the kind of weekend we read of in Henry James' *Sacred Fount,* when couples and individuals wander about weaving their innermost destinies with one another in what superficially looks like leisure and relaxation.

Bolm performs with a parasol while Ratan Devi, Ananda Coomaraswamy's wife, plays a Hindu musical instrument; other groups, following their own activities or amusements, are Steichen photographing Duchamp while Ettie keeps others out of view (one detects a gentle satire on the latter's officiousness), Marie Sterner watching Paul Thévenaz' handstand, and Mrs. Stettheimer, forming a duality with her card table, playing Patience. Though Baron de Meyer is seen only by the back of his head visible above the armchair at the lower margin, one senses that he is preoccupied in the same way as Florine; he is an observer and thus detached even while participating. Some social destinies, like a novelist's or a painter's, are eminently private. But Florine's truthfulness did not wish to leave this factor, in regard to herself, merely tacit; hence, the symbolic figure of the Faun is meant to depict the subjectiveness of her social interest at this time. While she paints, she too is absorbed with a private fantasy.

A similar device of revealing symbolically the nature of an artist's social relation to the world was conceived by Aubrey Beardsley in a self-portrait as original as Florine's own, or as her portraits of Duchamp and his *persona*. Archly disregarding the viewer, Beardsley drew himself dressed in a fantastic simplicity while a string attaches one ankle to a herm of Pan in the background. As different as Beardsley's and Florine's lines are from each other, both are calligraphic and (in strong affinity with the Art Nouveau movement) preoccupied with tendrils and linear arabesques; indeed, Duchamp's spring elevating Rrose Sélavy and an actual string coiled beneath the feet of Adolfo Best-Maugard in Florine's portrait have a way of suggesting Beardsley's device in his self portrait.

The portrait of the Mexican artist contains a number of features whose significance Florine respected by her own creative example. The subject holds in his hand, palm up, a purely linear, vertical form which might seem mysterious to those uninitiated into his teachings. This form is a Florinesque invention combining, as though it were a flower, the seven motifs shown and named by Best-Maugard in his *Method of Creative Design* as basic to all natural forms. Starting at the top of Florine's little arabesque, these are identifiable as the full circle, the half circle, the wavy line, the S-form, the zigzag, the straight line, and the spiral. The huge cornucopia behind Best-Maugard (who is close to the convention of the "pretty young men") stands for the spiral cone which is compared in his book with the actual pine-cone, something Florine transformed here into a pineapple perhaps because of the latter's comestible status. Of course, the large bird involved with the snake

in the background is a sign for Quetzalcoatl, his native land's
"Plumed Serpent." The ribbon, on which Florine wrote her signature and her dedication to the subject, echoes technical preoccupa-
tions of Best-Maugard's book and has a prominent place, indeed,
in Florine's heraldry. But the most Florinesque piece of wit in this
portrait is somewhat esoteric: the casual, stringlike form on which
the subject stands can be safely identified as his central device for
drawing a "bowknot"—"Make a circle with an S in it."

In portraying Best-Maugard's *ambiance,* as was her custom,
Florine also projected familiar characteristics of her own private
world of vision. At no time can she be accused of leaning too
heavily on another painter's example. Like Aubrey Beardsley, she
was an artist of deep originality as well as of subtle perversity.
So it is not unsuggestive that both she and Beardsley should have
portrayed self-images in close contact with the pagan. In *Sunday
Afternoon in the Country,* I believe that Florine has expressed, in a
manner as calculated in the mise-en-scène as *sotto voce* on the
stage, her affinity with a simple "beastliness" of nature which was
as much that of St. Francis as of an archaic, and implicitly erotic,
Faun. Surely, nothing could be more winsomely naïve than the
transmuted Faun-Nijinsky sitting at Florine's feet with as much
innocence as Duchamp at Fania Marinoff's (in the incident given
above) or, for that matter, as a pet monkey might have sat there.
It is a masquerade-Faun: the archaic beastliness of Nijinsky
turned into a mere costume. At the same time, its presence in this
context has a certain impudence. Florine's faun is critic as well as
self-critic: "High society," she is saying, "is a masquerade ball."

I HAVE ALREADY mentioned Watteau in relation to Florine Stettheimer's art. Florine seldom showed lovers as lovers (the most
explicit exception being the dancing partners in *Love Flight*) and
this neglect places her at a distance from the great French painter.
Yet Watteau—and not only in his large *Gilles*—could isolate the
self-contemplator in the midst of society. It is true that Gilles is a
theatrical performer, but there is a posturing dandy in one of the
fêtes galantes, *Réunion en Plein Air,* whose figure at once reminded
me, after I grew to know Florine's paintings, of the Marquis de
Buenavista idly attitudinizing on the raft in *Lake Placid.* It is true
that he seems to have one observer, Carrie, who is seated under a
parasol on this raft, but he is just as absorbed in semi-nude self-

sufficiency as Watteau's fabulous dandy in fully attired self-sufficiency. In terms of differing styles, whether calculated or not,
Florine's dandy is an equivalent of Watteau's—even to the self-
conscious placement of the right arm. This is an aspect of Buenavista quite different from the head-hanging one found in *Sunday
Afternoon in the Country;* perhaps the head-hanging figure against
the tree is the *anima,* the posturing dandy the nearer, Narcissean
persona, and so comparable to the Follies Beauty in Florine's per-
sonality-complex. Florine found the Naples *Narcissus*—a shapely
youth whose every pore seems self-regarding—"as pretty as
ever." She would never forget just how pretty he could be, or
that, as he was antiquity's prime example of how privacy could be
exploited in the midst of publicity, modernity might imitate his
exemplary conduct.

WHEN, IN 1906, Florine revisited Santa Maria Maggiore, she remembered that when last on those magnificent premises, she was
"flirting." By 1923, the year of the recumbent self-portrait,
Florine the coquette dared to think of herself, in her boudoir
imagination, as a beauty reclining somewhat like a showgirl in her
"aquacade" fantasy, *Natatorium Undine,* a painting completed
four years later. Though, more than a decade after that, she found
the Aquacade at the New York World's Fair "great fun," and indeed (according to Ettie) planned to paint the Fair itself, she had
invoked its atmosphere already in *Natatorium.* The voluptuousness
of this painting, filled with quasi-nudity, is suggested by the minor
datum that the showgirl just mentioned is exactly in the pose of an
odalisque by Matisse. Yet, though the nudity here is the work's
most striking human feature, it holds an atmosphere of anatomic
insistence that is formalistically rather than anatomically nude;
I mean the sort of streamlining of the clothed figure that the
fashion silhouette of the period emphasized: the female as the
letter "I."

The best way of characterizing this laconic image, the artist
understood, was to make it active, to make it dance, and that is what
it is doing here whenever not posturing in arabesques. The canon
of Futurism, with its adaptation of material forms to arcs of
motion, is easily perceptible in the divers in *Natatorium,* one of
whom, emerging from a visibilized spiral twist, is almost a pure
curve on one side, and the other of whom, about to disappear into

the water, makes a moderate S-curve. The Bacchante-like attitudes of the kicking dancers, on the balcony to the left, are wonderfully angular and vivacious and reveal, as do similar figures in *Beauty Contest,* Florine's complete success with mere physical movement. Fania Marinoff, seen writing at a table, though in a short clinging dress, seems as nude as anyone else in the picture, while Florine's image of herself, in fancy beach blouse, breeches, and coolie hat, is simply the "I" silhouette split into two extremities, one of which forms a triangle.

One might think, despite this analysis, that Florine Stettheimer was not a woman to be conscious of exactly how her own figure looked, that all her images of herself came from a detached sort of fantasy which she did not relate to reality—to what she saw in a mirror after her bath if she ever looked then. I confess that one might so insist, with some plausibility, had we not a certain entry from the diary of 1916, made after Duchamp had taken her to a film starring Annette Kellerman's shape and based on the Undine legend. I am not sure how much of the diving star's anatomy was visible (I know she wore skintight dark underwear in the ads for it) but it was enough to make Florine write: "I shall no longer say I think I am shaped somewhat like Annette Kellerman. Having nothing on, it was easy to judge her looks."

One should beware of overrating Florine's conscious naïveté about the human figure. In Italy, she could admire an undressed male lead in D'Annunzio's *Fedora* without the least affectation of coyness, and in the whole length of her diaries and the breadth of her work, it was never shyness that conditioned her view of human anatomy. True enough, the following was addressed to her diary, but it represents the innate and impersonal wit she could bring to bear when contemplating nudity in the opposite or the same sex. It pertains to a sojourn on the New Jersey coast: "July 4th, 1924: Sherwood Anderson / paternally / dutifully / naïvely nude."

WE FIND THAT the "Parisian dollishness" of Florine's figures as mentioned by Paul Rosenfeld, who also invoked their trait as "archaic popular images," is notably dynamic, modern, and uninhibited. Their dollishness is a form of idealization rather than of mechanization, and seldom detracts from their essential humanity. One might think that her version of the Statue of Liberty (gold leaf on putty impasto) would be a minimization of the heroic. But it is not. Liberty is the largest figure in *New York 1918,* celebrating President Wilson's trip to the Peace Conference; one feels the upward thrust of her torch-carrying arm and the weight of the book in her other arm.

So far as characterization of the human race goes, Florine's super-dolls are individually far more flexible than, on reading Rosenfeld's descriptive term, one might imagine. Take the frieze of figures daringly spread across the left side of *Cathedrals of Wall Street:* Mrs. Roosevelt, Mayor LaGuardia, Michael Ericson in American Legion uniform, Michael J. Sullivan (a Civil War Veteran), Clagett Wilson in Marine uniform, an Indian Chief, and the artist in the act of presenting a bouquet to Washington's statue. Grace Moore, her skirt touching Wilson's and the Indian Chief's heads, may also be considered part of the frieze; however, as she is so far above and not on so vertical an axis as the rest, she does not form part of the musical phrase, the melody in visual form, made by the others. Generally on a transverse line, their standpoints are actually on five levels, two of the seven figures being on (roughly) the same level as another.

The degree of individual differentiation in the series of verticals relates to character-traits as well as formal variations. Mrs. Roosevelt becomes a sort of triangle, with one side curved, because of her long train. Mayor LaGuardia, second in line and moderately S-shaped, echoes the more emphatic "S" of Florine, who is seventh in line at the end. Third in line, the erect American Legionnaire, as the simplest vertical, mediates between the Mayor and the variant-S of the Civil War Veteran, whose age and caste are happily indicated by his posture leaning back from the waist. Fifth in line, Clagett Wilson qualifies his strict vertical by folded arms and a right leg in "fatigue" while, next, the Indian Chief echoes him with folded arms and allows his war bonnet subtly to echo Florine's S-curve behind him; between them, the long streamers of the artist's bouquet complicate this end of the "melody" with serpentine accents. A further accent is that all seven figures are in strict profile except Florine and Mayor LaGuardia (respectively seventh and second), she slightly turning away but looking back at us, he with head turned three-quarters to the picture plane. The whole painting, as a matter of fact, is a triumph of curves and verticals as well as of profile and full views, and the frieze I have just de-

rather curious pejorative, considering that one of Florine's fortes was theatrical costuming. Moreover, one might speak automatically of Florine's "society portraits," and yet we have only to turn to the traditional school of society portraiture—to, pertinently, a lady arrayed to go to the opera, such as the Duchess of Portland in Sargent's portrait—to gauge how important was Florine's choice of portrait subjects together with her imaginative treatment of them. The Duchess of Portland is "operatic" simply because she is dressed to go to the Opera, while Carrie is "operatic" not because she is dressed to go to *Four Saints,* but because she is palpably the heroine of a chamber opera of her own or at least the portrait-painter's imagination. No doubt, each sister had her own brand of fantasy, and Carrie's was certainly incorporated in Florine's portrait of her, for by reputation she was the most formal and "regal" dresser of the family.

BUT ANOTHER SUBJECTIVE trait inheres in Carrie's portrait as well as in Florine's portrait of her mother, who appears in black with black lace panniers. Before I noticed it myself, my friend Charles Boultenhouse pointed out that Mrs. Stettheimer's long full black dress, curving to a point at her feet, viewed in conjunction with the transparent lace panniers, looks like the body of a bee and its wings. This immediately brought to my mind how Florine (in the above-quoted poem) called upon her maid for "the honey jar" to revive the dying yellow flutterby; that is, I thought of the insect-totem so indubitable in the artist's self-portrait and of the fact that Carrie's portrait is characterized by two long black antennae rising from her close-fitted white hat. I have searched for a comparable characterization of Ettie but have failed to find it.

One may wonder if there was not a curious blockage in Florine's sisterly affection for Ettie to prevent a characterization such as symbolized a gauzy and wingèd race. I thought that perhaps the bow-tie and lace collar of which (according to various images of her by Florine) Ettie was fond, might be a "dragonfly" symbol since in two cases it has the "mayfly tails" and a set of "wings": the bow. But the very word, dragonfly, brought me up, for I remembered the so-called portrait of Ettie as Medusa, the only previous reproduction of which, I believe, was included in the Duchamp issue of *View.* * That Florine's "dragonfly" might be so

* Series V, No. 1.

named for dragonish qualities I hazarded above on one basis, among others, that she had made the blackness of a butterfly stand for the night as evil.

A curious parallel occurred to me as I studied the Medusa portrait of Ettie, done by Florine in 1908—according to Ettie's note on the back of a reproduction—as a bookplate: my parallel was simply one between the snakes twisting about beneath Ettie-Medusa's chin and the string bow-ties actually worn by Ettie. As much evidence indicates, Florine's mind must have worked in this associational way. Certainly, there was no reasonable and conscious basis for visualizing a loved sister as a mythical image associated with deadly evil. There is playfulness in the Medusa-Ettie portrait, the kind of ''amusement'' that was to become a poetic element of Florine's great quality-of-qualities: the Commère-*persona*. In play there is wit, and in wit, of course, malice has taken up permanent residence as an entertaining guest. Carl Van Vechten, in fact, has already recognized malice as an ingredient of Florine's portraits. I think her malice always a harmless one: a sting with its own anodyne.

THE ARTIST'S USE of couture and haute couture, by implication, was always amenable to flexible uses as symbolic characterization. Why not, then, the opposite?—why should not the symbols of Classical Myth—Apollo, Eros, Narcissus and Medusa—appear as a kind of witty costuming? Ettie's level-browed gaze, as I have noted, was the antithesis of Mrs. Stettheimer's gaze. The latter's naturally lifted eyebrows—her daughter being prompt to exploit this in her portrait—helped make her a symbol of innocence and goodness. Florine's self-portraits tend to lift her own brows in an artless sort of wonder and amusement at the spectacle of life. But Ettie's levelness of gaze, italicized by the unrelenting closeness of her brows to her eyes, suggests a criticism of the world that portends little indulgence for it; this much is clear from the photograph forming her memorial volume's frontispiece as well as from Florine's portrait of her, where they curve like a printer's bracket. At the same time, perhaps this very gaze has more bark than bite.

It would have been logical for the fanciful Florine to have seen in Ettie's mature aspect a hint for a costume mask of Medusa, as though they were going to one of the balls in Germany where they danced with resplendent officers, and if it were to be a masquerade, Florine had remarked, "Ettie, why don't you go as Medusa?" Ettie would have thought the idea, I imagine, delightful, for she wrote of the bookplate after Florine's death, "In those days I much admired it." Its face has the look of a mask and seems as suited for a Mask of Tragedy as for a Gorgon-mask. One day, Florine was looking at a Medusa (which example she does not say) in a museum in Italy when a custodian approached to tell her that the object of her contemplation was a Medusa. "Yes," returned Florine, with one of her dry-sweet smiles, "I am well acquainted with her."

AS TO THE facts of life, as Virgil Thomson says of the Stettheimer sisters, "They knew everything." But an artist (as many artists have said) never stops learning. Florine was always one to know how she felt at any given moment, but she could feel doubt about the world and its data, and like many highly subjective personalities, she grew impatient with a world that was needlessly withholding as well as often misguiding and misguided. She kept going abroad and touring Italy and criticizing the methods of the Masters. She claimed of a "golden-haired Venus" (in all probability the one in Botticelli's *Birth of Venus* since the artist was then in Florence) that she ought not to hang in a "light-chocolate colored room" and that if she—Florine—"ever grew rich" she would donate a new gold frame for her with the stipulation that the painting be hung against white walls. Apparently, though Florine did grow richer, nothing was ever done about it. She wrote that the Flora of the same painting was "too fat to move," that her bust had not enough "curve," and that her underarm curvature ("a most attractive muscle") was defective.

From this criticism, we can select what Florine was to eliminate from her own creed of anatomy and what she was to aggrandize for it. The "curve" was to be aggrandized, and the stark musculature was virtually to disappear—except, I believe, on one occasion: when she included a lifeguard in *Natatorium Undine*, but even then he was made nearly all silhouette. Internal modelling, when shadow, became for Florine extremely conventional on the Cubist side; her painting language was primarily line, contour, and color. Thus we can grasp the standards by which she portrayed men and women, especially the former, who typically became stylized dolls like the ones she eloquently composed of wire and cloth. One fancies that she secretly deplored the fact that men did not use make-up, only her sense of humor imparting a healthy equilibrium on this point. But on the stage, in ballet, it was natural for men to use make-up—and there, as she had proven to Bolm, she was an expert.

Temperament flourishes on prejudice, and it was a long-nurtured prejudice for white and gold that enabled Florine to criticize the way the Uffizi Gallery had hung the *Birth of Venus*. Through the large windows in the portrait of Fraulein von Prieser, of the Berlin-Stuttgart schooldays, one can see the Royal Palace at Stuttgart; very likely there, and in the white of antique statues, she first conceived her prejudice for white and gold. Part of Florine's originality was that, for her, art was anecdote in an era when all the modern schools had decided that anecdote was what art was not. Duchamp suggested, considering Florine, "Why not revive the anecdote in painting?" Well, why not? An anecdotalism such as Florine's draws upon a highly cultivated symbolism so that her work echoes the humanist revival in being a miniature Renaissance of one artist.

FLORINE STETTHEIMER CERTAINLY invented creatures in the mythological sense that the ancients did and reinvented them as did the neo-Classic centuries—there are her "dragonfly," her balletic angel, her anthropomorphic bouquet, her heraldry, her image in the self-portrait. Whatever was put in her pictures was "known" in the Classic sense of that word: it has an explicit identity and is never mere form; her decorativeness, thus, is never abstract in feeling. However it was that, ultimately, she portrayed Grace Moore and Mrs. Roosevelt, Louis Bouché and Nijinsky, she had a concrete reason for every bit of the characterizations. Lace, for example, is not the arabesque it is in Bouché's portrait only because Florine was partial to draped lace. Since among the New York art groups, then, was one undergoing a "Victorian Period," many putting lace in their paintings, it was also because Bouché himself painted lace. And if lace crosses his lap in Florine's portrait, it was because of a certain effect in Bouché's own painting of a Russian dancer performing in Central Park.

Florine's art is thus ideal for iconographic criticism because each object in it, no matter how small, has an identity and a history, assigned with what I suspect was usually a maximum consciousness on the painter's own part. Yet specificity in Florine's art varies in type. An unfinished painting, *Christmas,* shows a masquerade party on a skating rink in Central Park and identifies Columbus Circle in the background by several unequivocal landmarks. Florine was a realist in being a fetichist but she was never a naturalist, assuming that a naturalist identifies an object all the way to its individuality. The sense in which her portraits are ideal and fancifully romantic has been amply notated here. In making her brother, Walter, one of the screen portraits, she classified him among the ''pretty young men,'' for his daughter, Mrs. Julius Ochs Adler, testifies that its likeness to him is virtually non-existent. Mrs. Adler, to whose charming drawing-room the screen in question lends a handsome decorative note, further asserts that while Walter Stettheimer had pure breeds of smooth- and wire-haired fox terriers, the dogs shown with him in this portrait are ''mongrel.'' This epithet may be true and just from the viewpoint of the dog-fancier, but in fairness to Florine it must be said that what she intended in the ''portraits'' of Walter's dogs was ''doggishness'' and, just because this doggishness was Florinesque, it sufficed an art so decorative as hers. In the *chinoiserie* decorations of Watteau and others—of which Florine did her own brilliant version now also belonging to Mrs. Adler—one does not wonder if the capering figures are ''real'' Chinamen.

Florine never dreamed of being a Leonardo toward either the surface facts or the inner secrets of nature. Once, in Italy, she attempted to sketch a bird she could not decide was a dove or a seagull. The point is not that she was ignorant of ornithology but that she began to think the bird itself did not look ''like anything in particular.'' She added then: ''So I certainly could not draw it.'' She could paint or draw, however, any identification of life she ever made, especially if she identified it with an art manifestation. On an Italian beach she admired a sunbather grown so dark that he seemed to be, her diary says, ''created by Gauguin.'' I rather think that, among ''the friends of her youth'' in *Love Flight of a Pink Candy Heart,* is this mere glimpse of a beautiful nude that was a memory of two decades; that is, of the two very dark young men lying on one side of the picnic cloth in that painting, one of them may well represent the Gauguinesque man on the beach; the other could easily be Louis Bernheimer, whose very ''Latin'' looks and large, heavy-lashed eyes seem to have inspired Florine to make him the subject of an early portrait.

Florine was never very far from painting as an apotheosis of humanity, its monuments, its costumes, its objects. As much palpable fantasy as her works have, she wished them to be based on fact and the distinct lineament of fact. For example, for *Cathedrals of Wall Street,* she demanded from her lawyer, Joseph Solomon, who then represented the firm of Alfred Cook, actual tickertape so that she could personally copy its apochryphal messages in her painting; for the same work, she visited the Stock Exchange and applied to the Navy Department for exact information about a uniform. Adjacent star-fish help us "place" the sunbather in *Love Flight:* the satellite was as essential to Florine's configurations as the planet. If, in her Golden God poem, she referred to "sunkissed" men as likenesses of a Pharaoh, the metaphor invoked is as significant as the immediate subject (which, after all, is the general point about symbolism). Other races are dark; the sunbather on the beach she thought of as Tahitian. But with a Pharaoh and his Queen she shared something subjectively: a vision of life, death, and eternity.

What are the *persona*-projections of her portraits but images parallel with those of the ancients who considered the tomb a place in which to continue life, a temporary home like a ship, in which one took with him all he would need for his voyage to the endless life after death? Florine's earliest desire—perhaps never quite allayed—was to have all her pictures, at death, placed with her in a mausoleum. The manner of her portraits may suggest to some the ex-votos, but in this capacity they would not yield their subtle flavor of profundity. Doubtless it is hard to reconcile the solemn mood of the mummy portraits with Carl Van Vechten's portrait and most of the others. Yet, allowing for Florine's lyric style, Van Vechten's amiable mouth and Ettie's stare are not far from the eager, greeting lips and eyes of the mummy portraits. The artist's own heavily mascara'd eyes in the self-portrait were probably encouraged by Best-Maugard's example; partly, that may have been because, he, too, had heeded the meaning of the Egyptian make-up for eternity, and even by way of the same vivid source: the haunting eyes of the Fayum portraits of the Roman period.

IN 1908 AND 1909, while she continued her Italian trips, Florine was still eliminating other painters' art from her blood: taking in "this" but often rejecting "that." In the International of 1909, she found but two works to her taste, one by Bernard and von Stuck's *Amazone,* which latter she recorded her wish to own. Florine's lifelong acquisition of major art works was practically nil. In part, doubtless, this was due to limited means, however otherwise useful these means were and would become, but it was due as well to a certain exclusivism of personality, the desire to make all form a highly personal web down to the smallest piece of décor or *objet d'art*. The Stettheimers, owning a number of the latter, bequeathed them to friends in their wills. Of ranking paintings, Florine seems to have owned—or at least held on to—only a supposed Claude Lorrain; in any case, she mentions having to repair damage done to "my Claude Lorrain" on its fall from a wall at the Alwyn Court.

Florine did not wish to be challenged in her own domain, especially when this domain, at last, became the large Beaux Arts studio, so much of which, including furniture, she had personally designed and initialled. I was taken aback to learn from Marcel Duchamp that, to Florine, even "Duche's" art was practically nonexistent. She could call him her "confrère" in her diary, but I have Duchamp's word that they never talked shop or discussed aesthetic values seriously. So far as her express taste for contemporary art went, the preponderance of available evidence points to a lively distaste.

Carl Van Vechten, on a certain occasion, found her so contrary on the subject of art that he demanded to know what artist in the world she did like. He claimed to me that she took ten minutes to answer: "Van Dyck—a little." I told him that the general impression was that her favorite painter was Hals (of course, both artists painted a great deal of lace). "Maybe," Van Vechten replied in the quaint judiciousness of his present-day speech, and regarding me elfishly from beneath his snow-white bangs, "she thought a little longer and found it was Hals." Her treatment of the big names of modernism showed little quarter to their vaunted merits. Virgil Thomson recalls being with her at the Museum of Modern Art when she was confronted by a Picasso bright enough to rival her own palette (I imagine it must have been *Girl Before a Mirror*). "What could you use them for but a sports suit?" she rhetorically asked him, meaning the color-patterns. When the Museum of Modern Art first opened the doors of its new quarters on 53rd Street, Florine and Robert Locher (forming a "tribuna" of two) attended only to find the works on the walls as disagreeable as the thousands of persons crowding the rooms. When adverse aesthetic feelings were aroused in the artist, she never compromised with them. Thomson is also witness to an occasion at the ballet, to which he took Florine when Balanchine's *Cotillon* was being performed; thinking the sets and costumes by Christian Bérard interesting, the composer had been eager to know what Florine thought of them. She satisfied his curiosity by averring that "dirty colors should not be mixed with clean ones."

One might have thought, as did Van Vechten, that she would look with favor on the work of choice contemporary naïfs. The novelist, on discovering that the Negro cook who worked for Mrs. Lachaise's sister did chalk paintings on tissue paper, enthusiastically acquired some, and almost at once it occurred to him to present Florine with a few of these "characteristic" works, whose people had huge heads and tiny feet. He was abashed to have them back in the next mail. The piquant legend of their creator held no charm for Florine and she thought the images themselves ugly. Evidently, her aversion to modern deformation was dogmatic. So let this be the place to distinguish, once and for all, Florine's picture-sense from that of the true naïfs and self-taughts.

It is not only that her compositions are not tight, her forms neither tiresomely upright nor stodgy, and her figures not static, all of which tends to be true of naïfs, but more significantly, she avoided an almost universal trait of theirs: the unvaried repetition of units. Take the familiar panorama of John Kane's *Industry's Increase* or some equivalent work of Joseph Pickett's; their houses, windows, and columns of smoke illustrate exactly what I mean. A similar opportunity for Florine was the equally panoramic *West Point,* whose ranks of cadets and tents were "naturals" for such uniform repetition. But how did Florine solve her problem even as she yielded to her typical, naïvely authentic device of showing us a side-elevation world? The fact is that no significant row of units in *West Point* stands clear without modulative superpositions. The conspicuous row of three tents in the middle ground is broken by an arch superimposing on one of them while a tree rises between two others to obscure the middle tent of the row of three standing behind. Even the row of six "toy" cadets directly between the tent-rows is modulated by the superposition of a tent's peak. In the background, two sets of three columns of marchers

Opposite: *Portrait of My Sister,* Carrie W. Stettheimer, 1923, oil on canvas; the subject (her typical elegance fantasized by the artist) is shown with her doll-house and family scenes in the background. Her monogram forms an outside motif for the carpet. *Estate of Ettie Stettheimer*

CARL SPRINCHORN -
Matagamon series - NR. 24 -
NOV. - DEC. 1944 -

Coll. the Artist

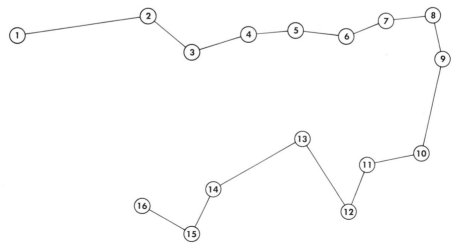

1 Beatrice Wanger (niece of the Misses Stettheimer and sister of Henry and Walter Wanger)

2 Elsa Brill (Mrs. N. E. Brill)

3 Florine Stettheimer

4 Beatrice Keyser (Mrs. Ernest Wise)

5 Charles Demuth

6 Carrie Stettheimer

7 Georgia O'Keeffe

8 Carl Van Vechten

9 Arnold Genthe

10 Carl Sprinchorn

11 Philip Moeller

12 Hilda Hellman (Mrs. George S. Hellman, mother of Geoffrey Hellman and sister of Elsa Brill)

13 Edna Lilienthal (Mrs. Joseph Lilienthal)

14 Fania Marinoff (Mrs. Carl Van Vechten)

15 Isabel Lachaise (Mme. Gaston Lachaise)

16 Ettie Stettheimer

Opposite: The Three Stettheimer Ladies and Some Friends, watercolor by Carl Sprinchorn, who first met his principal subjects here at one of his one-man shows. Executed in 1944, this work is a recollection of the Stettheimer home at the Alwyn Court during the early thirties; a chart identifying those represented will be found below the picture.

Portrait of Florine Stettheimer, *circa* the late twenties, pencil, by Marguerite Zorach, a friend of the Stettheimer sisters.

Ink drawing by Pavel Tchelitchew, who met Florine in 1935 and the same year whimsically sketched a phase of the milieu they shared; left to right, the late George Platt Lynes photographing, Monroe Wheeler behind his desk at the Museum of Modern Art, Barbara Wescott paddling; below them, Lloyd Wescott sunbathing, Glenway Wescott writing.

leafy gestures,'' is an excellent impression of him. A certain diary entry, however, is in a soberer, more objective mood: ''To Pavlik's studio to see his great chef-d'oeuvre [*Hide and Seek* (1940-42)]. The Museum of M. A. has acquired it. Peacocky self-interpretation and as brilliantly colored and done as he could make it.'' Palpably, Florine was never oblivious to any little flaws presumed to lurk in another's crystal.

A PORTRAIT PAINTER to rival her own originality was Virgil Thomson in his musical portraits. As was previously mentioned, he did a commissioned portrait of each of the Stettheimer sisters. Florine's reaction to hers, noted when she first heard it some months after its composition, was of a negativity unusually impressive because given as directly and unaffectedly as the time when her reaction to this composer at the piano had been so different: ''Virgil played my portrait to me on his piano in his apartment with M[aurice Grosser] present. Afternoon tea. I am not at all what I thought I was in his eyes and ears. I am very sad and dreary and suddenly become boisterous and even modernly screeching. He said the noisy quality is the color I use. That's that.'' It is true that at this time, Florine was approaching her fatal illness and may have been disposed to interpret the *triste* or meditative as the ''dreary'' and the lively or loud as the ''boisterous.'' She always saw life from under the exclusive canopy of a very personal imagination, subtly altering it as décor alters the walls of a room or a façade the aspect of a building.

Actually, she had ''sat'' for Thomson's portrait the afternoon of October 5th, 1941, when she was quietly at the classic occupation of stringing beads, and her diary also records that as he worked, the music of a band reaching them from Fifth Avenue, a block away, ''disturbed'' him. But the truth was that the composer, attuned to the modern artistic creed that consciously utilizes ''hazards'' while engaged in creative work, had seized upon the ''intrusive'' martial music as a theme expressing the sitter's known patriotism and her flair for her country's colors. It may be that Florine entertained a certain naïve incomprehension of special manners belonging to any art other than her own; hence, her recorded verdict of ''screeching'' on a phase of Thomson's musical portrait may be valued as unduly . . . Florinesque.

FOR THIS ARTIST, form may have been a flutterby, but as the flutterby's architect she was also the architect of its domain, airy space. If the ghostly presence of the trellises in the garden at André Brook necessarily root the painting, *Music,* in Florine's external life, her own image as its dreamy heroine roots it also on the stage. Superficially one of the most casually composed of pictures, its lack of defined perspective and artificial landscape give it the look of a backdrop. Likewise, it has the side-elevation illusion of which Florine was fond and only the highly decorative trees (Chinese-into-Modern) have any integrative rôle in relating the widely spaced figures: Nijinsky as the Rose, an unidentified master pianist, and Adolph Bolm as the Moor in *Petrouchka* when he lies on the divan tossing a cocoanut in the air. Undoubtedly, here as in other works, Florine was inspired to emulate Chinese painting by way of Bakst's designs for the Russian Ballet.

The principle of isolating the individual in the house of his dream—which is only life itself—is seen in this painting like so many botanical specimens. It is true that the Rose, the Girl, and the Pianist are united by the plot and musical accompaniment of Fokine's ballet and that the single décor of this ballet had, I believe, a profound influence on Florine's painting. Yet each individual here, not only the Girl, exists primarily in his own dream. The general principle forms a kind of democracy in artistic vision, and is oddly like the socialist ideal of a society which becomes cohesive through complete individuality in all its members. The canopy of the bed of the Girl (enacted by the artist) is not like the drapery, or the canopy, of the bed in Diaghileff's production seen by Florine in Paris, but rather is like the fringed or scalloped garden parasols of which the artist did many versions in her pictures. What does it signify here? It is the instrument of magic itself and as sacred a symbol as the priest's canopy, the saint's or the god's halo, and as elegant as a parasol placed by a painter over a Venetian aristocrat. In *Cathedrals of Art,* the canopy signifies that what we see there is the artist's own vision, while the Commère is her surrogate within the work itself. Primarily, then, *Music* is Florine's memory of her most treasured ballet legend, as reconstructed from the viewpoint of her canopied bed identified with a theatre-box.

MEN, WOMEN, AND things never appear in any other way in this artist's eyes but as vehicles of self-regard blended with other-regard, formal individuals seen as both units and parts, taking meaning from themselves as well as from what surrounds and connects them. Inevitably, this unified visual attitude was reflected in terms of a style formula, which I suspect was nothing but Best-Maugard's seven linear geometric motifs. But an art is never, strictly speaking, a formula; hence Florine's art, as a personal style, owed nothing to her preceptors. Her avoidance of superposition was a device to give us, without loss, the individual's integrity. Even in the very crowded pictures, our eye goes around him as easily as around the body of a Paleolithic animal; he is pure in space, his own and universal space. Florine speeded this process of grasping a man's or woman's figure by the activist concept of her anatomy, imparting character primarily by silhouette and dispensing with muscular definition to attain utter simplicity. In principle (look at her own figure in *Family Portrait No. 2*), it is the same as the style of marionettes meant for shadow plays: a hieroglyph to portray, with a minimum of adjustment, either motion or stillness. That Florine's men and women actually convey more than such shadow-people is a fact for which to be grateful. If her persons were not so Florinesque, they would be—as I hinted above —Egyptian.

Tchelitchew saw in Florine's style the delicate silhouetting of the Persian miniatures, and truly, in the light elegance of her human figures we see a resemblance to those paintings, especially in the self-hypnotized pride or sweet serenity of a face or an attitude. Of course, a dazzling rapidity is often perceptible in Florine's accomplishment of a figure (like her own image in *Asbury Park South* or the ladies trying on dresses in *Spring Sale*) that is Far Eastern rather than Persian, and in the best style of Impressionist economy. It would be foolish to evaluate the "dollishness" of Florine's human beings as either subhuman or inhuman; at their least expressive, they approach the comicstrip and the illustration; at their most, they are as finely hieroglyphic as a human attitude in Bosch or Japanese painting. The Chinese wall painting, *The Eight Perils,** bears a striking resemblance to the layout of *Spring Sale* and is to that work of Florine's as *The Moon King and His People* is to her *Asbury Park South*. In some ways suggestive of Quattro-

* Plate 15: *Chinese Painting,* by Arthur Waley.

cento figures or those of the great French tapestries, Florine's are never so stiff as the former or so anatomically self-conscious as the latter. Her flatness of manner and nervous outlines buoy up even ovalish and seated figures, and her generally negative emphasis on perspective-values tends to make her personnel as flighty as arrows. This likewise applies to things. Not only the airships but also the battleships are "aloft" in *New York 1918,* and there Manhattan Island itself (each building individualized) is a "city in the skies."

THOSE WHO FEEL that Florine Stettheimer's human world is too subjective and internal, that, in brief, it is too artificial and removed from reality, ought to study *Spring Sale* for its objective suite of the human body in willed motion, and concerned entirely with common, external objects—in this case, articles of apparel. There is nothing in the least unrealistic, humanly speaking, about this work. Formulating the frenzy for clothes, it is a little epic of timelessly comic femaledom and a perfect achievement of style. It is also a most meaningful instance of the fact that Florine's special province was the figure suited to its clothes. Her basic conception of the costume, no matter how ornamental, was as a functional unit inseparable from the body (indeed as some dolls are made): a principle that is copiously demonstrated in *Natatorium Undine.*

As careful as she was of the integrity of the figure in space and its necessary relation to things, Florine was cavalier about perspectival proportions, often reducing only about 1/5 figures that would seem to demand, scientifically, a 4/5 or 1/2 reduction. In large scenes, toward which she took a notably aërial view, she dealt little in perspectival lines as such (i.e., the garden path almost parallel with the line of vision in *La Fête à Duchamp*) until she came to the architectural arrangements of the *Cathedrals*; or, if she was faced inevitably with the problem of such lines by choice of subject, as true of the panoramic *West Point,* she handled them in an arbitrary way. There is intimacy in all Florine's works and not only because, as in *West Point* again, they are in general toylike, but also because whatever is distant in them, owing to the small ratio of perspectival reduction as well as to the general lack of superposition, tends to come forward and make "a small party." It was hard for Florine to exceed the dimensions of the large salon, and when she decided to do so, she simply made walls and the earth itself disappear—as in her and Ettie's portraits. Her *Cathedrals* are window-display versions of real cathedrals, being about the literal dimensions of many jewelry-displays.

I THINK THAT the artist's most beautiful conquest of the picture surface is in the beatific *Picnic at Bedford Hills,* where the individuals are magnetized to the delightfully handled picnic cloth, its interrupted sidewise diamond placed so as to accent the rise of the ground toward the two trees at the top. With earth, Florine achieved here the same thing she achieved with water in *Lake Placid,* a sense of its organic nature, and neither achievement seems to have been quite duplicated anywhere else in her oeuvre. The high activation of Carrie and "Duche" spreading out the lunch in the lower part pushes the uppermost angle of the white cloth toward the inert quadrangle of Ettie supine on the black rug; at the same time, the pronely attentive Nadelman at the corner of Ettie's rug duplicates the thrust of Carrie's relation to the cloth below them; all of which hints of hilliness and yet also of the gravity centering in the picnic cloth, whose pivot is marked by a layer cake. Each shape about the cloth, thing and person alike, has its local integrity and each has a rôle in echoing and contradicting the forms near it or opposite. One feels that these world-loving people are waiting to imitate the society of the food and the regularly patterned flowers on the cloth, eager to align themselves with the picnic-spread's four sides. Whether vertical or horizontal, angular or round, diagonal or parallel to the sides of the frame holding them, they revolve about the same center of interest as attracted McBride to this same picture soon after it was painted. Love also is a food, though a phantom one . . . As Watteau had his way of showing this great truth, Florine had hers.

canopist
blazonist
symbolist

WHILE CATALOGUING THE different types of canopy Florine used, I realized how wide the references were—from the sacred canopy over the bridal couple in *Cathedrals of Fifth Avenue* to the profane awnings over the veranda and the motorboat in *Lake Placid;* from the casual and delicate canopies over numerous bouquets and vases of flowers to the sumptuous, conic, symbolically weighted canopy sheltering the Commère in *Cathedrals of Art.* Noting the scalloped paper-lace about one bouquet, I reflected that these scallops, some-

times fringed like those of the huge canopy over the balcony in
Love Flight of a Pink Candy Heart, were, after all, echoes of
flower petals, stamens and stems, and that the canopies themselves,
as inverted flowers, were phases of Florine's "universal" bouquet:
a kind of *milles-fleurs* surface varied with artificially arranged
clusters; in other words, I was actually getting at Florine's
iconology as a kind of heraldry, which is obvious enough and which
I have already ascribed to her. But now the question would be:
what is the structure of this heraldry and what its meaning?

SURELY IT IS concentrated in the bouquet or at least the bouquet-
idea. The bouquet-with-the-snake motif, appearing in *Sun, Family
Portrait No. 2* (where supposedly it is a fern-frond) and *Flowers
with Snake,* is disproportionately large in relation to the other
figuration in these paintings, and thus appears as a deliberate coat-
of-arms. In a sense, it is equivalent to Florine's signature and in
line with the custom of incorporating a coat-of-arms in those decorative panels of the seventeenth and eighteenth centuries to which
I previously compared the screen portraits of Florine, Walter,
Carrie, and Ettie. The three hearts that dangle from the bouquet
held by Florine in *Cathedrals of Art,* and that represent the three
sisters, have predecessors in the four hearts attached to a bouquet
in one of the destroyed paintings—indeed, the same as that having
the scalloped paper lace mentioned above. The fourth heart in that
work may be either Walter or Mrs. Stettheimer. The four ladies,
of course, are in the official family portraits labelled "1" and "2."
The mother and three daughters, as I have consistently assumed,
represent the ultimate family nucleus owing to the marriages of
Walter and Stella. But the heraldic bouquet in the *Portrait No. 2,*
composed of three large flowers loosely held together by a serpentine fern, identifies the snake-motif mysteriously with one of the
four. Originally I speculated that it symbolizes Mrs. Stettheimer
for two reasons.

1) Because, as snakelike, it harks back to Eve's original surrender to the Serpent's persuasion in Eden, and thus signifies the
marriage that the three daughters have helped transform into a
cult of immaculacy (Mrs. Stettheimer was, after all, an "elegante"
who usually wore black); and 2) because in functioning as a ribbon,
the fern holds the three flower-symbolized daughters together; in
fact, after her death, the trio became domestically, if not spiritually,

I adored gay uniforms
I thought they contained superforms
Though they did not quite conform
To my beauty norm
The Belvedere Apollo

How could she know they did not so conform except by assuming, a priori, that real human flesh cannot compare with ideal human flesh?

A marble statue is as aesthetically intangible as an abstraction. Without doubt, Florine's proneness to flatness in the portrayal of depth has something to do with the theatrical illusion of reality, in which the actual dimensions remain untouchable because they exist behind an impenetrable barrier: the proscenium. Very few paintings of Florine's (at least after 1916) give the window illusion of a contemplated world of three dimensions; normally, her work is decorative in the mural sense, images appearing in the character of an illusive surface to which the wall itself is basic. In this regard, Florine is modern in the twentieth-century manner, which accounts for some of her paintings suggesting almost as much flatness as many of Miró's—for example, *Spring Sale,* where the staircase and drape make clean, typically Miróesque curves.

THE MAGICAL EFFECTS to which Rosenfeld referred in Florine's work pertain to those trick illusions in the theatre where things look suspended in air. Such are the heraldic bouquets that seem magnetized to the surfaces of the recumbent self-portrait, *Family Portrait No. 2,* and *Cathedrals of Art.* The bouquet in her recumbent self-portrait, a typical one seen in earlier and later works, is made of relatively few flowers (often single specimens), is never "bunched," and emerges from a conic vase or slender cone of paper, in the case of paper being tied with a ribbon. Florine at first does not seem, in the recumbent self-portrait, to be holding her bouquet, but there exists an appearance of her daintily dangling it from the fingertips of both hands as though it were a swing or a drape. Sometimes this typical or heraldic bouquet emerges from a receptacle that is itself like a flower.

Here is established Florine's connection with the Art Nouveau movement in decoration. The vase in her delightfully arabesque *Flowers with Blue Curtain* (1927) seems directly inspired by a

flower-shaped vase (1915) designed by Michael Powolny; this bouquet, incidentally, contains the heraldic four bleeding hearts in
their botanical rather than symbolic manifestation (the latter appearing in *Cathedrals of Art*). The lip of the vase in the just-
mentioned picture curves back in formalized "petals" and the
conic cup rises from an attenuating tail resting on two small legs
and ending in an upcurving split that instantly recalls the Mayfly-
Dragonfly tails and the fleur-de-lys motif. We can deduce from
Florine's bouquets alone that, to her, nature—however sensitively
organic or roughly asymmetrical—must be contained or framed
by a device of craft; by, in short, artifice. Her bouquets (as in *My
Birthday Eyegay*) constantly suggest St. Valentine's decorations,
and in *Delphinium and Columbine,* as in the self-portrait, the bouquet is surmounted by two flowering sprays touching at the top in
a Gothic Arch pattern. The vase in *Sun* seems a tight spiral and
echoes the spiral columns that illusively supported the canopy of
Florine's Alwyn Court bed: the one partly visible in *Family Portrait No. 2.*

Previously, I discussed the mannikin bouquet (its stems tied
with a fringed ribbon) which exists suspended in rays of light as
does Florine in her self-portrait. This suspension is bound to suggest, in the context of the artist's life and work, religious elevation:
both assumption and resurrection. The Mayfly-Dragonfly, Florine's
own symbol, is undoubtedly her *anima;* or generally speaking, her
soul. In the same way that the heraldic, or family, bouquet is magnetized rather than grasped, the soul is magnetized to the body
rather than held *in* or *by* it. This is plain from the recumbent self-
portrait; we should not forget that, even if Florine portrays herself here as an insect-woman, she is (as her very name proclaims)
essentially flowerlike, so that the insect-flower-woman represents
a compact series that is Florine Stettheimer symbolically suspended in the light of the world. The couch on which she reclines
is a sensual note; yet observe that the long points of its border are
petal-like.

A DISTINCT EFFECT of the mannikin-bouquet is the morning glory
serving as a canopy. In this exploration of Florine's icons, I am
compelled to think of the canopy's *histoire* as her *histoire* for a
reason which must be unfolded gradually. The zinnia-face in the
mannikin bouquet is orthodox Florinesque to the extent of having

a little halo of pencilled zigzag. The halo-technique of the artist's portraits is a conception of the frame, and thus, in the specially designed frames of most of Florine's pictures lies an element of the strict devotion she gave her work as an expression of the sacredness at its center, which (as the portraits so eloquently tell us) is nothing but the human individual. In the Conversation Pieces, the individual is usually given an isolated contour expressing his separateness within society; it is an ideal not only of democracy but also of the best society, where individuality is the value earning a distinguished place amid an elite group.

However, when the individual (as in the mannikin bouquet and Florine's recumbent self-portrait) is, as it were, unmoored from social contexts, he is unmoored from all diurnal reality, which is relative, and exists in absolute relation to himself and the world —lives in Eternity and Infinity. This is consistent with the psychology of heraldry as a family tradition: it is the sign of an uncut, and presumably endless, genealogical line. In Florine's world, the Stettheimer family could expect mortal continuity, on the other hand, only from its peripheral members—only from Stella and Walter, who had married. These two, of course, like relatives more distant, could not partake of the sacred honor of Florine's escutcheon. The way in which the artist, her mother and two sisters, are silhouetted in blacks, reds, and golds against the blue infinity of sky and sea in *Family Portrait No. 2,* excludes anyone not visibly present. As though suspended in space, a dragonlike beast, itself wearing a suspended crown, emerges from the margin back of the elegantly gathered, gold-fringed red curtain at the right. This beast is part of the elaborate relief façade of the Alwyn Court, and may be seen there today. It was identified by Florine as a salamander,* and unquestionably is presented in this climactic portrait as in "amusing" analogy with the beasts seen on coats-of-arms. The fabled aspect of the salamander as a fire spirit would likewise be of importance to Florine because, as immune to fire, it is a symbol of resurrection and immortality.

TWO ICONOGRAPHIC SYMBOLS are worth mentioning in the very significant *Portrait No. 2.* The star-shaped base of the Statue of Liberty is alignable with the sunburst-halo of which Florine used several variations, while at the same time it is a formalized flower,

* See color illustration: *Family Portrait No. 2.*

its points being especially like the petals of the lily family: a fact suggested by the adjacence of the lily-like flower in the great heraldic bouquet in the picture's center. On the side opposite to the salamander, the crystal chandelier, in suggestive juxtaposition with both the conic tower of the Chrysler Building and Cleopatra's Needle, makes with its companions variant forms of the vases and bouquet-holders so frequent in Florine's oeuvre. The star-points are echoed in the carpet's central circle in a pinwheel version, on four of whose spokes "Mother" and the first names of the three sisters are printed. We may consult a work previously mentioned only by name, *Cathedrals of Broadway,* which has one of Florine's two images of Stella—though the only one with her face visible, as in *Heat* she is turning away. This work has numerous variations of the halo, the star, the arch (i.e., the canopy's contour), and the drape.

Impressively, in its very center at bottom, is a railed-off circle with a halo-effect in its own center, out of whose axial spot rises a formalized lily whose middle projection is a more or less botanical calla lily; demurely emerging from its cup is a tiny nude with a finger at her lips and in the large circle on the floor is written "Silence." It is the insignia of the Silent Film at a moment when the Talkies (as we may find from the same picture) were already here; in other words, Silence Is Sacred. I mention the device in such detail in order to point out the constant renewal, even in this "commercial" Conversation Piece, of Florine's heraldic bouquet, but even more specifically of its peculiar structure. Here the complex trisula is strongly reminiscent not only of the mannikin bouquet, with its explicit canopy-flower at top, but also of the mechanism seen in Duchamp's portrait: the spiral-spring elevating his *persona.*

I had long been struck in Duchamp's portrait by the flower-like form on the floor, in whose center the narrow vertical base of the spiral is planted. The form of this spiral, as functionally a spring, is mechanically absurd. It looks flat (i.e., like Apollo's snake mimicked by Florine's ribbons) and therefore is only a token-spring, not being curved in three dimensions like a real spring.

Here, once more, I posit Florine's derivation from Best-Maugard's example because of photographs in one of his books showing "spiragraphs" or shadows projected by actual spirals onto a flat surface. "Such," wrote the Mexican artist, "can be seen in the zigzag projected by the coiled wire, or the scallop line made by the shadow of the spiragraph." But in drawing her scallops, spirals, and ribbons, the creative "student" who was Florine had perversely torn a leaf from her friend's yet unwritten textbook; she always flattened objects in the round at will, and did so partly, I suspect, from impish humor and her instinctive desire to build an illusive world: a world made of articulate side-elevations. She pulled the carpet of reality from under the feet of the world and yet left it magically standing!

In any case, she had not the least intrinsic interest in Best-Maugard's technical demonstrations of how three-dimensional forms are "betrayed" by their shadow-versions, but rather, grasping the principle of conversion from the round to the flat as true of the very art of painting, she experienced an independent—virtually mythical—sensation akin to the Impressionists' when they sought to represent on canvas the optical sensation of objects instead of their volume and mass. Strictly speaking, as soon as I began to be conscious of the structure of Florine's canopies, I noted that the earliest had the scallops of a covered garden hammock, as seen in a destroyed picture as well as in *La Fête à Duchamp* and in *Lake Placid* on the motorboat's canopy and the veranda's awning. This resemblance indicates an associationism of image that in itself has symbolic value. That Florine was aware of the scallop form as so named because of its source in nature, a seashell, and of the fact that legendarily Venus was born from the sea on a scallop shell, are points self-evident in *Natatorium Undine,* where the central image is a nude woman outstretched on this kind of shell. Repetition of units such as those of the scallop-spring in Duchamp's portrait can mean only a drive toward symbolistic statement in a style showing objects. The flower form from which the scallop-spring arises was suggested to Florine, probably, by carpet flowers of the kind appearing in Carrie's portrait. Yet one committed to the symbolistic theory of this artist's work would also notice that the round seat on which Rrose Sélavy rests could easily be an abstract flower and a version of the canopy.

The sacred tradition of the canopy as a protection ritually given holy objects (and the priest himself) is anciently connected with the canopic jars and vases which housed the ashes or the organs of the dead, and which in Egyptian custom were a set of four containing the chief organs of the deceased—ritually preserved for his use in the afterlife. Wolf's *Dictionary of the Arts* has this definition of the canopic vases: "The general form is that of a reversed truncated cone rounded off hemispherically, with the opening at the top, which was closed by the head as a lid . . . The Etruscan examples," the same source proceeds, "have handles, and bear human arms as well as the head . . ."

Florine's mannikin bouquet is a structural paradigm for such a vase (of which she is quite likely to have seen examples in Italy) especially because the zinnia-head and the morning glory-canopy respectively represent the mouth of the "vase" and its lid. The corresponding structural relation of these two flowers, in addition, is precisely the same as that of the table and canopy-umbrella in Hergesheimer's portrait, and the flower-base and flower-seat in Duchamp's portrait, since all are connected by a generic stem or generic handle, accordingly as one looks botanically or mechanically at the double image.

FLORINE'S EVENTUAL GENIUS burgeoned into improvisations on given themes. There can be no question that whatever she *imaged* she also *imagined,* and that the whole function of her method can be expressed by the formula of subconscious inspiration transforming the visible. It is the kind of Romanticism that documents the psyche —as a great deal of Romanticism (though some are reluctant to admit it) has done. Virgil Thomson believes axiomatically in Florine's sense of place in painting, even her fantasies having, as it were, geographic authenticity. Yes—because she was always aware of *where* she was dreaming, and of the relation of the dream to the living environment and the individual's actual range of habits. She and her sisters, according to the evidence of a couple of small (unfinished?) works, had had rigged-up an outdoor shower in a secluded part of the grounds at André Brook, where like Bathsheba they could believe themselves protected from observation. A watercolor sketch shows what apparently the *plein-air* shower, occupied, was actually like. A more elaborate work shows it gilded with the imagination and suggesting a ritual canopy. Now what is such an imagined object—whether, indeed, really so decorated or not—but a sheltered sky that rains? Perhaps Bathsheba was too modest a predecessor for the pagan Florine. In such a setting, the artist could have been a suburban "Diana" ready to quail and forthwith punish an intruding "Acteon."

The mental structure of fantasy is first of all an intuition of the imagination projected into something already given and real. The showerbath is not merely a modern household convenience; it is also a metaphor for the actual canopy of clouds that produces showers in a world of which man himself is only one natural development, and moreover (if all we are told is true) a development later than rain. In the same sense, an umbrella is an artificial sky whose mood is dry rather than moist. It is very possible that, one warm sunny day, Florine discovered this when raising a parasol and thinking of the canopies that have protected sacred queens as suddenly behaving like a supersaturated sky and "raining inside." As we shall see, there was a basis for such a fantasy in her intimate daily life . . .

MY OWN PREJUDICE is to assume in Florine the presence of automatic association and subconscious metaphor, rather than of continuously conscious symbolism because, from the poetic viewpoint, the former is theoretically sounder. Her heraldic motif alone, which is explicit enough, not to mention also the allegorism that was developed for the climax of the *Cathedrals,* would establish a conscious use of symbolism. Yet associationism implies a greater flexibility and an opportunity for subtler forms of invention than does a thoroughly conscious system of symbols; this greater flexibility and these subtler forms, I think, are truly characteristic of Florine Stettheimer's art.

A moment comes when a painter never really listens to anything but what his eye, and his eye alone, tells him. If a purely optical associationism is to be emphasized in Florine's oeuvre, nothing seems to illustrate this better than the fact—classifiable as psychologically automatic—that the explicit canopy over the bed of the Girl (Florine) in *Music,* as she lies dreaming of the dancing Rose (Nijinsky), is perspectively the same tapering oval as the bed below it; in other words, it is an especially striking confirmation of the canopic structure of vase and lid already defined, a mechanical arm rising from the head of the Girl's bed and so stamping the canopic image as authentic Florinesque: the connecting arm is the visibilizing of the real, but invisible, relation.

IF FLORINE BE a symbolist, what does she symbolize? The obvious clue is in the religious use of the canopy in church ceremonies as well as the jars of Egyptian tombs and the funerary urns of Latin peoples. We may note that the "umbrella arm" holding its canopy from above rather than underneath is of the pulpit type, something which Florine had an opportunity to observe even in the chapel where she saw the image of Herr Gott. She could not possibly have been unaware of the ceremonial connotation of her canopic images, for even had she been so before 1929—when she made friends with St. Theresa and her holy ecstasies—she could not have been so afterwards. We could indeed trace, if we wanted to, a perfectly conscious and poetically humorous secularization of sacred images by Florine, and we could start with the three loudspeakers seen in *Love Flight,* which patently are hybrids obtained by crossbreeding with the Easter Lily, the visible sound issuing from them corresponding to stamens. This particular congress of icons, moreover, is the converse of the silence-enjoining, trisulated lily-group in *Cathedrals of Broadway.* And we might go on to note of the latter that a miniscule image, in one of the niches of the display columns of the Paramount Theatre, is that of a nun on her bier from Lillian Gish's film, *The White Sister,* surely being Florine's expression of a lurking religious taste. In turn, we could say that these "niches" themselves are puns for the canopied niches in cathedrals, containing the statues of saints. There is an explicit example of such a canopy in *Cathedrals of Fifth Avenue,* serving in this mixture of the sacred and profane to represent St. Patrick's Cathedral.

All such observations symbolize Florine's comic sensibility— her keenly poetic sense of the comedy of commercialism. But I want to prepare for the tragic end of all life, *death,* as Florine herself prepared for it, with an ecstatic consciousness of the idea of resurrection that is always at the heart of religious experience, especially the saint's. The artist's most expressive paradigms of the canopic idea as visible in nature, and artificialized in terms of vases and all forms of the canopy itself, seem to me the decorative panels which she once exhibited at the Belmaison Gallery (Wanamaker's) and which I have mentioned as portraits of herself, Carrie, Ettie, and Walter. The base of each is in itself a vase resting on a low pedestal, on whose frontal sides are respectively printed "Florine," "Walter," "Henrietta," and "Caroline." They include Florine's family totemizing and reduce the halo-technique of her

Exterior façade (opposite) : the Beaux Arts studio building at the corner of Sixth Avenue and 40th Street in New York City, where Florine Stettheimer made her private residence after the death of her mother in 1935.

Interior cocoon: Florine's fabulous lace boudoir at the Beaux Arts, decorated by herself. A portrait of her mother is on the top shelf of the whatnot to the right. At the right margin, an oblique view of *Flowers with Snake*.

View of Florine's residence at the Beaux Arts; foreground: the great sky-lighted studio; beyond: the Salon with George Washington's bust in a niche. The artist's visible works are: far left (above) right side of *Beauty Contest*, far left (below) right side of fire screen titled *Persiana;* next to it, a standing screen, with panels showing portraits of Ettie and Carrie Stettheimer; on wall above, *Asbury Park South;* on easel, in frame designed by the artist, *Cathedrals of Wall Street*. The arched windows above the curtained colonnade are those of the lace boudoir.

is elongated in consonance with the highly vertical style of the whole panel. In each case the aërially situated canopy is the "lid" of the extended vase whose "mouth" is the flower-platform. The analogy with the anthropomorphic vases of Canopus and the Etruscan tombs becomes plain: Florine would paint death in the very gesture she painted life. This may be inferred from the fact that the whole image of each panel represents the flowering of something released by lifting a lid. The human is the "artificial flower" of life resurrected: the doll of diurnity turned into the elf of the everlasting . . .

Florine Stettheimer's high instinct for joy made even her most satiric aims lyrical, while at the same time the funerary connotation of her canopies automatically translated itself into hymns of faith in resurrection. As I have indicated, the light gayety of her style bears a basic relation, at all times, to the Rococo mood of old-fashioned valentines, distinguished by lace as these frequently were. Moreover, the altar-effects of her portraits—as well as the side-elevation effects of *Cathedrals of Fifth Avenue*—are much like the multi-dimensional décors of mechanical valentines. One such in the noted Norcross Collection has dove-borne flowers (Thomson's portrait), white, gold-fringed curtains draped in its arch (the Commère's canopy and a curtain thus draped in *Four Saints*), flower-twined columns (many bouquets and the Compère's column), and the "arch" pattern used by Florine so variously.

The tradition of the canopic vase was comically inflected by another sort of nineteenth-century valentine: striped jars of the urn type had detachable lids which, when lifted by a ribbon at top, drew up with them ladies respectively identifiable as one's sweetheart (or "wife") and "mother-in-law"; the opposite emotions of the masculine heart are signified by "Preserves" written on the pretty girl's jar and "Pickles" on the homely mother-in-law's.* In such ways, the most ancient religious superstitions are translated into the profane emotions of a much later people. So the popular tradition of funerary urns was a wide one to which Florine brought, in her four screen portraits, her own individualized imagination.

SHE APPEARS THERE (as also in the *Portrait No. 2*) as a painter, with palette and brush in hand and wearing a fantastic bohemian out-

* Collection of the Museum of the City of New York.

fit, including (as in the recumbent self-portrait) an opulent beret. Florine's is a dance posture, Carrie's is a fashion pose, Walter in sporting clothes teaches his dogs tricks, while Ettie postures with a quill pen in one hand and a mirror, surmounted by a parrot, in the other. The bird totem for Ettie (denoting a rather ambiguous form of conversation) suggests why Florine may have decided not to give her sister, in the later portrait, an insect totem. Through a hole in the canopy above Ettie, in the panel-portrait, hangs a drape to which two masks are attached, thus recalling the Gorgon-mask which (as I mentioned above) seems to be the subject's face conceived as a theatre mask no less than as a Medusa. Two of the flowers in Ettie's panel are stylizations of bleeding-hearts. The correspondence in Walter's and Ettie's portraits between "lid" (the canopy) and the vessel's "mouth" (the platform) is emphasized by duplication of shape in the same way as Florine's canopy and bed in *Music,* and as Rrose Sélavy's highstool-flower and its floral base in Duchamp's portrait. In the latter, the religious image of assumption is clearly parodied by a profane parallel: the artist's supposed "advertisement" of his social *imago,* the *persona.* Thus Florine's tragi-comic version of the professional artist's "assumption" of celestial heights takes its deepest meaning from the iconology of her canopies. The closest religious analogy happens to be Oriental: Buddha seated on his Lotus and sheltered by a lotus-canopy. There is insouciant satire in Florine's device of seating Duchamp *on* the canopic feature rather than *under* it: he wants to be even higher and swivels himself up on the arm of the canopy as if it were a piano-stool . . . Consult the real piano-stools in *Music* and in Florine's portrait of her mother, where each "leg" has exactly the same spiral-form as Duchamp's spring.

We have seen that part of Florine's understanding of the art world's commercial comedy was her own peculiar position as an artist desiring fame but never consenting to "buy" it with self-advertisement. Her intuition of the canopy as lid of a funerary urn gives us reason to suppose that she anticipated the true height of her fame would be posthumous. The theme of the screen portraits as resurrective is confirmed by a further metaphoric dimension in the recumbent self-portrait. Etruscan cinerary urns of terracotta were rectangular and carried on their lids reclining, and usually cushioned, effigies of the departed which easily bring to mind this self-portrait of Florine's and her portrait of Ettie; both of these resemble a sculpture with which, as I have mentioned, Florine was familiar: that of Pauline Borghese at the Borghese Gallery in Rome; Florine's couch also has scallops. The Etruscan effigies, moreover, sometimes hold a wreath (one such, with which the artist could easily have been acquainted, is in the Metropolitan Museum) and in the recumbent self-portrait Florine holds one of her heraldic bouquets. On the side of the urn at the Metropolitan is carved the head of a Medusa, a further indication that the *couchante* figures of both Florine's portraits represent herself and her sister resurrected from the time of their lives into the endless spaces of eternity.

V *Apotheosis in Daily Rhythm*

F SHEER FACTS—toward which our society rushes like children in the direction taken by fire engines—there seem in Florine Stettheimer's life more than enough, and not *fact* enough. For the purposes of biography, there are never quite *image* enough in *anyone's* life. For if a fact be not trued in its idea as *idea* well as its image, it must stick out—and who shall present the essentially imperfect, man himself, as the perfect idea? Before anything be said and after everything is said, a human being is and remains a fact: a real image yet a potential idea which he himself must complete. The rhythm of Florine's outward life has been perceived here as it interwove with the rhythm of her inward life, from the center of which she expressed the vision that is and can only be—however much it registers outward things—inner and subjective.

But, incontestably, she lived meanwhile in a world, a country, a city, a house. She was just as much aware of this as anybody in New York, as anybody at the Beaux Arts, where commercial photographers as well as artists lived and worked. Pathetically, a kind of light came to her—external, ambiguous—that had nothing to do with heart or spirit, and from which previously, a fringed sunshade or a canopy had been adequate to protect her. Like the sun itself, it was meant to be beneficial, curative, but even as with the sun, it was eventually futile and its function was inverted. It *burned* . . .

DAILINESS IS AN inalienable pulsebeat. Flowers bloomed and gave forth their odors for Florine Stettheimer: sweet or the natural odor of green things. All things had their perfume for her: people knew it and acted accordingly. Sometimes her thanks, as for a bunch of flowers from Carl Sprinchorn, left in her hall when she was out, was the simplest of one-line notes; sometimes, as for Charles Henri Ford's book of poems, *The Overturned Lake,* one of her spontaneous versified notes. No mere formal thanks were extended in reply to a poet's gift, but critical thanks, charmingly personal, and closing: "Amazedly / Florine St." *

"Florine St." knew the ontological symbolism of the eye that binds all artists together. Thus, on August 19th, 1929, one of the birthdays that came and went like a scented breeze, she christened a new work *My Birthday Eyegay,* replacing one sense-organ with another. That was the year of her first acquaintance with St. Theresa, and the later note to the poet, Ford, came as another testament of her "sainted" signature that was by then a habit. The title of the birthday painting appears on an heraldic serpentine ribbon below a vase-heart—St. Valentinish . . . "amusing." But her own, irreplaceable description is more serious: "A heart ablaze," says her diary "from which flowers blaze." Though such a reference to her own work was rare, let no one claim that Florine Stettheimer was unaware of her pictorial metaphors. The framing lace-curtain

* See *Crystal Flowers,* page 67.

above is in subtle relief and the whole impasto surface has an unusually beautiful palpitation that alternates ridge and graffito. The vase, of course, is a virgin's heart, burning alone.

TO HIS BED, everyone goes for the final answer to doubts and dilemmas, and even to solve an obstinate fate that at one time may seem less impregnable than at another. Yet just to lie down and sleep is a token submission to fate: a premonition of the everlasting submission . . . At the same time, sleep pacifies nagging desires in one form only to revive them in another: *dreams*. To her bed, like many another, Florine retired hoping for the fire from heaven but getting, according to the harsh fact, water from a ceiling . . .

It was in the "lace bedroom," where the four bed pillows were arranged, when "made," like half a sunburst halo, upright on their sides in wheel-formation from the headboard. If Florine lay there, like St. Theresa, with "heart ablaze," she also lay there as the occupant of a studio, fearing another attack on her by water from the commercial photographers' tanks upstairs. Twice, damage was done, though not enough water leaked through to make a rain; the third time, she came home to find the ceiling ruined and some of her lace wet. Thus the fires of the earth are to be quieted and thus the primordial flood dismayed man and sent him running! But, as St. Ignatius sang of the fire of transfiguration in *Four Saints,* "Last act, which is a fact." There are all sorts of facts!

THE WATER THAT ruined her ceiling was certainly not the "last act" in Florine's life if only because it was literally an accident, a diurnal externality; if only because it was wholly irrelevant (like those fumes of smoke in Carnegie Hall) and disturbed the play itself. Usually, life seems not to be coming out like a play, but somehow, despite all the extraneousness and all the surprises, it does —"just like the book says." And if not flood, then fire sounds the real, and perhaps symbolic, alarm. During Florine's residence at the Beaux Arts, fire struck twice in the building in gross emulation of the fever and the fret of actuality. Once the occupant was away, but the other time she was at home, at night, alone. A studio on the eighth floor entirely burned and it was fortunate that a knight-errant, Glenn Anders, an actor friend, "came to [her] rescue." Florine wrote in her diary, nevertheless, that the experience had been "unnerving."

BY THAT TIME she was a "bachelor" artist, living exclusively at the Beaux Arts, for it was after 1935. Though no pages concerning Mrs. Stettheimer's death remain in the diary of that year, Florine left there a recipe for a plaque which today, appropriately, might be placed in the apartment at the Alwyn Court so gloomily vacated by the Stettheimer daughters. It reads, in its original arrangement, as follows:

Sept. 30, 1935
The Collapse of Our Home
Goodbye Home
182 West 58th St.
the Allwyn [*sic*] Court

———

Salamanders, Crowns,
Cupids and Fleur-de-lys
farewell

There were, as Florine knew, other salamanders, cupids and fleurs-de-lys besides these stone ones . . . Of course . . . But the point was that these, such as they were, were unique. Though fashioned after those on the Chateaus of Blois and Chambord, none were "like" them as there is nothing like the houses where we are born, where we die, and where we achieve our great moments of life. The New Year's Eve following the move from Alwyn Court found Florine nostalgically inclined to make—in Ettie's own words—"a concession to family feeling" by sleeping over at the Dorset so as to spend New Year's "in the bosom of her family." And yet, ironically, as Florine and her sisters had reached maturity, they must have felt a curious, rootless feeling of being what they were: a matriarchy that was basically a tour-de-force of family self-sufficiency since further generations were not to come from this division of the Stettheimers. The "matriarchic" homes themselves were perpetually rented, not owned, and as such they were passing illusions that gave way only to other passing illusions. Feeling royalty in their bones, the Stettheimers (even at André Brook where they spent the war years) were still only tenants, not landed proprietors; only summer boarders, not the heirs of green estates . . .

AS WITH ALL self-creators, Florine's spiritual ancestors were partly invented. Whenever she glanced at George Washington's bust in its niche, she sensed a unique configuration, purged of purple in a constellation of red, white and blue—a reassuringly abstract and paternal image, benign as only the Washington of schoolbooks can be, the Father of His Country, and subtly without sex except in a secondary, angelic sense; far more a votive image than a man, and thus with a sexlessness that allied him, to Florine, with other white images just as Classical of face. There was her aunt, Caroline Walter Neustater, of whom she did a portrait in 1928, a grande dame of the last century in a formal black, embroidered dress trimmed with black lace, including a lace collar in form exactly like Washington's in the famous Stuart portrait. Aunt Caroline is in a palatial if not ostentatious setting, but more than that, her face and white hair, waving close to her head, have a matriarchal severity and a look remarkably like Washington's.

This portrait, a sophisticated, gilded version of the American Colonial portraits that imitated those of the English Court, gives us an image of female authority, Classical in its majesty, as Junoesque as that of Fraulein von Prieser. In Florine's portrait of the latter, we see a sculptured head of Juno, sitting large on the mantelpiece near a mirror-reflection of Florine herself as a child. The Fraulein, we learn from a notation by Ettie, considered that she resembled Juno. Oh, yes, the goddess wife of a *god!* But for the child in the mirror, the god would become "President" rather than "Herr." Finally, she looked to him for an implicit authority to preside over her home at the Beaux Arts. He was like a household god of Rome, a sign against fire and flood, and "domestic" where Apollo—who had stood on the bedroom mantelpiece with the snake he had charmed—was so . . . so *vaguely* universal . . .

Inevitably there were days and weeks, before and after 1935, when neither Washington's bust nor Apollo's porcelain statue was regarded by the artist, such as those days when she was preoccupied with a painting or with distractions from a painting. If her eyes did envelop either of the votive images, it was with the automatic second sight, purblind, in which one regards objects fixed in place forever. About all that Florine loved fluttered the "dragonfly" of her spirit: the Mayfly-*anima*. Thus, when she was painting *Cathedrals of Broadway* in 1929 and included in the dance spectacle, half lost in light in the far central distance of the Paramount stage, a domed and columned "belvedere," her mental eye at least must have turned to the Apollo on the mantelpiece. Or, when she had least reason to think of Washington, or his bust in her studio, she would be deliciously surprised by a photograph of a Washington image, mailed to her by Carl Van Vechten, who religiously photographed such images for Florine whenever he encountered one.

Indeed, Florine herself kept the mails busy with succinct exchanges of postcards, joking ones that pointed to funny things (such as the howling menagerie that the family found near them one summer in New Jersey); or, in the city, she relaxed from work at the easel by slipping down next to the phone and hearing the voice of Sprinchorn or Tchelitchew, both of whom were fond of long, heartfelt commitments sent electrically, and lingeringly, through vague, anonymous space "from person to person."

At whatever time, Florine found it hard to detach herself from the human image as such. The *Fourth of July No. 1*—similar to another fireworks piece called *Fête on the Lake*—is one of the few works, aside from early landscapes and the majority of the flower pieces, not to show people: the explosives are juxtaposed to moon, stars, and flag in an abstractly decorative manner. The *Fourth of July No. 2*, a small still-life with a palmetto fan, is an epigram on a holiday. Similar, though larger, is the sketchy *George Washington and New York*, with Washington's bust looming centrally in Florine's studio window overlooking the city and with the hands of living persons entering on either side. One is reminded how the tips of skyscrapers, in *Family Portrait No. 2*, merge so valiantly with the blue void.

WHAT WAS THE real cathedral in Florine's life? Undoubtedly her own home, and in the *Family Portrait No. 2* the spectator is part of the altar, gazing down the aisle of space to the entrance, and instantaneously beyond to the very poles of the earth. This is why Florine's suspended bouquets seem magically upheld by light only: notice that the chandelier in the same work simply reverses the reach of the Chrysler Building. Florine's world was "relativist," created whole out of a vacuum (a treadmill-world both moving and not moving), and hence her art was the daily record of a fantasy-life, a "little theatre" like one at a royal court, where all life was reduced to a private midway with fanfares, lights, and dancers. To these, as a reflection of her day and age, Florine added billboards and electric signs. Her symbolic formula for reality was emphatically "synthetic": the great rug in the *Portrait No. 2* is curved like the apron of a stage. And notice that the doubled eyes in the Follies Beauty *persona* is a guide to this double vision of agglomerate, in-pressing sensation and transcendent, outgoing spirit.

Part of what the spirit perpetually searches for is the "new" which is to transcend the "old." The artist did not altogether escape the normal human allusion that new scenery and new people, just because they're new, will make a material difference in one's life. I don't know that Florine ever had a nervous breakdown, but it was in the family psyche to escape from the circumscribed monotony of its seasonal routine by travelling, as though travelling would liberate—and "amuse" as never before. They drove by car throughout New York State and New England as far as Boston. But Florine's diary at these times is mostly the repository of complaints about the dullness of the cities and towns where they stopped and the inadequacy of hotel service. A trip to Canada one summer was a total failure. Always a critic of people and their clothes, Florine ruthlessly condemned any infringement of how to dress for dinner. If the encroaching vulgarity of other tourists spoiled these excursions, they must have reminded her of similar distresses felt abroad, but if so, the memory could only have awakened also a nostalgia for the charms of Europe, such as its treasures of Classical art which this country, at its very best, could hardly duplicate.

Florine never returned to Europe after leaving it in 1914. Duchamp, however, shuttling regularly between this country and France, was one of those to appear less frequently at the Stettheimers'. Unlike Proust's Madame Verdurin, Florine noticeably does not seem to have repined at such gaps or cherished any rancor toward the "unfaithful." She heard from Carrie, during that sister's solo trip to Paris, that "Duche" had married "a fat girl," and was sufficiently stirred to dream about the news. Flesh displayed in ungainly quantities provoked her disfavor as much as sloppy dressing in either sex. First she dreamed that "Duche" was getting bald and that the fine top of his head was made of smoky-hued milk-glass; she then asked him about his wife, and he replied that she looked "about 8 or 9 years old."

Tchelitchew, knowing the way Florine felt about stout clubwomen, decided to spring a surprise on her by also asking to tea their arch chronicler, Helen Hokinson. Florine, sensing the perfection of incongruity in being entertained with such a guest, noted her friend's joke appreciatively in her diary. There was, in the sisters, a vein of risible eccentricity which at times they did not flinch at exploiting for their own giddy benefit. For many years, Carrie patronized only one butcher shop, which was situated on Third Avenue, but neither she nor, of course, Florine or Ettie had ever set foot there. However, they happened to be in its vicinity one afternoon when their only remaining destination was home, to which, as they then had their car, they were on the point of driving. But Carrie thought of the butcher shop nearby and suggested they all pay it a visit; her sisters acquiesced, and when they made their appearance, the red carpet—as they all enjoyed telling afterwards —was rolled out and they played their grand roles with infinite gayety.

BUT, OH, HOW the world could press in! Parties of a typical style, full of delicacies, effected terms with the in-pressing world, dinner parties and tea parties, when the distinguished of the intimate earth would partake of the transmuted fare of a Muse. But best of all, for Florine, was a solitary lunch of pastries by her easel, ordered from the downstairs restaurant that used to be attached to the Beaux Arts. *Only* of pastries. Why? Because she liked their pretty, whited colors ("things mean their colors") and to have combined them with anything else would have spoiled the ritual. Florine was never so full of risqué laughter as when she wrote her poems personifying delicacies of the table as sensibilities longing to be adored and submitting like ritual victims to the exterminative passion of the gourmet. Into the following poem, as the most significant, one may read what one likes, but inevitably to be read there is a kind of erotic wit which the patrons of the poets around Charles I of England would have applauded; the "Paul" could be either Thévénaz, Reimers, or Chalfin, all of whom are identifiable in parties painted by Florine:

TO P.

Paul you are my Valentine
You have a passion for me
Because you ignored me

For six long months
You look haggard
Your eye is wild
You are emaciated
You pine for me
My memory gives you no peace
Night and day you think of me
You are consumed with longing
For me
    La Cuisine française

The inclusion of a line based on a popular torch-song was part of Florine's subdued waggery.

Dali was not the first artist to find the work of artisans edible. It was the decoration on the pastries, as well as their flesh, that aroused the artist's truly epicurean palate. Their frosting was like snow and ice . . . the opposite of fire . . . But water, and frozen water, can be malign! New York is a city of treacherously iced sidewalks on which, like others, Florine had her slips. When a lady falls, a gentleman comes to her rescue. Once, finding herself down on a glass pavement after a bad slip, Florine was aware of men crowding toward her "from nowhere." On her feet with someone's help, she "smiled them away." Alone, she rested against a fire hydrant, wondering if she had broken a rib. Deciding, finally, that she hadn't, she walked home. "A body that gets damaged," she wrote that night in her diary, "should be able to turn on a healing apparatus—it's strangers that the body, at least my body, resents."

Infallible pattern of symbols! Acceptance of *food as love* and rejection of *love as food* . . . As she smiled away her cavaliers, what had the double eyes of the lady-in-distress seen behind the statistical surface of the incident? I suggest that flirtation on water which she wrote of in a poem, some of whose lines curiously resemble a famous (more earnestly moral) passage in *The Waste Land;* Florine wrote:

We flirted
On the Rotterdam
We passed the Narrows
Flirting
We passed French Liberty
Flirting

Wedding gifts are visualized in the next few lines: "Crystal things / Diamonds / Venetian glass . . . Perhaps / we could build / a treasure house / all of glass." But how does this shipboard romance end?

> His glasses
> strangely
> dulled
> his eyes
> They became
> An opaque barrier
> on which our flirtation
> Shattered
> In a thousand
> Splinters

She had probably observed the ocean mist frosting his eyeglasses. Men had double vision, too, and could be "double dealers." Rain . . . ice . . . disillusionment! Not surprising, then, the soothing self-possession, cloistrally safe and sure, "lying between perfumed sheets" while "it is raining warm rain in Bryant Park." Then a fire scare . . . and, inevitably, smoke . . . necessary water . . . *irrelevant* water . . . No matter what one does, life repeats itself.

FOR WEEKS, THE sisters would contend about where the approaching summer would be spent. Various arguments from all three arose and subsided. Florine usually gave in from ennui and packed her bags with the rest, but sometimes she just sat on her contrariness and wouldn't budge. They would go without her and she might or might not follow them. These were the summers of the fêtes and the weekends at André Brook, the country residence in Tarrytown, which Florine loved and whose arched trellises of rambler roses are visible actually and as a motif in numerous works, including the rear view of André Brook, *Sunday Afternoon in the Country, La Fête à Duchamp,* and *Russian Bank.* Observe these works, and see how really "feudal" was the life led by this branch of the Stettheimers. On days when the family was alone, games would be played, and in these Florine would sometimes join. In the last of the twenties, Parchesi "came back into their lives"—the "pink, blue, yellow markers" recalling to Florine her childhood. This game several could play, but more frequently the mother would be engaged in a Russian Bank duel with one of the daughters while the others gardened, read, painted, wrote (or worked on her doll-house).

The recourse to nature and sunny warmth provided a dual rhythm in Florine's life, one whose chronological sequence irked her as she approached the days of her more cosmic vision: the aisle up the center of the *Cathedrals.* The "commercial" Conversation Pieces, even as the Lake Placid and Asbury Park "class" Conversation Pieces, went by; the portrait period came and burgeoned, finally bringing Father Hoff in New Jersey as a diverting and prophetic incarnation. His portrait, not especially eloquent on the whole, and a trifle wooden in figure, has the literal religious motif, while his face (which one fancies Florine thought "handsome") looks like the Classic family-face found on Aunt Caroline and George Washington: an image at once Apollonian and Juno-esque. Though in Father Hoff's face and figure there is no leading evidence for Marsden Hartley's already quoted remark (unless it be the cassock itself), this painter had called the priest, or at least Florine's image of him, a "feminine man." Florine must have flirted with Father Hoff as St. Theresa does with St. Ignatius in *Four Saints,* with an irresponsible, quite transfigured, sort of innocence. "Padre Carlos" she would refer to him whimsically, and was distressed when, a few years after they had exchanged visits for tea one summer, and the portrait had been done, she heard of his death by drowning: he had lived by the sea and been a swimmer. He had also loved flowers and been a gardener.

ONE FEELS INSTINCTIVELY, from the more or less continuous record of the diary, that it was never men, per se, that unsettled Florine's contentment with life and with herself. Sometimes it was, first and foremost, the weather; or rather, as with original life on the planet, it *began* with the weather. In the following diary image of 1919, we see for all time the individual's relation with his environment—whether saint or artist or neither: "Every morning I seem to start up into the day—and the day comes down on me and we go fast on our separate ways." It is a perfect poem of the creative or spiritual being's alienation from the external world of nature, which may be just as sharp as his union with it. He is aware of reality and himself, as ever, but he feels drained: the cosmic pulse has eluded him; he is threatened by demons, by boredom's naked face . . .

On such days—especially, for instance, if fighting a cold— Florine would turn to the past rather than the future. Once, in uneasy nostalgia, she reread the letters from friends of her schooldays and tore them up in a mood of elegiac morbidity: "They are all gone now. I reread most of them. Those were my girl friends. My boy friends and swains will be destroyed the next time I have an ache." The once living and tangible individuals had been reduced to mere handwriting, something in thin, thin black-and-white, and so were eminently perishable. All of them ended in the fire— or in the wastebasket that preceded the fire.

FAMILY BIRTHDAYS, NATURALLY, were notable and appropriately sentimental events, though never the occasions of big parties. One may guess the reason for the intimacy of such celebrations. A large ritual would have demanded a cake with candles and thus a decision on the mathematical validity of this symbolic form of annuation. It is oddly suggestive that, while the birthdays of Mrs. Stettheimer, Carrie, and Ettie came close together in the last week of July, Florine's was relegated to August 19th. Sometimes the mutual celebrations of the sisters' birthdays were slight and casual, only a telephone call or a bottle of wine, while at others it was a traditional ritual of lobster *Américaine* and champagne at a restaurant. Florine was happy to find her mother, on the latter's birthday, July 22nd, 1921, "well, strong, and happy." The daughters chose to make this one "golden with gold paint and gold paper," probably meaning special decorations of the house and the festal board. Two days before her own birthday in 1923, Florine celebrated by beginning her recumbent self-portrait. A few years before, on August 19th, she had wistfully anticipated a *fête à Florine* comparable to the *fête à Duchamp,* but it had not materialized (she did not write how it was spent).

Rituals attached to dates are fleeting and ambiguous: more so than any other kind of ritual! The irony is that it is hard to find a ritual not attached to a date. As flowers fade, birthdays do. All Florine's nosegays, ritually picked in the country on every birthday, became ashes: only her "eyegays" remain. Christmases and New Years, like everything else, came and went. Only one of them

Tulips, around 1925, oil on canvas, one of the artist's very direct flower pieces, might be thought to lack her distinguishing style, but patient study reveals the indelible "flutterby" stroke she gave the world of nature.

After her death in 1944, Florine Stettheimer was given a Memorial Exhibition at the Museum of Modern Art in 1946; on its walls are visible: (upper photograph) *Family Portrait No. 2, Sun, Portrait of My Teacher, Fraulein von Prieser, Love Flight of a Pink Candy Heart;* (lower photograph) a typical flower piece, *Picnic at Bedford Hills,* (very obliquely) *Beauty Contest, Portrait of Henry McBride, La Fête à Duchamp, New York 1918;* all decorative frames were designed by the artist.

Mannikin for an unproduced ballet, *Orpheus of the Four Arts*, conceived
by the artist. Made by Florine from plaster, metals and paint, this dynamic
figure of Mars is seen above as he appeared, in the Memorial Exhibition,
along with other mannikins; and below, with reliefed costume designs for
the same ballet; the designs are painted with tinsel, gauze and other stuffs
to suggest the intended costumes.

That particular "vacation" was troubled by inability to paint and a residence that sprang so many leaks during rains that she longed for a different house, but none could be found. She was suffering a little from separation from André Brook, where she now went only as a guest. For a while, they rented the Gould Estate in Tarrytown but the proximity to their old home only made Florine feel nostalgic. Sometimes the furnace there hadn't worked but . . . Shortly before returning to the city, that Larchmont summer, the feverish diarist wrote one day: "I finished a history of my life that takes five minutes to read." Such were the intermittences of the heart, wretched in an enforced idleness that desired creativity and creativity only. By September 15th, she was back at the Alwyn Court— "Thank goodness," the diary frankly, almost blasphemously, comments.

PARTIES, HOWEVER, MADE a steady rhythm, a rhythm sanctified by long custom. Time after time, Florine, when she entertained in her own house after 1935, reshuffled the menus devised by Carrie and listed them along with the guests. Time after time, furniture would be repainted, new bouquets invented, or fresh cellophane curtains, always with luxuriant bouffantes and trailing on the floor, installed in the doorway between the small and the big salons. Perennially, the art-salon was the true measure of fame in Florine's eyes: the measure of her living, lasting communion with fellow artists. This measure did not itself depend on worldly or objective standards, such as those she had originally imagined in Paris, but rather embodied an hermetic milieu of glamor—an induplicable milieu that remained the artist's hallowed way of surpassing the New York of "speakeasy bars and motor cars / columnists and movie stars," whose provocative noises rose just beyond her front windows.

Not that, in the twenties and thirties, Florine declined to go to parties; she did go. But as time wore on, hosts saw distinctly less of her. Truth to tell, there was a point at which her "amusement's" inner laughter was vanquished by the hard facts of her disaffection. A loyal personal friend of Van Vechten's, she was yet uncompromising enough to confide to her diary her notions of "the rich fast set" to be found at his house, where the colorfully mixed bohemia that amused the host left "Miss Stettheimer" cold. Society's true spell existed for Florine only at home or wherever she could be an unobserved observer, free to mentally record those human charms and idiosyncrasies she thought precious enough to paint.

Her vocation of artist never gave her complacence—most abhorrent of traits!—nor could it fill her life. The premises at the Beaux Arts, deserted after a glittering evening party, presented more than once to their tenant a haunting image of barrenness, paradoxical and tantalizing. How many times she must have hovered, quite alone, unwilling to extinguish the downstairs light that would plunge everything into darkness and quell the last dazzling ghost of the evening! Then—at least once—she must have stepped to a covered easel, unveiled it, and brought to the light for a long, unscheduled moment that richly unique climate of identified individuals which, parallel to the fabled races of fauns and mermaids, were part-human and part-Florinesque . . . As she finally made her way to the lace-bedroom (having stood there as in the silence of a cathedral), she saw the phantom images of her friends troop back into her mind—and naïvely, joyously, full of inarticulate longing, she then ascended the red-carpeted stairs, looking forward to her next party . . . Knowing the urgent pulse of parties, Florine knew their full, incomparable fever. Characteristically, she liked the verve of Van Vechten's novel, *Parties*—which grew out of Joseph Hergesheimer's phenomenal shindigs—and confidently predicted to its author that "all young America" would soon be reading it.

WHEN *Four Saints in Three Acts* nominally identified Florine with the great world of theatrical entertainment, Broadway itself, she conceived the *Cathedral* series, the first of these being the *Broadway*. This meant that she now frequented commercial amusements more deliberately and judged them more consciously. In the center of the *Broadway,* beneath the Romanesque arch of the Paramount's proscenium, Jimmy Walker, then Mayor of New York, is seen in the act of throwing on the field the first baseball of the season: doubtless a newsreel shot. His image—since the movies were still nicknamed the Silver Screen—was accomplished by Florine in silver paint. With her sister, Stella, and Stella's son, Henry Wanger, who appear with Florine in the *Broadway,* the artist would "go to the movies" occasionally.

Of course, the legitimate theatre was an alternative at such times. During May, 1924, it was "for Stella and Mother" that

Florine "went out of the house" despite the fact that Marcel Proust's great work had been her "whole entertainment" the previous winter, and by then she had reached the eighth volume. This time Stella treated them to *Abie's Irish Rose,* to which Florine must have gone as a supreme, if unspoken, concession. "I am back with Proust," she wrote in her diary the following day, "and look at last evening's boredom with amazed horror." Attached to "horror," amazement could not be coterminous with amusement. She seems never to have been pleased in the popular theatre except by Disney's cartoons and Chaplin's films, feeling impelled to note, after seeing *The Great Dictator,* that Chaplin was "a great actor." She found color photography in the films (circa 1938) "as bad as ever," and felt that the movie version of *Wuthering Heights,* with Laurence Olivier, was "too tame." Sacha Guitry's film, *Pearls of the Crown,* went down in the diary as "a sample card of historic costumes and bon mots"—a description having considerable point.

The serious stage fared no better with her, apparently, than did *Abie's Irish Rose,* on which she could not walk out because of her mother's presence, but she felt no such restraint when going to a matinée of *Winterset* with Carrie and Ettie, who took her to it on her birthday. "From the minute the curtain rose," she pitilessly recorded, "I wanted to leave. Carrie said she wanted to also. So Ettie agreed that she would prefer reading it. I found it offensive from the girl's hair that covered her front as well as her back to the men's voices. So we went out into the sunshine after the first act. We had lobster *Américaine* and champagne cocktails and—we are all well—." It was the judgment of a professional authority on the theatre. But likewise it was one lyric occasion added to the debonair Stettheimer habit of just celebrating being a Stettheimer.

THE ARTIST KNEW public triumph as a paean and an ordeal. She knew its illusive nature and its spell; she felt that she had "manipulated" it and now, whenever she wielded the brush and palette knife, her fingers knew it too. She was headed straight into Eternity and nothing could deflect her course. The Ephémère that had been dazzled by the world's sun and, dazed and singed, fluttered helplessly in its rays, saw everything at this point as culminating in an altar. The heart of the Commère, bleeding in emulation of St. Theresa's, was to be worn permanently on the streamer of a bouquet. It all seemed as fixed as the façade of St. Patrick's, a feature of which had gone into *Cathedrals of Fifth Avenue* in 1931.

In this work, we see marriage as pricelessly conventional; the groom is fantastically "typed" like a fashion drawing, though somewhat more solemn; the bride's face is in the white-pink light inside the Commère's canopy, but utterly vague and characterless, which is its point. This is the world's marriage, and meaningless to Florine, a spectacle of which she was a witness exactly in the sense that the three Stettheimers (elegantly detached at the right) might stumble onto an actual wedding spilling out onto Fifth Avenue . . . then on to Sherry's for tea . . . a stop at Tappé's, whose windows Florine admired . . . and, en route, an order placed for a bunch of Pierson's "biggest, best zinnias" . . . Such was dailiness . . . precious dailiness.

FLORINE HAD SEEN the first Armistice Day of the two world wars, but she would not see the second. At five in the morning, 1918, the whistles had told her the Armistice was signed; at seven, she had gotten up, going to the Red Cross headquarters, opposite the Library on Fifth Avenue, to serve refreshments. Being thus humble on the frantic scene, she doubtless devoted some unspoken thoughts to Walter Wanger, her nephew. After entering the Air Force the year before, Wanger had come to Florine and remembered her birthday with a token. She could not have helped feeling that their "long talk" then might be their last. What was said can probably never be known, because the pages referring to it were deleted from Florine's diary by Ettie, who allowed us to keep only these words of the artist's: "I was awfully upset. I feel more peaceful now, and I don't know why, excepting that I suppose it's impossible to keep up being awfully upset. We are very good friends." He had promised to keep a diary for her, and it was then that he responded to her desire to do his portrait by saying he would "love to pose." Apprised of the fatal news taking him away to fight, Florine went into town to see him at Stella's. This diary entry was one of those she reread in 1941, and it was in December of that year that she wrote just these words as one day's entry: "Japan has started a war—with us."

IN THE INTERIM marked by the end of one war and the beginning of another, everything would be decided for Florine, the painter. The year after the United States declared war on Japan would see the last *Cathedral* come into being. It was December of still the next year that she somewhat mysteriously wrote in the diary: "I thought of doing Paradise [presumably *Cathedrals of Art*] last December. It became Purgatory which I have done instead." Her reference must have been to a notion derived from Tchelitchew, who considered that in *Hide and Seek* (1940-42) he had painted "Purgatory" after having finished *Phenomena*—or "Hell"—in 1938, and therefore he was obliged, after 1942, to paint "Paradise." Florine's allusion meant something fatal. At the beginning of the previous July, she had returned to the studio after almost three months in Roosevelt Hospital, and another three at the Dorset next door to her sisters. The name of the hospital might have had something to do with the choice of it. As Florine's personal choice, it would have been thoroughly like her.

In *Cathedrals of Wall Street,* where she seemed never to tire of putting more gold on Washington's statue, she had deified her quasi-paternal hero, the Father of her genius's Country, and in the same work she had placed Franklin D. Roosevelt's coin-image, very large and conventionalized into looking like the pseudo-Classical face of Duchamp, filled out and actually a masculinized version of the Junoesque Aunt Caroline and Fraulein von Prieser: revered aunt and revered teacher. The Eros?—the pretty boy of romance, that wingless "worm" of her satiric piece of Cavalier Verse?—his "day" was over except for the apotheosis of Robert Locher into the Apollo-Compère of *Cathedrals of Art:* God of Beauty and God-parent in one. Faithless to the purple of tyrants, she was faithful only to Apollo's impersonator and the red, white, and blue of a political father worthy of Washington: "Franklin D." (as he would have been called by her erstwhile collaborator, Gertrude Stein).

Up to the last party, everybody's name, and some new names, went down on her guest lists. Yet inevitably many had fallen away. Of Virgil Thomson, she noted principally that he was "writing brilliantly" as the *Herald-Tribune's* music critic. But Duchamp (who spent so much time in Europe) was almost never mentioned any more, nor Henry McBride. Somehow, these had become figures of another era, surviving as old friends whom one didn't have the energy to see much, whom habit had cloyed a bit, whose edge had been dulled by time. It was much more remarkable that Roosevelt should be reëlected than that a celebrated friend should again come to dinner. There was something of a democratic socialist in the diarist who could write of a spectacular party, given in honor of her birthday (at Aix-les-Bains) before the first world war, "enough to make a socialist of any human being with a mind."

The long-loyal McBride must have lost prestige with her on the disclosure of a certain aberration, noticed unflinchingly in her diary before the election November of 1940: "McBride and Clagett [Wilson] for Willkie—oh, horrors! Showed them *Cathedrals of Wall Street*." It was a delicious stroke: Roosevelt as Wall Street's managerial angel, exposed in an expensively gold setting to adherents of art who were faithless to New Deal Democracy in a political crisis . . . Her reward, not many hours after a constitutional among the 57th Street galleries, was this surprisingly delightful incident: "I took off my telephone receiver at 7 A.M. 'Roosevelt,' said the voice, instead of 'Good morning.'"

THOSE WERE THE days of her friendship with Tchelitchew and her admiration for his achievement as seen in the Museum of Modern Art retrospective in 1942. "It was very impressive," she wrote, "even grandiose." How honestly she must have envied her good friend's illustrious fortune! With him, she had been as one in being both otherworldly and of-this-world. Then the blow—the complaint that grew sinister, the doctors' examinations, the inevitable diagnosis . . . and the operation . . . Through it all, her sisters, since they took rooms at the hospital, were constantly at her side. Her return home in July was succeeded by an event whose superstitious character held an ominous note. Ten days later, she recorded: "*Natatorium Undine* fell off the wall. Second painting to thus behave." She was probably living in fear of a second operation. But despite pain and a strength that was returning only slowly, New Year's Day, 1944, was an occasion for the expression of optimism. As nominally she was again a healthy and independent being, Carrie and Ettie telephoned their holiday greetings to her instead of appearing in person. "Happy for us," the artist wrote in her diary, "after months of staying away owing to ill health." Carrie and Ettie, too, were indulging in the pleasure of refound privacy and time exclusively at their own disposal.

WHILE PAIN—THE pain of a persistent illness—mounted in Florine, she continued to work on the *Art*. It was hard for destiny to quell so enduringly vivacious a spirit, armed with palette knife and brush as with weapons of survival . . . Not to go into the field where an empty, a merely sketched, or an incompletely filled canvas stood like a mortal dare? This was the unthinkable part of the human condition to Florine, as it is to all artists who remain vital to the last. In the intaglio of her surface plane, and its tendency to support plateaus of paint and painted putty, there was a nervously incessant play with the creative ground which invoked the world and expressed the artist's grasp of the basic physical experience of space. Painting is above all arts that of illusion; that of a concretely fictitious realm. In its naïve emulation of mass and the third dimension—echoed in Florine's career by her actual manni-kins that seem so "translatable" into two dimensions—her paint-ing reveals that curious pulse which made her boudoir seem flatly "porous" with lace, like a plane surface which is only illusively penetrable . . . But not to lift her head, once again, from her boudoir's deceptively round pillows!—this was finally to vacate the great illusion, to abandon those images whose airy "tangi-bility" challenged her strength to move, her strength to load the palette knife with paint . . .

"MY LONG LIFE," says a refrain by the sculptured image of Susan B. Anthony, the heroine of Virgil Thomson's other masterful opera, *The Mother of Us All*, "my long, long life!" He might have been thinking of another virginal yet fruitful American: Florine St. The aesthetic demon, Apollo-Eros, that made her self-image as the Commère a masterpiece of lyric impressionism, was still active, still turned her eyes outward on the beloved world with its fasci-nating people—"candidates," that is, people who had not yet been in her canvases, who had never been in her life really, who might never have been, even once, in her drawing-room, but who belonged to the world, and somehow to the future: the art dealers of 57th Street and the rival artists whose fame so much overshadowed her own . . .

Though ill on January 30th, 1944, she went to Bernard Lin-stott's *vernissage* at the British American Art Center, hopeful of finding there some of her "victims." She found at least a hundred people milling about, poised, gossiping, possibly "interesting peo-ple," too, but since they were not the right ones, they represented only smoke and drink. She had wished merely to refresh her memory as to the appearance of certain ones. Soon she had to return home, tired and frustrated: a little grey-white shadow in which almost no pink was left, and on whom powder looked ghostly. It was the end. The last nakedness had to be endured, the ultimate surrender to the inquisition of light! The Ephémère, shrivelled by the glare of the infra-red lamp treatments that had been prescribed by her physician, was bit by bit burning up . . .

FLORINE STETTHEIMER DIED without having had that ultimate one-man show that would have been a successor to the first one at Knoedler's. Sublimely, in her way of being a saint, she had set her face against anything so worldly, and yet she had yearned for it with every ounce of her manifest worldliness. It was the contradiction that had produced the strange luminosity of her art: its "divine comedy" as well as its comedy of manners. Her lawyer and friend, Joseph Solomon, was with her at eleven o'clock on the night of May 11th, 1944, and her sisters had left her side only ten minutes before, when the artist passed away forever as a living image on earth. Transposed to a vocabulary with which her destiny had always been involved, she was now, infallibly, a "work of art" . . .

In a sense, the translation from human mortality to artistic immortality hoards its grain of grossness: its unbearable pathos that must be indescribable. Yet it is the same prospect that lies ahead of every far-looking artist (which one, indeed, is not far-looking?), and for Florine the prospect had been filled with a curious inward agony. For long there had been the inherent, anachronistic impulse toward the burial of her works with herself . . . This had been a mysterious (if not mystic) voice, never quite stilled or forgotten. At the moment of death, a standing impasse had been reached with this issue even though (according to a memorandum for an unexecuted will of Florine's) ten years of family discussion had been devoted to it—that is, it had thrust itself once again to the foreground of the painter's life on her becoming a bachelor artist in the large Beaux Arts studio.

From then on, there arose currents and cross-currents of discussion among the three sisters while living in sickness and in health. Ettie, alone, was later to take the burden the most seriously of all—logically, literally, practically. During the period of Florine's last decline, the artist seems to have abandoned everything of material consequence to her sisters as if her interest, as well as her strength, was at an end. At the time of the legal memorandum mentioned above, her uppermost wish was to keep her oeuvre perfectly intact as a legacy to the world, with the hope of finding a suitable setting for it as a suite of some museum, which would also display the furnishings of her studio. So enterprising a dream, however, inspired no real corresponding confidence in its practicality: at least one blankly received hint had been made to an eminent museum director. Thus, when Florine died, her fame before her eyes was still hazy: a bonanza of fancy . . . Yet she had certainly reconciled herself to that division of art and artist that means a clean, bisymmetrical split: the Ephémère had suddenly had to resign the contest and dive, wings open, into the heart of the sun.

AT HER EXPRESS desire, Florine's body was cremated. But this did not mean an end to the phantom of incertitude hovering about the perpetuation of that other Florine: the Commère. The artist had committed everything to the world by the rather ghostly smile of glamor she had bestowed on her lips in *Cathedrals of Art*. As a matter of fact, Kirk Askew, in his relations with the living artist, had never permitted the subject of another one-man show to drop. Now, on the question of the future course regarding his late friend's oeuvre—left, with all her other property, entirely to her sisters— Askew took the practical stand that this painter's art could not gain the recognition it deserved at any imminent date unless, duly offered for sale, her works brought higher prices. A letter from Florine to Askew indicates the atmosphere in which latterday discussions of this issue revolved.

"Pavlik * got going," she wrote Askew, "when I confided to him that a very stylish exhibition—elegant—had been offered me. So far I have not accepted although it would be very chic. However, now that I have had a warning that I am not immortal and my paintings may disappear with me, if a pleasing disposition of them cannot be found, I have a few unrealistic ideas for their future which I should like to tell you about." But these the letter did not reveal. Whatever they were, now that everything has been settled, makes no difference. All that matters as we take in the past of this artist is the vividness with which, at last, she turned her face to the

* Familiar for Pavel (Tchelitchew).

simple publicity of the picture plane, where we can see not merely her, but also the world as she saw it.

In the plain sequence of events following her death, a certain uncomfortable hiatus was apparent. But this was to be filled one day by a ritual of which no one, then, had any notion, saving probably Carrie and Ettie. After the funeral services and the cremation, Florine's ashes were deposited exclusively under the eyes of her sisters and of Joseph Solomon, no others. Only a few intimate friends had attended the funeral, which had been quite private and unnoised in keeping with the Stettheimer canon of unpretentiousness. Yet the future hung low and large in the image of an insistent question-mark that somehow modulated the gay glow and ebullient painted figures that still dominated Florine's (otherwise vacant) studio.

THE ARTIST WAS gone. Her art remained: it was a responsibility which at once drew the two remaining Stettheimers' bowed heads together and broke out on their lips in phrases both rapt and questioning, phrases principally addressed to Kirk Askew and Joseph Solomon, phrases which reverberated and induced, through influential friends of the artist in key places, the great show that set a title on Florine Stettheimer's ideal forehead: the Museum of Modern Art retrospective, actually a memorial. Standing in the midst of it, Ettie Stettheimer (the last of the sisters because, with unexpected rapidity, Carrie had followed Florine out of the world in a matter of weeks) remarked to Glenway Wescott: "I think that this is the beginning of something."

It was the proud "Egyptian" note, abstracted from antiquity and projected into the swift, conglomerate, unpausing future. Out there, Ettie also saw her forthcoming book, her own memorial . . . All would be done, the sister must have said to herself; one sees her body stiffen in an attitude from one of Florine's paintings: a pose practiced but not self-conscious. Did not art and its dazzle make a plateau around whose feet the shadows of the real cluster and fume, mixing with one's daily bread? The clock now took absolute command. The quotidian set up its iron tent at the Dorset, where desolately the last of the Stettheimer matriarchy became a secluded invalid, always attended by a companion.

The temporal form of immortality grew to be a loud voice in Ettie Stettheimer's most secret ear as she lay under an oxygen tent

in 1950, the light in her eyes scarcely a light at all, reaching out
to ask Joseph Solomon if the clause in her will, dealing with the
conditions by which the body of Florine's art would be preserved
and resuscitated, was right—was the best!—would satisfy the
image of yearning in the small white mask she still remembered as
her sister's gaze . . . As if some inspiration might suddenly well up
from another source, a mutual friend of hers and her lawyer's,
James N. Rosenberg, was sent an urgent message; only a codicil was
needed! Again, Solomon reviewed the crucial clause with Rosenberg, and again the supreme sum set aside was altered.

WITH MIGHT AND main, Florine's art dragged one and all into the
future; did not even let one die in an orderly way. Ettie felt that
the final ends would simply have to be caught up: Florine's diaries
edited, all the documents inspected, collated, sifted; the priceless
souvenirs of the artist's studio-suite photographed at the top of
their form: in full season. Florine's mind had ever fixed itself on
the reconstitution of the present in the future tense: all the beauties
and laughters and changeless mementoes in one chamber—one
"cathedral" interior floating on the future like an ark . . . This
brought more than one piercing twinge to the suffering Ettie's
breast as she lay in her hospital bed.

ON THE HUDSON River, one day in 1948, she had exposed her being
to all the reality which the weather might muster. The family flesh,
so exquisitely reticent under time's fingers, bared itself in Ettie
with the ultimate bluntness of the desperate. As it was an Indian
Summer day, smiling, utterly benign, both Solomon and Ettie had
been copiously grateful, panting a little with thanksgiving. The
lawyer had known of it for some time, had known that it would
have to be October and the fourteenth day of the month. Now for
the first time, he understands why, and assumes that Ettie post-
poned it from one year to the next, while Florine's ashes rested in
the urn, in order to seize an October when she would be well enough
to make the venture. She had asked him to hire a motorboat and
have it waiting by the dock at Nyack, to which they drove on
schedule, that October 14th, in Solomon's car. The lawyer had pro-
cured a light cardboard box for the ashes in his arms, leaving their
original repository, the cumbrous urn, at the local chapel to which

they had been transferred (after two years) from the Ferncliff Crematory.

His client looked quite composed and had even brought along sandwiches for their lunch. They were long on the river, snug at the back of the tilted craft, and buzzing along as though all were right with the world because the weather was sublime. Then Ettie had elected to preside over the long-delayed ritual. Remaining seated, she had simply opened the box and begun gently, without emotion, strewing the silvery-grey mass of flakes onto the idiosyncrasies of the passing river. For a few seconds, they made a ribbony mist, dissolving upon the churning water with alarming suddenness. Drawing back in deference, Solomon had expressly declined to join in the strewing and then assented. He felt, as he saw the box really empty, a kind of bright ache in the overwhelming sunshine and a quiver in the great mountain by them, which seemed like Florine's mausoleum . . .

The ritualistic instinct of the artist had survived in her sister and prompted, as though with a pinch or a proud peremptory word, the traditional figure of fame to rise upon the glowing graves of the endlessly passing minutes. No monument in some rightfully accommodating museum?—Florine's creative home nothing but a nest of large photographs?—So be it!—There was an inflexible irony in the Stettheimer nature, ever gallant, ever with an unaffected shining and a regal calm. The frailty and the tears: these together belong to women and sink in whatever sand surrounds their visible memorials. Ettie had known just when the strewing of the ashes would have the right portent, would call most effectively upon the latent ghosts of the past to stir themselves, spanning in one leap the pulse of the present to bear up the catafalque of the future . . . Florine's first (frustrated) one-man show had taken place on October 14th, 1916, and now, thirty-two years later, its anniversary must celebrate a death and a resurrection.

INDEX

An asterisk before an entry indicates a work of art by Florine Stettheimer.

ETTIE   CARRIE